BLAST

Vorticism 1914–1918

William Roberts, *The Vorticists at the Restaurant de la Tour Eiffel: Spring 1915*, 1961–2, oil on canvas, 1830 x 2135 mm (72 x 84 in)

BLAST

Vorticism 1914–1918

Edited by
PAUL EDWARDS

With contributions by
JANE BECKETT and DEBORAH CHERRY
RICHARD CORK
KARIN ORCHARD
ANDREW WILSON

ASHGATE

Published by
Ashgate Publishing Limited
Gower House
Croft Road
Aldershot
Hampshire GU11 3HR
England

Ashgate Publishing Company
131 Main Street
Burlington
VT 05401 – 5600
USA

British Library Cataloguing-in-Publication Data
A catalogue record for this book is available from the British Library

Library of Congress Card Number: 00-107422

ISBN 1 84014 647 8

Produced for the publisher by
John Taylor Book Ventures
Faringdon, Oxfordshire

Typeset in Stempel Garamond by
Tom Knott, Mears Ashby, Northampton

Printed in Singapore
under the supervision of MRM Graphics

10048661997

ILLUSTRATION ACKNOWLEDGEMENTS

The editor and publisher wish to thank all those owners credited
in the list of illustrations for permission to reproduce their works.

Works by the following artists are copyright as follows:

David Bomberg (except for Plates XII and XX)
© The Artist's family

David Bomberg (Plates XII and XX)
© Tate Gallery, London 2000

Jacob Epstein
© Tate Gallery, London 2000

C.R.W. Nevinson
© Anne Patterson

William Roberts
Reproduced by permission of the Estate of John Roberts

Helen Saunders
© Brigid Peppin

Dorothy Shakespear
© Omar S. Pound/Emerson Gallery, Hamilton College

Edward Wadsworth
© Estate of Edward Wadsworth 2000. All Rights Reserved, DACS

Percy Wyndham Lewis
© Estate of Mrs G.A. Wyndham Lewis. By permission of the
Wyndham Lewis Memorial Trust (a registered charity)

This volume is an English-language adaptation of the publication
which accompanied the exhibition BLAST: Vortizismus – Die erste
Avantgarde in England 1914–1918 held at the Sprengel Museum,
Hanover and the Haus der Kunst, Munich in 1996–7. The publisher
thanks the Sprengel Museum for its generous cooperation.

Contents

List of Illustrations

Introduction

In the four years from 1910 to 1914, in parallel with the social and political ferment of the times, radically new ideas and practices in the visual arts were introduced in Britain. The exhibition organized by Roger Fry in December 1910, 'Manet and the Post-Impressionists', is conventionally taken as the starting-point, while the climax came in the late spring of 1914, with the emergence of a genuine avant-garde movement having its own identifiable form of geometric abstraction and its own vibrant and aggressive magazine, *Blast*. The movement was 'Vorticism' (belatedly christened by the American poet Ezra Pound even while *Blast* was in production), now recognized as the high-water mark of modernism in England at least until the 1930s. A Vorticist exhibition was held at the Doré Galleries in London in June 1915, and another in New York in January 1917. Despite the efforts of Pound to maintain the movement's momentum during the First World War, when its leading figures were in the services or working as war artists, by 1919 it was clear that Vorticism could no longer be sustained. The last 'blast' of Vorticism was Wyndham Lewis's 1919 pamphlet, *The Caliph's Design: Architects! Where is your Vortex?*, which called for the initiation of a modernist architecture in London based on the formal innovations of Vorticist painting, and excoriated both the reactionary classicism of the Parisian *rappel à l'ordre* and the domesticated formalism of the followers of Roger Fry. But the spirit of 1910–14 could not be revived. Some of the old Vorticist artists, allied to others who shared their dislike of Bloomsbury, formed 'Group X' (which held one exhibition in March 1920), but, aside from some individual, character-istically idiosyncratic, efforts by Lewis in the early 1920s, this was the end of modernism in British art until it was re-imported from Europe by a younger generation in the 1930s.

Vorticism, while remaining important in the careers of the artists and writers who were associated with it, retro-spectively took on the image of a false start. Its works – particularly its paintings, by their nature less physically robust than stone or metal sculptures – vanished or were destroyed. Paintings by Helen Saunders, for example, were used as oilcloth or lino in her family's larder; all Edward Wadsworth's oil paintings disappeared; Wyndham Lewis's huge canvas, *Plan of War*, somehow went missing after Lewis in 1930 satirized its owner (who had paid $20 for it in 1927), and Lewis himself evidently cut up some of his large Vorticist works and recycled the canvas.[1] Interest in the movement briefly revived when the Tate Gallery held what was really a Wyndham Lewis retrospective in 1956. It was called 'Wyndham Lewis and Vorticism' and included a small and somewhat haphazard section entitled 'Other Vorticists'.[2] No one was pleased: the achievements of the 'other Vorticists' (among whom were included people who had never been or called themselves Vorticists) were slighted by being cast so obviously in Lewis's shadow, while the impact of Lewis's own achievement was somewhat dissipated by the inclusion of forty works by these other artists. Wyndham Lewis was a notoriously tactless and aggressive self-publicist. Understand-ably anxious to locate the centre of the exhibition in his own development as a visual artist (which continued until 1949, when deteriorating sight prevented further production of works of quality), Lewis made a statement in the catalogue introduction which has overshadowed all subsequent writing about Vorticism:

> Vorticism, in fact, was what I, personally, did, and said, at a certain period. This may be expanded into a certain theory

regarding visual art; and (much less theoretically) a view of
what was excellent in literary art. *The Enemy of the Stars*, and
the first version of the novel *Tarr* [both by Lewis] exemplified
the latter of these two intellectual novelties ...[3]

In a series of angry 'Vortex pamphlets' William Roberts
rebutted the claim, but Lewis was too ill to reply.[4]

Only in the late 1960s and early 1970s did serious work
begin to recover the lost history of the movement and to trace
its dispersed and lost works. In keeping with the priorities of
the time, its avant-garde credentials tended to be evaluated
according to the degree that the group members approached
total abstraction in their work. When introducing the ground-
breaking 1969 exhibition 'Abstract Art in England 1913–
1915', Anthony d'Offay could legitimately claim that the
movement remained 'largely unknown', but subordinated
further historical enquiry to contemporary relevance: 'our
interest in the movement today must be centred on the degree
of abstraction it achieved'.[5] Other historical reconstructions
were under way, however, notably Richard Cork's large
study, *Vorticism and Abstract Art in the First Machine Age*,
which is currently the standard account of the movement.[6]
For Cork, Vorticism was an exemplary group movement of
artists co-operating in a communal progressive enterprise,
rather than the 'only a couple of women and one or two not
very reliable men' claimed by Lewis as having been grouped
under the Vortex banner he had held aloft. The death of the
movement was epitomized in the retreat from abstraction in
the paintings some of its members produced as War Artists.
Richard Cork was also responsible in 1974 for the largest
exhibition yet held of the Vorticists' work, 'Vorticism and
its Allies', in which nearly 500 exhibits (by no means all
avowedly 'Vorticist') substantiated his claim for Vorticism
as a movement of major significance in the history of art in
Britain. A complementary and equally valuable account of
the movement, *Vorticism and the English Avant-Garde*, by
William C. Wees, was published in 1972, placing the
movement's aggressive radicalism in the context of the social
upheaval that occurred in Edwardian London and continued
until the outbreak of war.[7]

In 1972, also, Hugh Kenner's monumental study of Anglo-
American high modernism in literature, *The Pound Era: The
Age of Ezra Pound, T. S. Eliot, James Joyce and Wyndham
Lewis*, was published.[8] It effectively announced its priorities
in its title. For many years in American criticism, 'Vorticism'
had been significant primarily as a stage in Ezra Pound's
progress towards composition of the major 'epic' poem of his
era, *The Cantos*. Now Hugh Kenner found in the movement's
dominant image of the Vortex (chosen by Pound) the concept
of patterned energies manifested through the varying
phenomena of nature, culture and history, a set of continuing
dynamics discernible as constants in the material they

ordered. This was a Vorticism quite different from, yet
recognizably akin to, what was described in the work of Wees
and Cork. Its conceptual framework would later be refined
by Reed Way Dasenbrock in *The Literary Vorticism of Ezra
Pound and Wyndham Lewis: Towards the Condition of
Painting* (1985) so as to encompass the visual aspects of
Vorticism.[9] Other studies of Vorticism, such as those by
Deborah Cherry and Jane Beckett, pursued a feminist cultural
analysis in order to illuminate the peculiar position of women
artists who allied themselves with what was, on the face of it,
an aggressively masculinist movement.[10] *Blast* endorsed
militant action in pursuit of female suffrage (so long as decent
works of art were spared), but did so with a patronizing air.
For a woman to be a member of this avant-garde grouping
was simultaneously to declare independence from the
hegemonic construction of womanhood and to place oneself
in awkward relation with a group of men whose gender-
politics remained relatively unexamined and hence
unreconstructed.

In 1996 Vorticism was at last granted international
recognition with an exhibition in Germany (curated by Karin
Orchard) devoted entirely to its visual legacy. It could now be
seen in its own right as an avant-garde movement fully part of
the Europe-wide rebellion against conventional bourgeois
canons of taste, and redefining, like other art movements of
the time, the function of the elements of painting and
sculpture so that they formed a new language whose relations
with the perceived world of common sense, and with the
invisible energies at work beneath its surface, were
unanchored and vertiginously unstable. In doing so,
Vorticism mirrored the exciting but threatening instability of
the multiple identities now seemingly transforming the
experience of humanity in the modern urban world of radio,
fast transport and heavy industry.

This brief history of the 'afterlife' of Vorticism shows, I
hope, that there can be no simple answer to such questions as
'What was Vorticism?' or 'To what extent should artists like
Bomberg or Epstein be considered as participants in the
movement?' For the original group members, and for those
who deliberately kept themselves independent despite
producing work that could have been called Vorticist (as
Bomberg and Epstein did), a variety of histories, motives and
objectives determined their decisions. And for later historians
the configuration of the movement, the relative prominence
of its different members and the degree of unity found in their
aesthetics equally depend on the starting-point from which
enquiry proceeds. Vorticism is itself like one of its own
characteristic products, unstable and dynamic, changing its
identity as it is viewed by different observers identifying
different elements as the ground from which a definite shape
must be picked out and reconstructed. The present multi-
authored study, therefore, focusing on sculpture, painting,

the women of Vorticism, the Rebel Art Centre, and on the dualities of Vorticist literature and aesthetics, attempts to do justice to this plural character of the movement and the field of alliance and enmity in which it operated. The remainder of this introduction will concentrate more directly on that alliance and enmity, briefly outlining the sequence of events that brought this first, and still most impressive, British avant-garde movement into existence.

If 1910 was important for the exhibition 'Manet and the Post-Impressionists', it was equally important for a much less publicized event earlier in the year, the first visit of the Futurist leader Filippo Tommaso Marinetti to London in April, to deliver his 'Futurist Address to the English' at the Lyceum Club. Marinetti praised the English for their bellicosity and individualism (found in their love of sport) but deplored their 'passéism'. In the audience was Wyndham Lewis. Futurism was not to have its full impact on visual art in England until the Futurist exhibition at the Sackville Gallery in 1912, for the simple reason that until then nobody knew what Futurist painting ought to look like; in the mean time, the chief effect of Marinetti's speech was to show Lewis the value of pugnacity.

Roger Fry had become seriously interested in modern French art ('Post-Impressionism') around 1909. A gentle, scholarly man – though not without ambition or egotism – he would never have sympathy with Marinettian bombast, or with the work of the Futurist painters. Fry was himself a painter, and after meeting Clive and Vanessa Bell in 1910, he became one of the 'Bloomsbury' group of painters (though as yet no identifiable group existed). Among future Vorticists who would be associated with Fry and this grouping were Edward Wadsworth, Frederick Etchells, Henri Gaudier-Brzeska, Cuthbert Hamilton and Wyndham Lewis. The other main group of painters was the Camden Town Group centred round Walter Sickert and Spencer Gore. It formed in 1911, and numbered Wyndham Lewis among its members, more because of his personal friendship with Gore than because of any shared aesthetic. One other grouping should be mentioned, that of the painters associated with the magazine *Rhythm*, which began publication in 1911. This was a 'Fauvist' group, subscribing to Bergsonian ideals of creativity. The future Vorticist Jessica Dismorr was a prominent and accomplished member.

All the future Vorticists, with the exceptions of Lawrence Atkinson and Jessica Dismorr, were associated in one way or another with Roger Fry, some through the Friday Club, some through the Grafton Group, and others later through the Omega Workshops. Of the 'non-Vorticists', David Bomberg and C.R.W. Nevinson also exhibited with the Friday Club; Epstein kept aloof. As the organizer of the Post-Impressionist exhibition, Fry was an important influence on public taste and

was able to raise the profile of artists he patronized: Frederick Etchells, Wyndham Lewis and Helen Saunders were able to exhibit in Paris under Fry's auspices in May 1912 at the Galeries Barbazanges as 'Quelques artistes indépendants anglais'.[11] Not that Fry was the only 'impresario' of innovative art in London. The critic Frank Rutter in 1908 had founded the Allied Artists' Association as an equivalent of the Parisian Salon des Indépendants, and in 1913, partly as a corrective to what he saw as the narrow focus of Fry's conception of Post-Impressionism, he organized a 'Post-Impressionist and Futurist Exhibition' at the Doré Galleries in London, including a wider range of European movements and artists than were represented in Fry's shows, as well as a wider range of British artists.

What was happening during this period in British art was a fairly unsystematic assimilation of the innovatory styles of European art, from Cézanne to Matisse, Picasso and Kandinsky.[12] For Roger Fry and his lieutenant Clive Bell, this progress was towards a realization that 'form' alone was significant in art, whether form was considered as a two-dimensional arrangement of line and colour on a surface, or as the three-dimensional forms those arrangements could be regarded as creating in the spectator's imagination. Any correspondence between such forms and those of nature was not of aesthetic significance. By 1912 only a few English painters were felt by Bell and Fry to have attained sufficient mastery of form to be represented in the 'Second Post-Impressionist Exhibition' in October to December 1912.[13] Of these, Bell singled out Lewis in his catalogue introduction, entitled 'The English Group', as someone whose work was independent of irrelevant non-formal associations: 'Hardly at all does it depend for its effect on association or suggestion. There is no reason why a mind sensitive to form and colour, though it inhabit another solar system, and a body altogether unlike our own, should fail to appreciate it.'[14]

The truth was that Lewis was now producing work that was in its form quite clearly deploying a 'cubo-futurist' style, and, though his artistic aims were not quite those of the Futurists, he was, as much as they or the painters associated with *Rhythm*, concerned with the exploration of Bergsonian and Nietzschean ideas of explosions of creative, Dionysian energy. Lewis had evidently been profoundly affected by the exhibition of Italian Futurist paintings held in March 1912 at the Sackville Gallery. It speaks a lot for Bell's appreciation of Lewis's work that he could ignore its concern with subject-matter and its Futurist affiliations in order to make it stand as an exemplar of his own fundamentally Platonic aesthetic. Fry may have felt differently about Lewis, either as a person or as a painter, for he did not include any of his works when a selection from the exhibition was sent for show in Liverpool. His explanation to Lewis, that he 'forgot to ask' if he had something to send (when other exhibitors were simply asked

to give permission for work already at the Grafton Gallery to
be sent on) puzzled Lewis, and he wrote asking Fry to 'give
me, quite roughly, my bearings'; Fry's response is not
recorded.[15]

Lewis's major Dionysian painting, a massive nine-foot-
square canvas entitled *Creation* and, later, *Kermesse* (now lost;
but see fig.11), was painted for Frida Strindberg's nightclub,
the Cave of the Golden Calf, which opened in June 1912.
Other artists involved in decorating the club included
Cuthbert Hamilton, Spencer Gore, Charles Ginner, Jacob
Epstein and Eric Gill. The 'primitivism' and savagery of the
décor here, particularly in the work of Lewis and Epstein,
answered much better to the idea of modernity that many
of the young artists wished to celebrate than did the more
cultivated and well-mannered gentility of the circle
surrounding Fry. Nevertheless when, in the spring of 1913,
Fry launched the Omega Workshops, his scheme for a
modernist arts and crafts workshop to design and (in some
cases) produce decorated textiles, furniture and objects of use
and ornament, Lewis, Hamilton, Wadsworth and Etchells all
joined the enterprise. The directors were Roger Fry, Duncan
Grant and Vanessa Bell (fig.1).

The event that precipitated the formation of a group which
would go on to form the core of the Vorticists was a quarrel
over a disputed commission for a decorated room at the
Daily Mail Ideal Home Exhibition. The full facts cannot be
recovered, and in an art historical context are less important
than their consequence. Lewis, Wadsworth, Hamilton and
Etchells broke away from the Bloomsbury Omega Workshops in October 1913, angered by what they considered to
be the duplicity of Fry in appropriating the commission for
the room's wall decorations. This had been intended for
Spencer Gore and Wyndham Lewis on the strength of the
decorations they had provided for the Cave of the Golden
Calf; Omega Workshops were to supply the furniture for the
room. Gore, who was contacted in July by the exhibition
organizers on the recommendation of P.G. Konody of the
Mail, was asked to organize a meeting of Fry, Lewis and
himself with them. He called at the Workshops and left a
message with Duncan Grant to this effect, but it was not
passed to Lewis. Fry received the message but, having
(according to his account) been contacted independently by
the *Mail*, met the Ideal Home officials on his own and took
on the whole commission for the Omega. As Spencer Gore
commented, 'of course the Ideal Home doesn't care [who
executes the commission] as long as it gets the room'.[16] Gore
was not especially interested in the commission himself, but
was surprised to have heard nothing from Fry or Lewis about
the affair. Lewis did not find out until too late what had been
envisaged. He met Gore on 4 or 5 October by chance after
the room had been completed. Having heard Gore's story he
confronted Fry with what he regarded as his shabby dealing, a

1 Omega Workshops on Opening Day

heated argument ensued, and Lewis walked out, accompanied
by Wadsworth, Etchells and Hamilton.[17] '*C'est trop fort!*',
shouted Fry as they clattered downstairs and slammed the
door.[18]

The incident brought out Lewis's talent for aggressive
rhetoric, and revealed a deeper and ultimately more important
quarrel with Bloomsbury, when he composed a denunciatory
'Round Robin', not only accusing Fry of shabby dealing, but
denouncing the Omega for its aesthetic tendencies:

> As to its tendencies in Art, they alone would be sufficient to
> make it very difficult for any vigorous art-instinct to long
> remain under that roof. The Idol is still Prettiness, with its
> mid-Victorian languish of the neck, and its skin is 'greenery-
> yallery', despite the Post-What-Not fashionableness of its
> draperies. This family of strayed and Dissenting Aesthetes,
> however, were compelled to call in as much modern talent as
> they could find, to do the rough and masculine work without
> which they knew their efforts would not rise above the level of
> a pleasant tea-party, or command more attention.[19]

The aggressive rhetoric was to set the tone for the Vorticist
movement that eventually emerged from this angry secession.

After the quarrel with Fry, Lewis formed a brief alliance
with C.R.W. Nevinson, organizing a dinner for the Futurist
Marinetti on 18 November, and planning a magazine to be a
vehicle for the new, more 'masculine', art. Nevinson suggested
the name *Blast*, and through his father's journalistic contacts
found a printer. Wadsworth also became involved in the
arrangements for the magazine. Progress was slow, and in the
mean time the artists who had walked out formed an uneasy
alliance with the old Camden Town painters (amongst whom
Gore was held in high esteem), and shared an exhibition
with them at Brighton Public Art Galleries ('English Post-

Impressionists, Cubists and Others', December 1913–January 1914), from which the Bloomsbury artists were excluded. They were joined by Bomberg, Epstein and Nevinson. The more 'advanced' artists had their own section, and Lewis wrote a separate piece in the catalogue, 'The Cubist Room', claiming that they formed a 'vertiginous but not exotic island, in the placid and respectable archipelago of English art'.[20] As yet, however, no name had been chosen for the grouping.

A new ally was found in the poet and philosophical journalist T. E. Hulme at about this time. Hulme had recently returned from a stay in Germany, where he had acquired a knowledge of the aesthetic ideas of Wilhelm Worringer. These ideas seemed to fit the developing style of abstraction better than the Fry–Bell aesthetic of pure form, for they linked 'form' with an attitude to the external world. This attitude, as Hulme interpreted it, involved a turning away from Romanticism towards a new Classicism, and, politically, a re-jection of the kind of 'liberalism' personified by Bloomsbury in favour of a more ordered and authoritarian political vision. Hulme had also been associated, somewhat uneasily, with Ezra Pound in the development of 'imagist' poetry, and both shared an enthusiasm for Epstein's sculpture. Lewis now asked Pound to provide poetry for *Blast*.

In January 1914 Kate Lechmere wrote to Lewis, whom she had met in 1911 or 1912, proposing the formation of a kind of *atelier* in London; a house was rented by her in Great Ormond Street, and the 'Rebel Art Centre', under Lewis's direction, opened in March 1914. Jessica Dismorr, Henri Gaudier-Brzeska, Helen Saunders and William Roberts were drawn in to the circle. The Centre was decorated with murals, paintings and hangings in a style now recognizably 'Vorticist'. But its ambitious programme of classes, lectures and pro-duction of applied arts was not fulfilled, although some lectures were given: one by Ford Madox Hueffer (later to become Ford Madox Ford), who would also contribute an instalment of the novel that became *The Good Soldier* to the first number of *Blast*. Marinetti also lectured, and in May Lewis published an article praising him as 'the intellectual Cromwell of our time'.[21] The always slightly paranoid Lewis suspected that Hulme, who struck up an affair with Kate Lechmere (and was engaged to be married to her when he was killed in the First World War), was plotting, probably with Epstein, to take over the direction of the Centre from him. Much of Lewis's energy was now going into *Blast*, for which he composed most of the theoretical essays and polemics. Though he had enlisted Pound on the literary side, he did not consider his poems anything like as radical as the visual art that was to be reproduced in the magazine, and wrote a prose-poem or play, *Enemy of the Stars*, as an example of what a

truly modern literature might be. Nevinson seems to have dropped out; Wadsworth, meanwhile, was working on a synoptic review of Wassily Kandinsky's *On the Spiritual in Art*, which was about to be issued in Michael Sadleir's translation.

Perhaps aware that he was falling into the background, and that *Blast* would, finally, appear, Nevinson joined with Marinetti in issuing a manifesto, 'Vital English Art', on 7 June. Anticipating *Blast*'s 'Blast' and 'Bless' pages, it was divided into 'Against' and 'We want' sections, and concluded with a call to the public to support the 'great Futurist painters or pioneers and advance-forces of vital English Art – ATKINSON, BOMBERG, EPSTEIN, ETCHELLS, HAMILTON, NEVINSON, ROBERTS, WADSWORTH, WYNDHAM LEWIS'. It was addressed from the Rebel Art Centre.[22] The effect of this was to present the English group as followers of the Futurists, who were about to hold another exhibition at the Doré Galleries. It is possible that the issuing of the manifesto was a pre-emptive strike by Nevinson, for the Rebel Art Centre artists had probably already decided to launch themselves as an independent avant-garde movement, and had agreed on Pound's coinage, 'Vorticism'.[23] Certainly, the name was bandied about in the heckling of Marinetti and Nevinson carried on by the new group in order to disrupt the launch of the Futurist exhibition on 12 June. On the next day a letter appeared in the press dissociating the future Vorticists from Futurism, and condemning Nevinson's use of the Rebel Art Centre address as 'unauthorised'.[24]

Much of *Blast* was already typeset and, perhaps, printed. But with a new name, new material and manifestos were required so that works of the various individual artists reproduced in the magazine could acquire a proper group-identity. A Vorticist Manifesto was composed and added to the front of the magazine. Its signatories were Richard Aldington, Arbuthnot (Malcolm Arbuthnot, a photographer), Atkinson, Gaudier-Brzeska, Dismorr, Hamilton, Pound, Roberts, 'Sanders' (Helen Saunders), Wadsworth and Lewis. Personal 'Vortex' statements by Pound and Gaudier were added at the back of the magazine. *Blast*, with its puce cover emblazoned diagonally with the title in thick black block letters (fig.2), finally appeared about the first week of July at much the same time that the Rebel Art Centre wound up its business. Within a month war was declared, and Vorticism's fate was sealed. But *Blast* itself, and the work produced by the Vorticists and those associated more or less closely with them, already constituted the initiation of a real avant garde in England. The work that survives from that turbulent period is the subject of the essays in this book.

'A Laugh Like a Bomb':
The History and the Ideas of the Vorticists

KARIN ORCHARD

'We hear from America and the Continent all sorts of disagreeable things about England: "the unmusical, anti-artistic, unphilosophic country" – we quite agree.'[1] Those are the opening words of the second part of the second Vorticist Manifesto, which appeared in July 1914, in the first issue of the journal *Blast*. Immediately afterwards came the self-confident assertion that England was now ready for 'the appearance of a great art', and it was precisely the signatories of the manifesto who had come together to put an end to this lamentable state of affairs and who were to spread the word of a new 'vital English art'.[2]

When in 1914 certain artists and writers gathered in London to commit to paper for the first time their ideas and projects, their action did not come out of the blue. A great deal had gone on before to prepare the way. It is important to know and understand the historical and social background to their meeting. Around 1910, Great Britain thought of itself as Europe's leading industrial and colonial power. The British Empire spanned the globe. The Industrial Revolution had come much earlier to Britain than to other European countries. This general supremacy was emphasized in the Vorticist Manifesto:

> The Modern World is due almost entirely to Anglo-Saxon genius, – its appearance and its spirit.
>
> Machinery, trains, steam-ships, all that distinguishes externally our time, came far more from here than anywhere else.
>
> In dress, manners, mechanical inventions, LIFE, that is ENGLAND, has influenced Europe in the same way that France has in Art.[3]

But national self-confidence had already to some extent been

shaken, and a certain measure of self-doubt had set in. Other countries, particularly Germany and the USA, had made enormous economic advances in the second half of the nineteenth century, and represented a real competitive threat. World industry was no longer exclusively British. A feeling of the decline of civilization, an apocalyptic mood, had set in, that came to be known as 'the English sickness'. There was a widespread impression that Great Britain had somehow missed out on the general modernization of the beginning of the twentieth century. Things were not going as well as they had done. One example was the success of rival nations, mentioned above, that threatened British hegemony.

At the same time, one cannot say that English society had ever wholeheartedly committed itself to the industrial system. Old England, with its idyllic country life and its ancient traditions, survives even into our own day, and was always more than an arty turn-of-the-century fantasy of a refuge from the big city. (London was then the largest city in the world, with six-and-a-half million inhabitants.)

Growing social unrest had brought the country close to civil war in the years leading up to the First World War. Not for decades had Britain known such general discontent as it experienced after the constitutional crisis of 1909–11. Three massive problems, and the movements that had sprung up with them, held public attention: the labour unrest of 1910–11, complete with strikes; the radical women's movement, which brought arson and bomb attacks; and the Irish question, which threatened to bring on armed conflict. It was only when the Great War broke out that domestic stability was restored. The war diverted people's attention and created a feeling of a shared national identity. The domestic crises nevertheless remained unresolved, and some of the interest groups achieved their aims only after the war, and then only partially.

Class war, gender war, and the threat of civil war, all contributed to the general uneasy mood throughout society, a feeling accompanied by rebellion and revolt in the world of culture. Various events and personalities of the international avant garde combined in the London of 1910–14 to form an explosive compound. The young artists who in 1914 came to be known as the Vorticists were ready for a sort of confrontation as yet unknown in England.

The break came at the end of 1913 when Wyndham Lewis, Frederick Etchells, Cuthbert Hamilton and Edward Wadsworth walked out of the Omega Workshops after their quarrel with Roger Fry. The ostensible cause of the quarrel, described in the introduction, was the dispute over the commission for a decorated room at the annual Ideal Home Exhibition. It was, of course, only a pretext for the rupture. The real issue concerned whose ideas were to prevail in the English avant-garde movement. Lewis certainly had the ambition and the drive to take over the direction of the new movement instead of leaving it to the older generation.

It was not only that the personalities of the two men were basically opposed. Their social backgrounds, and those of the artists gathered around them, could not have been more different. The artists of the Bloomsbury Group, and others associated with it, were of the cultivated middle classes and led comfortable Bohemian lives. They were politically liberal, and included among their number a fair few homosexuals. Most of the rebels, on the other hand, had emerged from humbler circumstances, or were foreigners, or of foreign background, all of which tended to make them outsiders. Such were Lewis himself, Pound, the American photographer Alvin Langdon Coburn, David Bomberg, Jacob Epstein and Henri Gaudier-Brzeska. While the rebels tended to volunteer for the army immediately on the outbreak of war, or allowed themselves to be conscripted, the Bloomsbury Group contained dedicated pacifists and other conscientious objectors. The liberal acceptance of homosexuality in the Bloomsbury circle was something directly opposed to Lewis's aggressive heterosexuality and anti-feminism. When we consider the nature of the Vorticist model and the images associated with it – dynamism, aggression and energy – it becomes increasingly obvious that these diverging conceptions of art could no longer live together. Lewis and his friends accused Fry of entering into compromise with the nineteenth century. The affinity of the Omega Workshops with the Arts and Crafts movement of William Morris, which flourished around the turn of the century, went against the grain for Lewis and those around him. The idea of the artist as an anonymous performer in a shop given over to crafts and handiwork as exemplified in the products displayed at the Ideal Home Exhibition did not correspond to their ideal, that of the autonomous artist making his way in an industrial world created by individualists and characterized by machines.

The time had come to seek new alliances and examples, and to find models for the new movement. What was needed was an English Marinetti – a role that Wyndham Lewis was to assume. A large Futurist exhibition entitled 'The Italian Futurist Painters' had opened in February 1912 in the Bernheim-Jeune Gallery in Paris.[4] An immediate *succès de scandale*, it drew large crowds – nothing unusual in the Paris of the second decade of the century, but there was this difference: the show had been carefully planned as a scandal from the very beginning, and its effect had been calculated well ahead of time. Filippo Tommaso Marinetti, the leader and general impresario of the Italian Futurists, had had pamphlets proclaiming the Futurist manifesto distributed weeks in advance. The year before, Futurist artists had visited Paris and had met the leading French modernists.

The Futurist exhibition then went on to London, where it opened on 1 March 1912 in the Sackville Gallery. Its third stop was Berlin, in the Sturm Gallery, arranged through the good offices of Herwarth Walden. 'Nightmares in Paint', or 'The New Terror', as it was indignantly labelled in the British press, drew in Berlin as in Paris a large and for the most part furiously outraged public. And, as in Paris, Marinetti approached the most advanced local artists directly, to recruit adherents to his Futurist movement. C.R.W. Nevinson was the only English artist to be lastingly impressed by Marinetti, and whom Marinetti was able to win over as a Futurist.

Marinetti's influence as a catalyst in cultural matters is not to be underestimated. He spread the word of Futurism in literature during his first visit to London, in 1910. In March 1912 he and the painters Umberto Boccioni, Carlo Carrà and Luigi Russolo attended the exhibition in the Sackville Gallery, and later the same year Gino Severini visited London. In November 1913 Lewis and Nevinson held a dinner for Marinetti in the Florence Restaurant, on the occasion of Marinetti's return to London. In 1914 London's second Futurist exhibition took place, in April and May, and in June London heard the Great Futurist Concert of Noises. Marinetti accompanied the exhibits with his provocative lectures and forcefully eloquent speeches that stamped his notions of art indelibly on the public consciousness. He was a constant visitor to London, which he hailed as a 'Futuristic city'. The colourful illuminated advertising signs and the fast-moving Underground, in particular, impressed him deeply. He wrote: 'I got what I wanted – not enjoyment, but a totally new idea of motion, of speed.'[5] Marinetti, a talented speaker and all-round impresario, provided a good example of how to go about organizing and leading an avant-garde movement.

Marinetti's artistic-political agitation only began to work fully on Lewis in the following year, when Lewis and his friends left the Omega Workshops in high dudgeon. Lewis found in Marinetti a kindred spirit, difficult and endlessly quarrelsome, but also well able to calculate how to place himself at the head of a group and how best to promote the group's interests and his own. Until Marinetti's appearance in London, Lewis and his Rebel Gang had heard of these avant-garde concepts mainly by hearsay and through the works themselves. To be initiated in these things by Marinetti himself, to learn from him the techniques of art-world public relations, made a deep and lasting impression on the young rebels. Marinetti's example showed them how the ceaseless presentation of oneself as theatre, and the distribution of pamphlets and other writings that cried aloud the author's concerns, could spread controversial ideas far and wide. Here were new techniques for a self-conscious avant garde to use in expressing its intentions: carefully timed appearances, declarations of opinion, and provocative announcements and manifestos.

But Lewis was not the only one in London interested in these tactics to the point of trying to put them into action. The American poet Ezra Pound, who had settled in London in 1908, in 1912 declared himself leader of the Imagists, a loose gathering of writers and poets that included Hilda Doolittle and Richard Aldington. Pound preached that the aims of Imagism were plain language, the creation of new forms of spoken rhythm, and an unconditionally free choice of subject in poetry. The main surviving result of their association is an anthology of poetry that appeared in 1914 under the title *Des Imagistes*. It contains contributions by Amy Lowell, William Carlos Williams, James Joyce and others. Pound's role as ringleader of the group, author of manifestos, publicist and general agitator, clearly drew on Marinetti as a model.

The Futurist manifestos, with their message of praise for the delights of violence, danger and speed, were translated into English for the catalogue of the Sackville Gallery exhibition, where they served as a stimulus to the younger English painters. 'We shall sing the love of danger, the habit of energy and boldness.'[6] The fascination that speed and aggression held for the Futurists ('There is no more beauty except in strife. No masterpiece without aggressiveness.'[7]), their glorification of war, the reckless destructive fury that they wished on museums, libraries and academies, all have become legendary. The Futurists celebrated the new Age of the Machine, with all its attendant clamour. Tradition, and indeed the entire past, was wholeheartedly condemned. Marinetti, and all the Futurists, had been strongly influenced by the French philosopher Henri Bergson. Bergson's idea of time as a dynamic, continuous process, in which living things develop, and in which the vital impulse (*élan vital*) strives constantly to bring about fresh creation, enjoyed great currency among European intellectuals in the second decade of the century. His ideas were paraphrased in the Manifesto of Futurist Painting in this way: 'The gesture which we would reproduce on canvas shall no longer be a fixed *moment* in universal dynamism. It shall simply be the *dynamic sensation* itself. Indeed, all things move, all things run, all things are rapidly changing.'[8] Lewis too was familiar with Bergson's philosophy, and had attended his lectures in Paris, presumably before returning to England in 1908.

Lewis, having observed the provocative and successful movement around Marinetti, proceeded to turn out a similar strategy for himself and his friends. The Rebel Art Centre opened its doors, in Great Ormond Street, after the group around Roger Fry and the Omega Workshops had broken up. A friend of Lewis's, the painter Kate Lechmere, had approached him with the idea in the first place. She supplied the money for the rent and other expenses, and officiated as director and business manager. Other founding members were Etchells, Wadsworth, Nevinson and Hamilton. The painters Helen Saunders and Jessica Dismorr joined shortly afterwards. Pound, a good friend of Lewis's, lent his full support to the new undertaking. He gave lectures in the Great Ormond Street premises on the relationship of his own movement in poetry, Imagism, to this new departure in art. He introduced his fellow-poet Richard Aldington to the Rebel Art Centre. The photographer Malcolm Arbuthnot and the painters Lawrence Atkinson and William Roberts found their way to the Centre in the same manner. The original concept, set out in its prospectus, envisaged the Centre as a place that could 'by public discussion, lectures and gatherings of people … familiarise those who are interested with the ideas of the great modern revolution in Art.'[9] The Centre was to serve as workshop–studio, meeting place, exhibition rooms and lecture hall, and as a place for painting classes.

The organizational abilities of the membership left a great deal to be desired, however, and all those active in the Centre, especially Lewis, were careful to attend to their own personal concerns. Lewis's overbearing personality and irascible temper, although somewhat alleviated by his undeniable charm, brilliant intellect and energy, came to be more and more of a drag on the organization, then and later. Under such circumstances, the overall harmonious atmosphere necessary for the pursuit of a common set of goals was not possible. Internal rivalries were the order of the day. It was for these reasons that some artists, Epstein and Bomberg among them, kept their distance from the group and did not let Lewis draw them into it, even though they were completely in agreement with the Vorticists on many points, and held many opinions in common with them. Bomberg in fact worked in a Vorticist vein, as can be seen in such paintings as *The Mud Bath* (plate xx), *Ju-Jitsu* (fig.19) and *In the Hold* (plate xii). Some of the most daring works ever produced in the Vorticist manner are his, although he never considered

himself a Vorticist. The only successful event that the Rebel
Art Centre did bring off was a collective exhibit of designs
for interior decoration that formed part of the Allied Artists'
Association salon of June 1914. The Centre closed at the end
of July 1914, a few months after it had opened. Lewis and his
circle had not managed to recruit enough new members and
students.

The Rebel Art Centre was an important milestone on the road
to the establishment of the original and independent movement in art that would be known as Vorticism. Vorticism was
able to bring into sharper focus its goals and ideas when,
during 1913 and 1914, people earnestly discussed whether one
should enter this or that alliance, which particular comrade-
in-arms was to be considered unsuitable, and so on. The break
with Marinetti was typical of what went on. Nevinson and
Marinetti collaborated on a manifesto in the Futurist style
that was published in some of the London newspapers in June
1914. This manifesto, entitled 'Vital English Art. Futurist
Manifesto', bore the address of the Rebel Art Centre. It called
for 'Art that is strong, virile and anti-sentimental'. The two
authors named a number of artists who they said were 'great
Futurist painters or pioneers and advance-forces of vital
English art'.[10] These were Atkinson, Bomberg, Epstein,
Etchells, Hamilton, Nevinson, Roberts, Wadsworth and
Lewis. Those artists, however, had not been asked whether
they considered themselves Futurists, or whether they were
in agreement with Marinetti's views.

Lewis in particular objected violently to being included
as part of Continental Futurism, and promptly set about
quarrelling with Marinetti. In his autobiography, *Blasting and
Bombardiering*, published in 1937, he described, referring to
some debate with Marinetti, the basic distinction between
Futurism and the newer movement then in the process of
formation. The Italians, he claimed, were too fixated on the
machine, and machines had long since ceased to be a novelty
in England. He said that in their obsession with speed, the
Futurists tended to lose sight of individual elements of the
scene, and perceived only a sort of kaleidoscopic blur. The
conflict culminated in this outcry, a quotation by Lewis from
Charles Baudelaire, who wrote in his poem, 'Les Chats', in
Les Fleurs du Mal: 'Je hais le mouvement qui déplace les
lignes.'[11] While it is true that the Italian Futurists drew on
the realm of technology for their subjects and on modern life
in general, they used the artistic idiom of Impressionism.
(Ezra Pound described Futurism as 'an accelerated sort of
impressionism'.[12]) The Vorticists, on the other hand, were
more interested in a formal vocabulary to best express the
spirit and feeling of the modern machine age. They called for
sharp edges, machine-like precision, efficiency, clarity, and
economy of artistic means.

Unlike the Futurists, the Vorticists sought the very centre

2 Wyndham Lewis, cover of *Blast* no.1, 1914

of the hurricane, the quiet eye of the storm, from which point
they could concentrate on the chaos raging around them, and
control it. The Vorticists brought all their energies to bear on
this point. 'At the heart of the whirlpool is a great silent place
where all the energy is concentrated. And there, at the point
of concentration, is the Vorticist.'[13] Pound said, 'The vortex
is the point of maximum energy'.[14] He had first used the
expression 'vortex' on 19 December 1913 in a letter to a
friend, the poet William Carlos Williams, to describe the
London artistic and literary scene. The idea of the vortex and
its use as a label for the artistic movement were first explicitly
discussed and given definite meaning in the original issue of
the journal *Blast*. This, the Vorticist journal, was first
announced on the back cover of the periodical *The Egoist* in
April of 1914, where the world learned that the new publication would appear on 15 July under the title *BLAST:
Review of the Great English Vortex*. The title was meant to
bear its ancillary meaning of 'to damn'. Its publication was
celebrated at a large *Blast* dinner that was intended to enforce
group spirit and hold the members together as much as to hail
the appearance of the new journal.

Lewis functioned as editor of *Blast*, wrote various articles
and manifestos for it, and was responsible for its general
appearance and typography. The title *Blast*, appeared
resplendent and diagonal on the puce cover (fig.2),

BLAST First (from politeness) **ENGLAND**

CURSE ITS CLIMATE FOR ITS SINS AND INFECTIONS

DISMAL SYMBOL, SET round our bodies,
of effeminate lout within.

VICTORIAN VAMPIRE, the LONDON cloud sucks
the TOWN'S heart.

A 1000 MILE LONG, 2 KILOMETER Deep

BODY OF WATER even, is pushed against us
from the Floridas, TO MAKE US MILD.

OFFICIOUS MOUNTAINS keep back DRASTIC WINDS

SO MUCH VAST MACHINERY TO PRODUCE

THE CURATE of "Eltham"
BRITANNIC ÆSTHETE
WILD NATURE CRANK
DOMESTICATED
                    POLICEMAN
LONDON COLISEUM
    SOCIALIST-PLAYWRIGHT
DALY'S MUSICAL COMEDY
GAIETY CHORUS GIRL
TONKS

BLAST HUMOUR

Quack ENGLISH drug for stupidity and sleepiness.
Arch enemy of REAL, conventionalizing like
                    gunshot, freezing supple
                    REAL in ferocious chemistry
                    of laughter.

BLAST SPORT

HUMOUR'S FIRST COUSIN AND ACCOMPLICE.

Impossibility for Englishman to be
    grave and keep his end up,
    psychologically.
Impossible for him to use Humour
    as well and be persistently
    grave.
Alas! necessity for big doll's show
    in front of mouth.
Visitation of Heaven on
    English Miss
gums, canines of **FIXED GRIN**
Death's Head symbol of Anti-Life.

CURSE those who will hang over this
Manifesto with SILLY CANINES exposed.

3 Page from *Blast* no. 1

4 Page from *Blast* no. 1

'screaming'.[15] The trim size was 12½ by 9½ inches (30.5 x 24 cm), large for a magazine, and the paper was thick and crude. Its most unusual feature, however, was the spectacular and imaginative typography used for the two manifestos that take up the first forty-three pages (see figs 3–6). The type on these pages was organized vertically as well as horizontally, and in varying point sizes. Crudely cut capital letters, also in various sizes, embellished every page. Each page was distinguished from the next by the stark contrast of large, full-bodied black type separated by gaping white spaces. El Lissitzky, writing later (after 1926), saw in the design of *Blast* a predecessor of the New Typography, which revolutionized graphic design in the 1920s and 1930s. Even when one realizes that the typography of *Blast* was clearly inspired by Guillaume Apollinaire's manifesto 'L'Antitradizione Futurista', which appeared in the journal *Lacerba* in 1913, and Marinetti's *Zang Tumb Tumb* of 1914, these bold sans serif capitals still give *Blast* a striking appearance and make of every page an abstract composition.

The first of the two manifestos in the first issue, 'Manifesto – I' is, despite its title, not a manifesto in the real sense of the word. It is more of a playful list of statements, names and

ideas, arranged under two headings, 'Blast' and 'Bless'. There seems to be no clearly recognizable system or context to either. Lewis damns England for its climate, consigns France to hell, curses Britain's aesthetes with the same energy as he curses its amateurs, its humour and sport, the years 1837–1900, the Post Office, Edward Elgar and the Bishop of London. Under the heading 'Bless', he praises England for its ships and all its harbours, and blesses its constantly busy machines, the institution of the hairdresser, English humour (citing Swift and Shakespeare as its main examples), Charlotte Corday, James Joyce and the Pope, various boxers and well-known London music-hall singers.

But if one looks closely at the two lists, the general orientation of the Vorticists becomes clear. England is damned for its mild climate, which produces only weaklings and waverers. Nordic blizzards build character. This desire for a bracing climate is of course easily translated into cultural terms, and serves as a metaphor for the cultural situation of the island. England is praised for its harbours, ships and seamen, which maintain connections with other countries and so guarantee a certain internationalism. The ocean is seen as a 'vast planetary abstraction'. The mechanisms and equipment

1

BLESS ENGLAND !

BLESS ENGLAND

FOR ITS SHIPS

which switchback on **Blue, Green** and
Red SEAS all around the **PINK
EARTH-BALL,**

BIG BETS ON EACH.

BLESS ALL SEAFARERS.

THEY exchange not one **LAND** for another, but one **ELEMENT**
for **ANOTHER.** The **MORE** against the **LESS ABSTRACT.**

BLESS the vast planetary abstraction of the **OCEAN.**

BLESS THE ARABS OF THE **ATLANTIC.**
THIS ISLAND MUST BE CONTRASTED WITH THE BLEAK WAVES.

22

3

BLESS ENGLISH HUMOUR

It is the great barbarous weapon of
the genius among races.
The wild **MOUNTAIN RAILWAY** from **IDEA**
to **IDEA,** in the ancient Fair of **LIFE.**

BLESS SWIFT for his solemn bleak
wisdom of laughter.

SHAKESPEARE for his bitter Northern
Rhetoric of humour.

BLESS ALL ENGLISH EYES
that grow crows-feet with their
FANCY and **ENERGY.**

BLESS this hysterical **WALL** built round
the **EGO.**

BLESS the solitude of **LAUGHTER.**

BLESS the separating, ungregarious
BRITISH GRIN.

26

5 Page from *Blast* no. 1

6 Page from *Blast* no. 1

of the harbours, especially the technically advanced apparatus, serve to distinguish Britain from other countries.

The ironic elements of the manifestos are revealed in its two opposing treatments of humour. On the one hand, humour is condemned as 'Quack English drug for stupidity and sleepiness', on the other it is praised when it comes in the form of sardonic English wit, which can be used as a weapon against foreigners. Humour, as an indication of fantasy and energy, produces laughter and the 'British Grin'. It is important not to take this manifesto with dogged literalness, without perceiving the underlying irony.

While the first manifesto contains a good deal of disguised nonsense, its casual, mocking tone gives way to a more serious note in the second. Here is where we find the Vorticist programme clearly set out, with its list of demands and the signatures of those making them. As well as Lewis himself, ten artists and writers associate themselves with this manifesto: Aldington, Arbuthnot, Atkinson, Gaudier-Brzeska, Dismorr, Hamilton, Pound, Roberts, Saunders and Wadsworth. In euphoric mood, they declare their allegiance to the modern. The artist of the modern movement is, however, a 'savage', and 'this enormous, jangling, journalistic,

fairy desert of modern life serves him as Nature did more technically primitive man', and his 'Art-instinct is permanently primitive'.[16] England is condemned for its class society, its indifference to art, its luxury, its love of sport, and its sense of humour. But at the same time, these unfavourable features of national life provide the right conditions for 'the appearance of a great art'. The 'northern flower' must remove itself from Paris, the metropolis of art gone soft, by dint of its own Nordic nature, and stand up for a proper English art. 'The English Character is based on the Sea.... That unexpected universality as well, found in the completest English artists, is due to this.'[17] The modern world is shaped by the industrial process, which is the main subject of Vorticist art. But the Vorticists note as well the uncontrolled growth of industry, which has effects more 'savage' than those of nature. 'Machinery is the greatest Earth-Medium', and everything that outwardly defines the age – machines, railways, steamships – derives mainly from England. Technology has created a new Nature surrounding humanity. Now it is up to Art to keep up with this revolutionary step forward.[18]

The Vorticists were vehement in their opposition to sentimentalism and romanticism; they favoured the ideas of energy, purity, clarity of thought, hardness and power. This cool detachment placed the mechanical and geometric ahead of the organic and the naturalistic. The efficiency and clarity of the machine, in the Vorticist view of things, were to provide the example for the artist and his work, which were to be at the same time dynamic, unyielding and rigid. The metaphor of the machine provided the Vorticists with the definitive vocabulary of their own artistic idiom. T. E. Hulme summarized these ideas as follows:

> There is ... a desire [among modern artists] to avoid those lines and surfaces which look pleasing and organic, and to use lines which are clean, clear-cut and mechanical. You will find artists expressing admiration for engineer's drawings, where the lines are clean, the curves all geometrical, and the colour, laid on to show the shape of a cylinder for example, gradated absolutely mechanically.[19]

The tone of the manifestos is polemical and aggressive, although the style is well crafted, and in certain parts ironic and bizarre. Other contributions in the first issue of *Blast* include poems by Ezra Pound; *Enemy of the Stars*, a one-act play by Lewis; fiction by Ford Madox Hueffer (later Ford Madox Ford) and Rebecca West; detailed discussion and a partial translation by Wadsworth of Wassily Kandinsky's *On the Spiritual in Art*; brief essays by Lewis on contemporary art under the general title 'Vortices and Notes'; a message of solidarity to the militant feminists, combined with the request that they spare any works of art they might come across in the course of their attacks on society's institutions; and programmatic essays by Pound and Gaudier-Brzeska on their understanding of the Vortex. The journal was copiously illustrated with Vorticist art by Wadsworth, Lewis, Etchells, Roberts, Epstein, Gaudier-Brzeska and Hamilton. There was also something not quite in keeping with the rest of the contents, a memorial to the painter Frederick Spencer Gore, who had died shortly before the appearance of the first issue. Most of the pictures that appeared in that issue no longer exist, or their whereabouts are unknown. It is the same with many other Vorticist works. One can have an idea of the scale and importance of the movement only when one considers how many of the paintings, especially the large ones, have been lost. Richard Cork, author of *Vorticism and Abstract Art in the First Machine Age*, estimates that roughly half the work of the Vorticists no longer exists.

The second issue of *Blast*, scheduled for October 1914, was deferred by the outbreak of the First World War in August 1914, and did not appear until July the following year. This issue was called a 'War Number' (fig. 7). While the first issue, which had appeared just before the beginning of hostilities, was loud, witty and stimulating, the second was a great deal

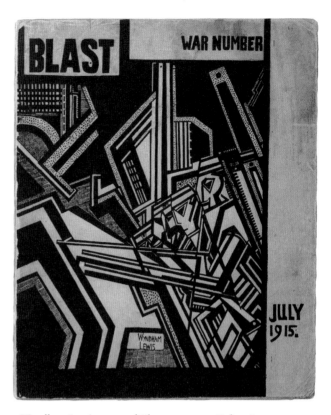

7 Wyndham Lewis, cover of *Blast* no. 2, 1915: *Before Antwerp*

less striking. The sand-coloured cover bore an angular wood-cut based on a sketch by Lewis of three soldiers, rifles at the ready, in a severely abstract composition, *Before Antwerp*. There was no programmatic material at all, and the 'Blast' and 'Bless' lists were reduced to two pages, printed in the conventional way. Only one of the contributions kept up the programmatic tone of the first issue: a piece from the Front by Henri Gaudier-Brzeska bearing the title 'Vortex Gaudier-Brzeska'. The announcement of Gaudier's death appears directly after this contribution; he had been killed near Neuville-Saint-Vaast on 5 June. T. S. Eliot made his first appearance in the pages of *Blast* with a series of poems. This issue makes up for its lack of striking textual material with numerous woodcuts and other illustrations that embody the Vorticist ideals of severity and geometrical clarity. Illustrations by Jacob Kramer, Dismorr, Nevinson, Saunders and Dorothy Shakespear appear for the first time in this second issue.

But *Blast* had come to an end; a third issue, planned for after the Armistice, never appeared. It was only in June 1915, a month before publication of the second issue, that the first exclusively Vorticist exhibition had opened, in the Doré Galleries in London. The last was to be in 1917, in the Penguin Club, New York, organized by Ezra Pound and John Quinn. Lewis wrote in his editorial to *Blast* no. 2: 'BLAST finds itself surrounded by a multitude of other Blasts of all sizes and descriptions…. The art of Pictures, the Theatre, Music, etc., has to spring up again with new questions and beauties when Europe has disposed of its difficulties.'[20] But a solution to these problems did not appear for quite some time, and afterwards Europe was not the same. The war had wrought fundamental changes in the European character and in the thinking of European intellectuals. Artistic life had practically come to a standstill during the war, and the spirit of the pre-war avant garde had simply not survived. The artists who returned from the war found that the movement no longer existed.

Lewis himself was ill, and so preoccupied with his novel *Tarr* while *Blast* no. 2 was in preparation that he completely missed the scheduled publication date. His personal goals had taken precedence over the interests of the group. He volunteered for the army in March 1916, and at the end of 1917 was appointed Official War Artist at Canadian Corps headquarters. He became part of a new and unusual art programme under the British Ministry of Information and the Canadian War Records Office. During the war years the programme took on almost all British artists of note, including members of the radical avant garde such as Lewis himself, Bomberg, Nevinson, Etchells, Roberts and Wadsworth.[21] The projects were especially uncommon in that they enlisted members purely in their capacity as artists, and sent them to the fighting as trained visual observers and analysts. The original aim of the programme was to bring back from the front pictorial documentary material for information and for propaganda purposes. With the passage of time, however, the projects changed, existing simply in order to encourage artists in their work. Commissions continued to be issued even after the war ended. Many of the works went into the collection of the Imperial War Museum in London. We have these war-art projects to thank for the preservation of some Vorticist paintings such as *A Battery Shelled* by Lewis (plate XXII) and Bomberg's *Sappers at Work*. The problem that arose in connection with these commissioned works is plain to see: some sort of compromise had to be found between the requirements of the official body that ordered the work, and the artist's own radical ideas. The first version of *Sappers at Work* (fig.8) was in fact rejected.

Since the Vorticists, unlike the declared pacifists of the Bloomsbury Group, regarded themselves from the very beginning as belligerents as well as artists, it comes as no surprise that a great many of them spent time at the Front, as volunteers or as conscripts, for shorter or longer periods. Gaudier-Brzeska and T.E.Hulme volunteered enthusiastically at the outbreak of war, and both died in battle, Gaudier-Brzeska in 1915 and Hulme in 1917. Others in uniform were Lewis, Nevinson, Wadsworth, Bomberg, Roberts, Hamilton, and Epstein. Of the ten male signatories of the Vorticist

8 David Bomberg, *Sappers at Work: A Canadian Tunnelling Company (First Version)*, 1918–19, oil on canvas, 3042 x 2438 mm (119¾ x 96 in)

manifesto of 1914, six took part in the war and four remained behind in London. Pound, a US citizen, was exempted from military service in Britain. It fell upon him to represent the interests of the Vorticists on the home front. He did in fact publish a geat many articles, reviews and essays on individual artists and on the Vorticist movement in general. But in the summer of 1916 he complained: 'I appear to be the only person of interest left in the world of art, London.'[22] And T.S.Eliot wrote, 'The Vorticists are non-existent.'[23] The pre-war avant garde, which had swept all before it with such effervescent energy, itself lay in pieces. The aesthetic war that it had foreseen and called for, and which had been waged on the battlefield of art, had become bleak, terrible reality on the world stage.

For the Futurist Nevinson, the war came as a sort of fulfilment. Through his war work he was able to extricate himself from Futurist doctrine and find his own style. A one-man show of his war pictures was held in the Leicester Galleries in September 1916. These paintings represented an important new direction in the portrayal of war. Nevinson had found a way to represent the mechanical and inhuman nature of modern industrial warfare. His marching soldiers, for example, are actually machines (plate XXIII).

Most of the Vorticist artists, with the exceptions of Atkinson and Hamilton, shared a tendency to return to a more traditional, representational style to convey the experience of war, rather than an abstract rendering. This later came to be regarded as an artistic step backwards. The extreme means of expression of the modern movement were not applicable to the horrors of war, could not appropriately overcome the terror of modern warfare, were not fitting means to assimilate 'real' experience and comment on it artistically. These artists, Lewis most of all, had over-subscribed to the rhetoric of aggression and the glorification of energy, that had now become obsolete faced with the real barbarity of a modern battlefield. Ezra Pound once accurately characterized Lewis in this way: 'He is a man at war.'[24] The ideals of energy, aggression and strength, once considered fitting attributes for 'modern life' in the new industrial world, had now to be re-examined in the light of the advanced weapons and techniques of war – machine-guns, tanks, more efficient bombs and shells.

This problem was made especially clear in Gaudier-Brzeska's piece called 'Vortex', written while he was in the trenches, which appeared posthumously in *Blast* no. 2.

I have made an experiment. Two days ago I pinched from an enemy a mauser rifle. Its heavy unwieldy shape swamped me with a powerful IMAGE of brutality.

I was in doubt for a long time whether it pleased or displeased me.

I found that I did not like it.

I broke the butt off and with my knife I carved in it a design, through which I tried to express a gentler order of feeling, which I preferred.[25]

The artist's eye, which goes on functioning even amidst the danger of the trenches, continues to look at things objectively, without emotion, from an aesthetic standpoint: 'I SHALL DERIVE MY EMOTIONS SOLELY FROM THE ARRANGEMENT OF SURFACES'.[26] This artist's eye now comes into question, because the artist understands that he does not like the main function of this deadly implement of war, the rifle, in spite of its mechanical character. The rifle must be transformed into an *objet d'art*.

It is true that Epstein was able to take a boring-machine direct and unaltered from the manufacturer and integrate it into his sculpture, *Rock Drill* (figs 44, 47). But he later distanced himself from this work, and destroyed it, acknowledging only the mutilated torso of the robot-like figure. The discrepancy between art and life had become too great for him. Unlike Marinetti and the Italian Futurists, the Vorticists were unable to fall under the spell of the destructive energy of mechanized war. They were too close to the reality of war to idealize or overdramatize it. Their breakdown as a group, and the silence of individual artists following the Armistice, are certainly to be traced back to the experience of war.

But precisely at this point, when the Vorticists were beginning to doubt whether their own artistic ways were altogether appropriate, their former critics encouraged them to continue in that direction. Who else, the reasoning went, would communicate to the civilian population the utterly alien and alienating landscape of the battlefield? The war had brought into being a new reality, and this demanded a new means of expression. At the same time, the type of representation required must provide a moral picture, a new sort of metaphor for the horrors of war. Only a distorted and alien means of expression could adequately express that horror. These artistic means were nothing new; they had been anticipated in the experimental art of the pre-war era. Now, in response to a new moral situation, these means were being used as a form of protest against the war.[27] Not the modern movement, but reality itself, had changed.

Artists had approached pure abstraction on the road to *Blast* nos 1 and 2 only with hesitation. Many of the works of these artists had for their starting-point the human form, in varying degrees of abstraction. Anthropomorphic, robotic forms from the world of the big cities, the harbours, industry and machinery, were frequent subjects. It was often left to the title of the work to arouse concrete and specific associations. Complete abstraction, which had been attained in a few Vorticist works around 1914, had been rudely interrupted by the war. Lewis wrote later:

The War, of course, had robbed me of four years, at the moment when, almost overnight, I had achieved the necessary notoriety to establish myself in London as a painter. It also caught me before I was quite through with my training. And although in the 'post-war' I was not starting from nothing, I had to some extent to begin all over again.[28]

The great dilemma of the art of the modern era, of the entire twentieth century in fact, lies in the constantly shifting to-and-fro struggle for predominance between abstraction and illustration, between pure form and literal representation. This conflict was particularly plain in the vision and experiments of the Vorticists. That they never lost sight of the human dimension may be a reflection of what is called the realistic, pragmatic side of the English national character. Artistically, the tendency towards concrete, conventional representation in the war scenes, especially after the war, is usually taken as a backward step. From the human point of view, this step is to be considered somewhat more sympathetically, and as one that takes some of the arrogant sting out of Lewis's biting polemical rhetoric of the pre-war years.

It is, however, important to note that there had been in England before the War a successful approach to abstraction. It is equally important to recognize that this episode in English art, if brief, was original and completely independent of outside influence, and that it occurred at the same time as similar developments in the great centres of European art, Paris, Munich, Berlin and Milan. Its critical acumen, exercised in the interpretation of the technologized industrial world and the mechanized war, with its power to dehumanize through danger, raised the Vorticists well above the Futurists'

anarchistic shouting and reflexive adoration of the machine and speed. The Vorticists were well aware of the alienating tendencies inherent in the machine; their view of the urban landscape was coolly analytical rather than euphoric. The chances were good that a real driving force in English art could have emerged from this circle of committed modern artists. But the outbreak of the First World War put an abrupt end to that endeavour. The mechanical barbarity of the war far exceeded all the worst fears of the Vorticists. Faced with the reality of the war, in which some of them fought, they saw that the world had changed in a basic way. In 1920 Wyndham Lewis declared Vorticism officially dead.

Rebels and Vorticists: 'Our Little Gang'[1]

ANDREW WILSON

The Vorticist movement is a movement of individuals, for individuals, for the protection of individuality. Humanity has been interesting, more interesting than the rest of the animal kingdom because the individual has been more easily discernible from the herd. The idiosyncracy is more salient.[2]

Blast presents an art of Individuals.[3]

Vorticism has always been a difficult movement to characterize. Dismissive of the crowd – personal identity lost in the face of massed unity – both Ezra Pound and Wyndham Lewis portrayed the Vorticist artist as a heroic individualist. The artists who found a home at the Rebel Art Centre in the spring of 1914 and between the pages of the first issue of *Blast* that June were a grouping of like-minded, yet strong-willed individuals. Even so, many of these artists had only just left art college and were open to influence; a point that the rapidly evolving nature of their work confirms. Contradictions abound when one is confronted by Vorticism, both in theory and practice. Its theoretical base can often seem at first reading to be either vague or esoteric, allegiances and influences become targets of enmity and vitriol and, furthermore, today it has become difficult, with so many major paintings having disappeared, even to reconstruct an accurate account of its history.[4]

Nevertheless, although Vorticism was indeed 'a movement of individuals', for a little over two years those individuals – Jessica Dismorr, Frederick Etchells, Henri Gaudier-Brzeska, William Roberts, Helen Saunders, Edward Wadsworth and Wyndham Lewis along with, variously, T.E. Hulme and Ezra Pound, Lawrence Atkinson, David Bomberg, Alvin Langdon Coburn, Jacob Epstein, Cuthbert Hamilton, Kate Lechmere, C.R.W. Nevinson and Dorothy Shakespear – succeeded in constructing a hard and coherent modernist vision that was quite distinct from the verdant and comforting bohemianism of the Bloomsbury painters, from the 'nature-mortism' of the Cubists and the 'automobilist' empty machine-fetishism of the Italian Futurists, each of which were, in their own way, 'Blasted' by Lewis and his compatriots. Although the 'Vortex' metaphor had been used by Pound as early as 1908 (the year

before he first met Lewis) in his poem 'Plotinus',[5] its use as a means of labelling Lewis and his cohorts as 'Vorticists' occurred rather late in the day in early June 1914,[6] shortly before *Blast*'s publication, as a means of proclaiming their identity as one that was different from Futurism.

Futurism first made its mark in England in 1910 when, in March, April and December Marinetti lectured at the Lyceum Club for Women in London[7] and was published in English for the first time in Douglas Goldring's magazine *The Tramp*.[8] A little over a year later these rather theatrical and publicity-seeking events were followed by the 'Italian Futurist Painters' exhibition at the Sackville Gallery in March 1912 that went on to spawn an exhibition of Gino Severini at the Marlborough Gallery in April 1913, Frank Rutter's 'Post-Impressionist and Futurist' exhibition in October 1913 at the Doré Galleries, and the 'Futurist Painters and Sculptors' exhibition also at the Doré Galleries between April and June 1914. Throughout this period Marinetti continued to give startling lectures which assured the Futurists a sensationalist stream of publicity which characterized their work at first as 'The New Terror',[9] until by 1914 almost anything that was challenging to contemporary orthodoxy or in any way perceived as new would be described as 'futurist'.

More to the point, however, was the effect that this polemical assault had on artists such as Lewis, coming, as it did, hot on the heels of exhibitions which had only just introduced Britain to Roger Fry's catch-all notion of Post-Impressionism. Framed by Fry's 'Manet and the Post-Impressionists' exhibition at the Grafton Galleries between November 1910 and January 1911 and the more international (in that it included British and Russian artists with the French) 'Second Post-Impressionist Exhibition' at the

Grafton Galleries between October 1912 and January 1913, the Post-Impressionists were characterized by Fry in 1910 as 'synthesists'[10] who were engaged in 'exploring and expressing that emotional significance which lies in things, and is the most important subject matter in art'.[11] To these ends he focused on the work of Cézanne, Gauguin and Van Gogh as artists who extended in different ways a reaction to the naturalism of Impressionism that was first registered in Manet's painting towards the end of his life. The work of Matisse, the only other artist to be mentioned in Fry's introduction, signalled a 'return to primitive, even perhaps of a return to barbaric, art…. Primitive art … consists not so much in an attempt to represent what the eye perceives, as to put a line round a mental conception of the object.'[12] Although Post-Impressionism could be explained through the simplification, also found in Oriental art, of the arrangement of vibrant flat colour surface, or in the more abstruse notion of 'sincerity to personal vision … in the place of sincerity to natural appearances',[13] it was Fry's grasp of the essentially conceptual nature of primitive art that acted as the greatest spur to artists such as Lewis. 'The Second Post-Impressionist Exhibition', in 1912, altered focus by drawing attention to 'contemporary development' instead of the 'old masters'. Fry typified the intentions of these artists as 'trying to find a pictorial language appropriate to the sensibilities of the modern outlook'.[14] Such vagueness continued throughout an introduction that gave an account of the creation by these artists 'of a new and definite reality'[15] in which they 'do not seek to imitate form, but to create form; not to imitate life, but to find an equivalent for life…. In fact they aim not at illusion but at reality,'[16] an aim that might even logically lead to the creation of a 'purely abstract language of form – a visual music'.[17] Clive Bell, in his introduction to 'The English Group', reiterated Fry's comments by marking the equation between 'significant form'[18] and an aesthetic disinterested 'emotion' which would become the subject of his book *Art*, published in 1914.

In its 'English Group' this second exhibition included a number of artists who would within the space of a little over a year and a half decisively distance themselves from such Bloomsbury theorizing. Lewis, the only one of this group named by Bell in his introduction, provided an exemplar of one type of Post-Impressionist artist who is 'certainly not descriptive',[19] and as such was at a distance from the Bloomsbury artists like Duncan Grant who were. Lewis's lost *Creation*, 1912,[20] or his drawings for *Timon of Athens*, 1912–13 (figs 9,13; plate II), reveal not only an awareness of Cubism that few of the other artists such as Etchells, Wadsworth or Hamilton could acknowledge in their pursuit of a Cézannism directed by Bell and Fry, but also a synthesis with Futurism; movement, within a narrative of ritual, is spatially structured.

9 Wyndham Lewis, cover of *Timon of Athens*, 1913, print, 387 x 272 mm (15¼ x 10¾ in)

The theorizing of Bell and Fry, with its talk of disinterested emotion, significant form and an unspecified new reality, was helpless when confronted by the histrionics of the Italian Futurists who extolled, in Marinetti's 'Initial Manifesto of Futurism', the virtues of

aggressive movement, feverish insomnia, the double quick step, the somersault, the box on the ear, the fisticuff.

We declare that the world's splendour has been enriched by a new beauty; the beauty of speed. A racing motor-car, its frame adorned with great pipes, like snakes with explosive breath: a roaring motor-car, which looks as though running on shrapnel, is more beautiful than the VICTORY OF SAMOTHRACE.

There is no more beauty except in strife. No masterpiece without aggressiveness.[21]

This document was reprinted in the catalogue to their 1912 Sackville Gallery exhibition along with the statement 'The Exhibitors to the Public' and the 'Manifesto of the Futurist

Painters'. This latter text codified and set out the concept of 'dynamism', which had only been alluded to in the 'Initial Manifesto', as the cornerstone of the Futurist aesthetic – its pictorial harnessing being the means by which their paean to Modernity could be freed from the past; 'The gesture which we would reproduce on canvas shall no longer be a fixed *moment* in universal dynamism. It shall simply be the dynamic sensation itself.... All is conventional in art. Nothing is absolute in painting. What was truth for the painters of yesterday is but a falsehood to-day.'[22]

Such Futurist rhetoric – more in touch with contemporary reality than Bloomsbury's Cézannism could ever be – would have been attractive to Lewis, as it was to a number of his contemporaries, and he was well prepared for it. Having left the Slade in 1901 Lewis had, until 1908, travelled extensively on the Continent – through Spain, France, Holland and Germany – at times in the company, variously, of Spencer Gore, Henry Lamb or Augustus John. Beyond Lewis's idolization of John and his adoption of John's image of the unconventional artist – large black hat and swagger – John was also, more fundamentally, instrumental in the transformation of Lewis from a Tonks-trained Slade student into an avant-garde artist who was able to assimilate the latest developments in painting. It was probably through John – who had visited Picasso's studio in the summer of 1907 and seen *Les Demoiselles d'Avignon*, 1907 – that Lewis first came into contact with the work of Picasso and Matisse.[23] However, by the time of Lewis's return to London he had turned on John, whose romantic bohemianism and invocation of a sentimental and idyllic fiction of pastoral life rendered him unsuitable not only as a guide to the recent work of Picasso but also as a model for an artist confronted by the modern urban reality praised by the Futurists.

As stimulating to Lewis was the world of philosophical thought that Paris opened up to him. Nietzsche, Georges Sorel, Charles Maurras and Henri Bergson all played a part in the formation of his artistic beliefs after his return to London. At some point during this period, probably 1903, Lewis, like T. E. Hulme later, became a 'Five o'clock Bergsonian'[24] and attended a number of Henri Bergson's influential public lectures at the Collège de France. By 1903 Bergson's popular reputation rested on his books *Time and Free Will* (1889), which held that the temporal dimension of human consciousness (duration) was synonymous with creative freedom, and *Matter and Memory* (1896) which applied those findings to an analysis of the relation of mind to body. His idealist notion of the 'vital impulse', the 'spring of life', the 'urge to create' was opposed to rationalism or voluntarism (reason or will) and especially to a mechanistic, structured and, to Bergson, a distorted view of life.

Despite Lewis's swift rejection, within a few years, of Bergsonian thought, its negative influence can be detected in his earliest writing that was later revised and collected as *The Wild Body*.[25] In these stories, and comparative drawings and paintings dating from 1912, can be detected an approach to image-construction and the position held by meaning and content that would mark out his own painting of the period, and the subsequent Vorticism, from the formalist structuring of the artists who followed Clive Bell's doctrine of significant form on a road towards abstraction, as much as away from the theatricality of Futurism. Although Lewis's early drawings of 1910–12 attest to the degree to which he had absorbed the formal lessons of primitive sculpture, he refused to submit to the portrayal of an idealized vision of primitive culture, such as Gauguin or John suggested. In the 'Wild Body' stories Lewis largely draws inspiration from the Norman and Breton country communities he passed through in his travels. The stories are peopled by animalistic figures that are depicted as raw, absurd and ultimately comic, engaged in carnivalesque, even pagan, ritual. Such people made obvious that split between mind and body registered in Bergson's vitalist philosophy. And yet, like puppets, they are slaves to those bodily urges over which they can exert no control, and this vitalism is observed and portrayed by Lewis in a detached, mechanistic way.

It is this stance that would become one of the organizing principles of Lewis's Vorticism. This equated the in-advisability of the merging of art and life with the loss of identity, just as when the human merges with the animal and the mind is split from the body. In this respect, Vorticism can be identified as vitalism controlled and stilled.[26] Furthermore, the 'Wild Body', amended to the Modern contemporary landscape, offered a continual subject for Lewis's Vorticism in which the identification of body with life delivers another sort of Body; a hard-edged, robotic manikin, part of the faceless unthinking crowd. Abstraction here is not the result of the formalization and simplification of a figurative motif but instead of its diagrammatic schematization, as Tom Normand has explained:

> Recognisable figures, acting in environments, gradually become absorbed into the pattern of the environment itself ... the figures are portrayed as abstract cyphers acting within an abstract environment.... The human grotesque, in the modern age, is viewed as a mechanical grotesque interacting with the environment after the manner of an absurd mechanistic dance.[27]

Throughout this process Lewis is not engaged in the formalist project of aesthetic disinterestedness but in one that is founded on a critical, intellectual detachment that is avowedly visual and spatially defined.

Lewis's rejection of Bergsonian thought in favour of the action of a detached, mechanistic intellect, and his awareness of both current philosophical thought and the artistic avant

10 Wyndham Lewis, *Creation*, 1912

11 Wyndham Lewis, *The Dancers (Study for 'Kermesse'?)*, 1912,
pen and watercolour on paper, 295 x 290 mm (11½ x 11½ in)

garde on the Continent, prepared him well for the effect of its reception in London between 1910 and 1912. For Lewis, as for many of his contemporaries, 1912 marks a turning point. *Sunset among the Michelangelos, c.*1912 (plate I), shows a group of grotesquely muscle-bound figures with minuscule heads, all body and no conscious mind, who are engaged in an ungraceful dance rooted within a landscape from which they cannot escape. Although the faceting and simplification of the forms of these figures and landscape bears little relationship to either Futurist or Cubist models, the implied attack on Michelangelo is all too Futurist.[28] Other works of this year such as *The Celibate*,[29] the lost *Creation* (fig.10), the various studies for *Kermesse* (fig.11) and the drawings for the *Timon of Athens*[30] portfolio all exhibit in one way or another the extension of the 'Wild Body' theme within a far more accomplished structural synthesis of Cubism and Futurism. *Kermesse*, and *Creation* with its fusion of animal and human naked bodies, takes Matisse's *Danse* and makes of it something unremittingly hard in which the head is lost to the ritual and the body becomes subsumed into nature by an all-encompassing geometry. This can also be observed in the designs executed in 1912 by Lewis for Frida Strindberg's Cabaret Theatre Club (fig.12).[31] Embodied in the *Timon* drawings exhibited, with *Creation*, at 'The Second Post-Impressionist Exhibition', is another, more involved, response to Futurism. In the portfolio Timon is typically shown as 'trapped within nature; his downfall is shown as a failure of consciousness. Timon's involvement in unconscious natural

life is a consequence of his lack of philosophical intelligence' (fig.13; plate 11),[32] and it was this failure of consciousness that Lewis discerned within the vitalist Futurist 'capture' of dynamism. Although the drawings evoke a Futurist simultaneity with no actual compositional centre, the eye moving in a dance from figure to figure, the notion of a Futurist dynamism is cut off by the insistent Cubist fracturing of space. Time, Bergson's 'duration', is here spatialized and cut up by the distorting mirror of Lewis's eye. Furthermore, Lewis, in a later study of Shakespearean tragic heroes, underlined the extent to which Timon was another form of Wild Body as 'a puppet, mechanically worked, and seeing nothing beyond his mechanism'.[33] In this respect the Shakespearean figure of Timon, as much as these drawings, represents a significant link between the drawings of 1911 and 1912 and the more abstract compositions of 1913 and 1914 that are related to the *Timon* project, such as *Composition* (plate III)[34] and *Timon of Athens* (plate IV), as well as *Portrait of an Englishwoman* (plate v), in which architecture and body are totally indistinguishable.

Despite this critical edge to his work, Lewis garnered praise for his paintings from both Clive Bell and Roger Fry. Characteristically Bell avoided the subject-matter of *Kermesse*, when it was exhibited at the Royal Albert Hall during the 1912 salon of the Allied Artists' Association, and expressed the ill-considered opinion that it should be judged by the viewer 'as he would judge music – that is to say, as pure formal expression. So judging, he cannot fail to be

12 Wyndham Lewis, *Abstract Design*, 1912, pen, watercolour and
    collage on paper, 240 x 390 mm (9½ x 15¼ in)

impressed by the solidity of the composition, to which the
colour is not an added charm, but of which it is an integral
part.'³⁵ Fry wrote more understandingly and singled out the
painting as 'the only thing that survives the ordeal of being
placed in such ample surroundings … [He] has built a design
which is tense and compact…. The rhythm is not merely
agreeable and harmonious, but definitively evocative of a
Dionysiac mood.'³⁶ As these assessments confirm, Lewis was
on good terms with Bell, Fry and the rest of the Bloomsbury
writers and artists, although his membership of the Camden
Town Group must have signalled that his allegiance was not
to their formalisms even if it was also at obvious variance
from the Camden Town Group's Impressionist-derived
recording of the city. Nevertheless, Bell had bought Lewis's
work, and at some point in 1913 Fry had accompanied Lewis
on a visit to Paris where they visited Gertrude Stein. In the
same year Lewis joined Fry's Omega Workshops before they
opened in July, to work on decorative commissions that
reflected Fry's evolving formalist theories carried out within
a communal environment. The earliest artists to join Omega
were drawn from the five members of the Grafton Group
(Fry, Vanessa Bell, Etchells, Grant and Lewis) and those
who were invited to exhibit with them in the group's first
exhibition at the Alpine Club with Kandinsky³⁷ and Max
Weber (Jessica Etchells, Winifred Gill, Gore, Hamilton and
Wadsworth), and the net was spread wider soon after. Lewis,
who had made a reputation with his contribution to the
decorations of the Cabaret Theatre Club the previous year,
found himself unhappily adapting his vision to approximate
Bloomsbury style – a state of affairs that the guarantee of
30 shillings a week did little to alleviate.

   Of the earliest group of artists at Omega, Lewis had been at
the Slade with Cuthbert Hamilton and had collaborated with
him at the Cabaret Theatre Club, while Frederick Etchells
and Edward Wadsworth had both only recently left the Slade.
Although Wadsworth had assisted Fry in his restoration of

13 Wyndham Lewis, *Timon of Athens: Timon*, 1913, print,
    387 x 272 mm (15¼ x 10¾ in)

the Mantegna cartoons at Hampton Court in 1912 he was
increasingly drawn towards the aesthetics of Futurism,
echoing, as they did, his own background in Yorkshire where
his family owned a worsted-spinning business. In 1913 his
painting moved from the decorative Cubist simplicity of
paintings that convey a languid pastoral impression, such as
(Reflections in Water) Pool with Trees and Punt (plate VI) or
Trees beside River, to the lost painting *L'Omnibus* (fig.14) in
which the stillness of the earlier paintings is fractured by the
movement of a bus through a resolutely sharply edged urban
landscape reminiscent of Severini.

   Etchells, who had left the Royal College of Art in 1911, was
considered by Fry to be touched, like Duncan Grant, with
genius,³⁸ and his early work, such as *The Dead Mole*, 1912,
stands as a catalogue of Post-Impressionist influence. Vestigial
signs of Cézanne, Van Gogh and Matisse can all be located in
this painting, along with a use of colour that moves from the
early pointillism of Matisse to full-blooded Fauvism. The
eccentric stiffness of the figure drawing points towards
Etchells's interest in the work of the Italian Quattrocento, and

14 Edward Wadsworth, *L'Omnibus*, 1913

15 Cuthbert Hamilton, *Group*, c.1913

instead of achieving a synthesis of styles, he is content merely by their juxtaposition. However, paintings like this do provide evidence of his independence from Bloomsbury despite his having worked with Fry (and lived near him in Surrey) and, as Richard Cork has pointed out, it was 'only when he rejected the patronage of Bloomsbury in favour of Lewis's more militant cause did his art manage to fulfil its most uncompromising leanings'.[39]

It would not take long for this to happen. Within the Omega organization Etchells, Wadsworth, Hamilton and Lewis identifiably moved away from the Bloomsbury notion of Post-Impressionism founded in Cézanne and Matisse, and towards the creation of a non-figurative and, apparently, non-referential idiom. That this was created within the context of decorative design offers some pointer to the extent to which they were all, ultimately, not only distrustful of the value of complete non-figuration in their own painting (later, as Vorticists, the majority of their paintings still carried a figurative basis), but also of the theoretical basis of Omega itself, founded as it was on the marriage of a disinterested aesthetic formalism and the values of C. R. Ashbee and the Arts and Crafts movement. These differences erupted over a commission from the *Daily Mail* to design a room decoration at the 1913 Ideal Home Exhibition, as described in the Introduction, above, p.12.

That the public display of acrimony and ill-will in the Round Robin denouncing the Omega's aesthetic outlook was strategic can hardly be denied. Lewis's aesthetic position was so far removed from that of Bloomsbury that such a parting of the ways was inevitable, and the Ideal Home Exhibition provided just the excuse that Lewis needed. An indication of how far Lewis had moved away from Omega can be gauged when one compares the surviving photographs of Lewis's decoration for Lady Drogheda's London house (December 1913–February 1914) with comparative work being carried out by Omega. Omega's bright, colourful, eclectic whimsies attempted to bring a fictional country pastoral, in the guise of bundles of flowers and fruit, into city drawing-rooms. Such a goal could hardly be discerned in Lewis's stark, darkly urban, totemic geometries and clashing colours.[40]

The rift with Omega was emphasized that same October by Frank Rutter's 'Post-Impressionist and Futurist Exhibition' at the Doré Galleries. Although the exhibition was broad ranging, Fry, Vanessa Bell and Grant were not included, while paintings by Lewis, Wadsworth, Hamilton (fig.15), Etchells and C. R. W. Nevinson amply justified the use of the term 'Futurist' in the exhibition's title even though no work by the Italians artists was included either. The contribution made by these five artists to the exhibition was recognized by Rutter when he singled them out in his foreword: 'That "cubism"

16 C.R.W. Nevinson, *The Departure of the Train de Luxe*, c.1913

and "futurism" have already stirred English artists is shown
by the contributions of Mr Wyndham Lewis, Mr Wadsworth,
Mr Nevinson and others'.[41]

For this exhibition Etchells contributed a number of recent
paintings and drawings of heads that exhibited a strong
Cubist faceting, while among the work Lewis exhibited
Kermesse and *Creation* were fast becoming icons of the nature
of his rebellion from the domination of Bloomsbury
aesthetics.[42] However, it was Futurism, excluded from 'The
Second Post-Impressionist Exhibition' for having evolved,
as was described by Fry, from a 'misapprehension of some
of Picasso's recondite and difficult works',[43] that was
particularly disliked by Bloomsbury and was gaining
affection among the rebels. The juxtaposition of Nevinson's
Waiting for the Robert E. Lee, c.1913, and *The Departure of
the Train de Luxe* (fig.16) with Wadsworth's *L'Omnibus*[44]
would have underlined the strength of these artists' detachment from the Bloomsbury notion of Post-Impressionism as
well as emphasizing the direct nature of the influence that the
Italian Futurists, and most specifically Severini, had exerted
on them.

When Nevinson left the Slade in 1912 and moved to Paris
he renewed an earlier acquaintance with Severini (in London
the most popular of the Italian Futurists) and, according to
his autobiography, formed a friendship with him and

Modigliani. He also met Boccioni, Kisling, Derain, Soffici and
Lenin, describing the latter as 'a revolutionary of some sort …
a cranky extremist'.[45] Quite apart from being an overt homage
to the paintings of Severini, the two paintings by Nevinson
exhibited at the Doré Galleries also encapsulated two of the
main Futurist subjects. The vigour and action of the modern
crowd acting as one body, about which Marinetti had proclaimed, 'We shall sing of the great crowds in the excitement
of labour, pleasure or rebellion',[46] was represented in *Waiting
for the Robert E. Lee*. Similarly *The Departure of the Train de
Luxe* portrayed the drama and action of the speeding modern
railway, described by Marinetti as 'greedy stations swallowing
smoking snakes … broad-chested locomotives prancing on
the rails, like huge steel horses bridled with long tubes',[47]
as the static geometries of both the cityscape and its Cubist
portrayal are fragmented into vectors of dynamism and force.

The following month the identification with Futurism of
the three artists – Etchells, Hamilton and Wadsworth – who
now clustered around Lewis was made clearer when, following Nevinson's invitation for Marinetti to give a series of
lectures in London,[48] they celebrated this event by organizing,
with Nevinson's help, a celebratory supper for him on 18
November at the Florence Restaurant. That Nevinson should
set about organizing Marinetti's arrival in London at the same
time that Lewis attacked Omega is no coincidence, as it was
at about this time that the two artists had first properly met.
Later, Nevinson remembered that evening as an 'extraordinary affair. Marinetti recited a poem about the siege of
Adrianople, with various kinds of onomatopoeic noises and
crashes in free verse, while all the time a band downstairs
played "You made me love you. I didn't want to do it." It was
grand if incoherent.'[49]

The Rebel artists' theatrical opposition to the tenets of Fry
and Clive Bell was maintained when, the following month,
they exhibited together for the first time in the 'Cubist Room'
of 'The Camden Town Group and Others' exhibition in
Brighton. This exhibition marked the founding of the London
Group, at a meeting on 15 November, as a merger between
the Camden Town Group, the Cumberland Market Group
of Robert Bevan and Harold Gilman, and the Fitzroy Street
Group. By February 1914 this new group, which excluded
artists associated with the Bloomsbury grouping, included
Lewis, Nevinson, Etchells, Hamilton, Wadsworth, Jacob
Epstein, Henri Gaudier-Brzeska and David Bomberg.[50] It
was intended that the Brighton exhibition would show how,
in the London Group, 'all modern methods may find a home.
Cubism meets Impressionism, Futurism and Sickertism join
hands and are not ashamed, the motto of the Group being
that sincerity of conviction has a right of expression.'[51]

Despite such a sentiment, Lewis's own catalogue
introduction to the room which separated the 'Cubists'[52]
from the other exhibitors, sharply rejected this spirit of

aesthetic compromise. He identified the artists gathered in the 'Cubist Room' as forming 'a vertiginous, but not exotic, island in the placid and respectable archipelago of English art',[53] and called for a 'revolutionary painting' that would have

> in common the rigid reflections of steel and stone in the spirit of the artist; that desire for stability as though a machine were being built to fly or kill with; an alienation from the traditional photographer's trade and realisation of the value of colour and form as such independently of what recognisable form it covers or encloses. People are invited … to entirely change their idea of the painter's mission, and penetrate, deferentially, with him into a transposed universe, as abstract as, though different to, the musician's.[54]

Such rhetoric certainly shows that Lewis had learned from Marinetti the effective use of theatrical hyperbole. However, although Lewis was content in the use of the term 'Futurist' to describe himself, he was not uncritical of Futurism – their subject-matter was not always 'of the future',[55] the machine had been too often praised by them without question,[56] and he finally suggested that the reality confronted and transformed by the vision of the contemporary artist was altogether more complicated than might be suggested by Futurism: 'Man with an aeroplane is still merely a bad bird. But a man who passes his days amid the rigid lines of houses, a plague of cheap ornamentation, noisy street locomotion, the Bedlam of the press, will evidently possess a different habit of vision to a man living amongst the lines of a landscape.'[57]

By the evidence of this text Lewis was already thinking ahead in carving out an identity for the Rebels that would be distinct from Futurism and Cubism as well as opposed to the Post-Impressionism of Fry. Nevertheless, the artists in the 'Cubist Room' were there as much as a result of their own aesthetic opposition to Fry or Sickert[58] as to any perceived allegiance to Lewis. Later in the spring of 1914 Lewis was able to provide what he hoped would be an alternative to Omega with the founding of the Rebel Art Centre. It was intended that artists could work both collaboratively towards an ideal of a New Art whilst also retaining their individual identity. However, as no commissions were gained by any of the artists apart from Lewis, and no guaranteed income was provided to artists working at the Centre (as had been Omega's practice), it only succeeded in providing an identity for artists opposed to Omega, and as such hardly lasted six months. By July 1914 it had closed.[59] The Centre was decorated, like Lady Drogheda's house, as the antithesis of Omega, a position that was clearly stated by an advertisement in the catalogue for the 1914 Allied Artists' Association salon in which the page is split between 'The Omega Lounge' and 'The Rebel Booth', the booth being their only group enterprise.[60]

However, despite the Centre only lasting a few months, in the first weeks of 1914 there would have been a sense of goodwill and camaraderie amongst the artists involved. Furthermore, other artists were drawn to, and allied themselves with, the Centre at this time, such as Helen Saunders, the photographer Malcolm Arbuthnot, Lawrence Atkinson, William Roberts, David Bomberg (who had exhibited in Brighton) and Henri Gaudier-Brzeska. Of these Roberts had been involved with Omega from the time of Lewis's 'Round Robin' in October 1913 until the founding of the Rebel Art Centre, while Gaudier used Omega from October 1913 until his death as a commercial outlet for his sculpture and rarely took part in collaborative decorative work. For Lewis, equally significant as this growing band of artists was his friendship during this period with T.E.Hulme who, with himself and Pound, would contribute to the theoretical formulation of a Vorticist aesthetic. As a result it was decided to produce a magazine – Blast[61] – that would discuss 'Cubism, Futurism, Imagisme and all Vital Forms of Modern Art. THE CUBE. THE PYRAMID … END OF THE CHRISTIAN ERA.'[62] However, within the space of two months such an all-inclusive aesthetic even-handedness had disappeared under another announcement for Blast declaring that it now constituted 'The manifesto of the Vorticists. The English parallel movement to Cubism and Expressionism. Imagism in poetry. Death blow to Impressionism and Futurism and all the refuse of naif science…. The artistic spirit of to-day is Blast.'[63]

What had happened between the end of March and June that transformed Blast from being a catch-all of the prevailing avant garde to being the specific mouthpiece of Vorticism alone? From the evidence[64] it would seem that the idea of Vorticism was only elaborated during this period, and that both as a group and as an aesthetic theory it was created to distance its members from the work of Nevinson and the Italian Futurists. Although his introduction to the 'Cubist Room' showed that Lewis was already critical of Futurism, events forced his hand. At the beginning of June Marinetti (in London following the second exhibition of Futurism that had opened at the end of April at the Doré Galleries) penned with the help of Nevinson a manifesto, 'Vital English Art',[65] that identified the Rebel Art Centre – and the artists associated with it, named as Atkinson, Bomberg, Epstein, Etchells, Hamilton, Lewis, Roberts and Wadsworth – as Futurist. Given that Lewis was increasingly critical of Futurism and wished to be identified as independent of it, such claims were enough not only to bring about a split with Nevinson but also to repudiate any link with Futurism and assert an independent identity such as Vorticism promised.[66]

Lewis's criticism of Futurism can best be understood as a consequence of his rejection of Bergson's vitalist philosophy towards a detached, more mechanical and structured thought that gave priority to space over time and the eye over the passing experience. Fifteen years later Lewis equated Bergson's vitalism with Marinetti's Futurists:

> with their evangile of *action*, and its concomitants, speed, violence, impressionism and sensation in all things – incessant movement with the impermanence associated with that, as the ideal of a kind of suicidal faith – they were thorough adepts of the Time-philosophy: and Marinetti, their prophet, was a *pur-sang* bergsonian.[67]

Although Lewis recognized the importance of the Machine Age he was unwilling to praise it unreservedly, and damned such Futurist adoration as sheer sentimental Romanticism and its concern with the pictorial representation of mechanized movement as a debased Impressionism. Similarly, Lewis was critical of Cubism partly for the static, unshifting nature of its formulations, but more crucially on account of its concern for the trivial subject-matter of the still life and autobiographical portrait: a worthless triviality that Lewis also located in the work of his Post-Impressionist contemporaries. In pursuit of a reality and an easy naturalism in painting, both Vanessa Bell and Duncan Grant had turned towards landscape and anecdotal portraiture for the subject of their paintings. One of Bell's more celebrated paintings, *Studland Beach*, c.1912, justifiably recognized as a high point of such painting in its use of flat non-descriptive expanses of colour, has as its subject-matter nothing more edifying than a day out at the seaside. The Fauvism of Matisse and the symbolic compositional structure of Gauguin is harnessed to record a bohemian tea-party. This shamelessly autobiographical approach continued in the more Cézannist paintings such as *Virginia Woolf at Asheham*, c.1910, or *Frederick and Jessie Etchells Painting*, 1912.

To a similar degree, their experimentation with abstraction also became little more than a stylistic option, within an outlook that would relegate it to hardly more than a decorative background. As far as can be ascertained no such work was attempted until the founding of Omega in 1913, and although the work produced there was often non-representational it was little more than a decorative backdrop to life lived. Within such a context a non-representational or abstract approach to painting could be equated wholly with 'design', there being little implied, qualitative or actual difference between work produced by Bell as, for example, a rug design and work produced as an abstract painting in its own right.[68] Just as the overlapping forms found in her *Abstract Painting*, c.1914 (echoing Kupka's *Vertical Planes III*, 1912–13, seen by her in Paris in 1913) are repeated as a decorative background in her portraits of *Mrs St John Hutchinson*, 1915, so also did Duncan Grant later alter a 1914 abstract painting by adding a lemon and a white jug (*The White Jug*,

17 Wyndham Lewis, *Vorticist Sketchbook: Composition No. 1*, 1914–15, watercolour, chalk, ink and pencil on paper, 324 x 460 mm (12¾ x 18 in)

1914–c.19). Neither painter was fully committed to the project of abstraction, just as neither was willing to marry the new formalisms with a content that was appropriate to the new cultural vision of which such painting was a part. Grant's major experiment in abstraction – *Abstract Kinetic Collage Painting with Sound*, 1914 – was abandoned; its scrolling mechanism was never built and it was never viewed to the accompaniment of music by Bach. The intention was not the creation of a painting that might stand as an equivalent to music's abstract qualities but instead the provision of an illustration, or even a representation of music. Non-representational painting, although recognized by both Clive Bell and Roger Fry as theoretically and aesthetically logical, was never wholeheartedly embraced by the Bloomsbury painters. Despite the formally uncompromising nature of *Studland Beach* and the rawness of Grant's reaction to the primitive paintings of Picasso in *The Tub*, 1912, or *Head of Eve*, c.1912, ultimately Bloomsbury enacted a domestication of such possibilities where Grant used a planar abstract simplification to picture an *Interior at Gordon Square*, c.1915.

Where the studio of the Post-Impressionist was replete with the materials for the creation of such inconsequential

18 Edward Wadsworth, *Abstract Composition*, 1915, pen, pencil and gouache on paper, 419 x 343 mm (16½ x 13½ in)

paintings, the workshop of the Vorticist was made up of the city itself, as Lewis's *Workshop* (plate VII) and *Composition 1* (fig.17) from his so-called Vorticist sketchbook, underline. *Workshop*'s bright clashing colour emphasizes the painting's uncompromising projection of an urban subject-matter through something more than just a formalist abstraction. Lewis's practice was well described by Pound in a letter to the American collector John Quinn: 'I think he is often experimenting in "unaccepted" colour, in colour that is often, at first sight, unacceptable. Just as he is often working in "unaccepted" form.'[69] This use of a composition and colour that appeared aberrant among their contemporaries was a distinguishing feature of much Vorticist work. Works such as Etchells's *Stilts* (plate VIII) and *Progression* (plate IX), Wadsworth's *Abstract Composition* (fig.18), Atkinson's *Abstract* (plate X) and Roberts's *Study for 'Twostep II'* (plate XI) all describe, with Lewis's *Workshop*, the basic elements of Vorticism's visual aesthetic. The colour is either high keyed and jarring or tastelessly sombre. Although the composition of each painting projects an architectural or sculptural sense of structural solidity, this is denied in their actual configuration – some, like *Progression*, chart a regular and restrained movement of pictorial development, but most depict forms that twist and expand, that appear top-heavy and

topple into and intersect with one another or that pile up repetitively. Such paintings chart a very different picture of the modern industrial world to that which the Futurists had been presenting.

The figurative basis for Vorticist abstraction is also distinct from that of David Bomberg's earlier paintings such as *In the Hold* (plate XII), in which the subject of a group of figures working in the hold of a ship is fragmented both by the imposition of a geometrical grid and the non-naturalistic and jarring use of colour that was also adopted by the Vorticists. The composition of Vorticist painting, unlike that of Bomberg, was constructed out of a depth of subject-matter that cannot be located in a direct process of abstraction or in the search of the Vorticists' Post-Impressionist contemporaries for aesthetic emotion or significant form. Instead the Vorticists took a more philosophical and radical view of the process of abstraction as it detached from its figurative source as much as it did from the demands of 'design'. In *Workshop*, Lewis creates a powerful image of the artist's relationship to the city; in *Twostep*, Roberts echoes Lewis so that the figures in his earlier work have now fallen away and merged with the abstract, mechanical, resolutely urban forms that make up the painting. Both paintings reveal the essential nature of Vorticist abstraction as analytical and an extension of Lewis's concern with the Wild Body in which 'Dehumanization' is recognized as 'the chief diagnostic of the Modern World'.[70]

Hulme, like Lewis, had grown through and against Bergson's philosophy,[71] and his interest in the work of the nascent Vorticists was mediated by the way in which they confirmed his own particular interpretation of Wilhelm Worringer's notion of 'Abstraction and Empathy' in which the creation of a new classical, geometric, abstract tendency in art was contrasted with what he termed a 'vital' naturalistic art. The strength of the abstract tendency signalled in Hulme's mind 'the break up of the Renaissance humanistic attitude';[72] the artist could no longer see himself as part of nature but instead realized his distance from it, the new art existing as evidence of such a decisive philosophical break with the past.

Hulme first saw this new art as best characterized in the sculpture and drawings of Epstein[73] and in the work of the artists around Lewis, most notably David Bomberg. To describe such work Hulme made reference to the archaic forms of Egyptian, Indian and Byzantine art in which, like the new art, 'everything tends to be angular, where curves tend to be hard and geometrical, where the representation of the human body, for example, is … distorted to fit into stiff lines and cubical shapes of various kinds.'[74] Although such art avoided 'those lines and surfaces which look pleasing and organic' in favour of 'lines which are clean, clear-cut and mechanical. You will find artists expressing admiration for engineer's drawings, where the lines are clean, the curves all geometrical, and the colour, laid on to show the shape of a cylinder for example, gradated absolutely mechanically,'[75] a view that would culminate in an art whose geometrical abstraction did not draw on archaic or primitive sources but on the contemporary machine. The art described here by Hulme, governed by stability and the communication of content over how something looked, was the antithesis of Futurism, 'the deification of the flux, the last efflorescence of impressionism'.[76]

Hulme's description of Lewis's painting as turning 'the organic into something not organic, it tries to translate the changing and limited, into something unlimited and necessary'[77] captures something of Lewis's goal in transcending Futurist impressionism and the triviality of Cubist subject-matter. However, although Lewis identified strongly with Hulme's writing,[78] it was actually closer to the work of other Vorticists. The foundation of Hulme's theory proposed a straightforward process of formally abstracting a visual subject, in which a figure is simplified through geometric form, and this does not adequately explain Lewis's motivation in works such as *Red Duet* (plate XIII). If *Red Duet* is compared with contemporary work of Bomberg's (plates XIV–XVII), it can be seen that of all the painters associated with the Vorticists it is Bomberg who provides the closest illustration of what Hulme wrote. Fiercely independent, Bomberg took little part in the activities of the Rebel Art Centre (when signing his name to the letter that replied to Nevinson and Marinetti's manifesto he stressed, in a footnote, his independence from the Centre) and even refused to allow any reproductions of his paintings within *Blast*. By 1912, and still at the Slade, he had achieved a level of abstraction and vivid use of flat clashing colour with *Vision of Ezekiel*[79] that was far ahead of Lewis; yet the painting's subject-matter, as well as its compositional structure, owed much to traditional Slade figure subjects (even if his treatment didn't) and hardly engaged with urban contemporary themes at all. Similarly, Bomberg's outlook can be compared with the angular simplification that his younger Slade contemporary, William Roberts, arrived at in 1913 in his *Study for a Nativity* (plate XVIII) or *The Return of Ulysses* (plate XIX).

Vision of Ezekiel marked Bomberg's entry into the contemporary avant garde, a position that he consolidated over the following year. In May 1913 he travelled to Paris with Jacob Epstein to select work for 'Twentieth Century Art: A Review of Modern Movements', an exhibition that was mounted at the Whitechapel Art Gallery in the summer of 1914 and included, shown on one wall, work from the Rebel Art Centre artists. While in Paris Bomberg met, among others, Picasso, Derain and Modigliani. Although Bomberg's painting was not noticeably influenced by any of the artists he met in Paris, this would have been a stimulating experience for him – just how stimulating was revealed by his first solo

19 David Bomberg, *Ju-Jitsu*, c.1913, oil on cardboard, 620 x 620 mm (24½ x 24½ in)

exhibition that opened at the Chenil Gallery in July 1914, in the same month that the first issue of *Blast* was finally published.

The fifty-five exhibits, many of which were executed at the Slade, did not display the same level of avant-garde intent, although works such as *Ju-Jitsu* (fig.19) and *The Mud Bath* (plates XV, XX) reveal that Hulme's belief in Bomberg's painting was fully justified. The optical fragmentation found in *Ju-Jitsu* contrasts strongly with the solid monumentality of *The Mud Bath*, but the extent to which both paintings are in sympathy with Hulme's outlook was stressed not only by Bomberg's explanatory introduction to the exhibition which paraphrases Hulme, but also by Hulme's own laudatory review of the exhibition published in *The New Age*. In these paintings Bomberg does not create completely non-figurative works (something Hulme could not countenance) but instead constructs a process of abstracting from nature that underlines a detachment from it – 'a separation in the face of outside nature'[80] – and in its final realized state an autonomy which Hulme felt registered the New Age as much as it did the New Art (plates XIV, XVI). In *Ju-Jitsu* the nature of this separation is markedly different in the drawing and the painting. The drawing shows a simplified group of figures wrestling within an arena, the whole squared and sectioned up for transfer to the painting where that overlaying geometry disembodies the figure composition as much as the spatial composition; as Richard Cork has cogently described, 'The real subject of the painting is not, as it was in the drawing, the relation between the figures and their confused, ambiguous surroundings. Now it is the tension set up by the jerking puppets and the grid which contains them, at once defining and confining their every movement.'[81]

When Hulme wrote of Bomberg's figure drawing *Chinnereth, c.*1914, that 'the pleasure you are intended to take in such a drawing is a pleasure not in representation, but in the relations between certain abstract forms'[82] he could also have been writing about *The Mud Bath*, which signals a change in Bomberg's practice away from the progressive abstracting and fragmenting carried out through a figural simplification and the action of a grid which shatters bodily resemblance, towards a more subjective and monumental process. Nevertheless, as Hulme wrote in his review of the exhibition,

> the first step towards the understanding of this process of genesis is to recognise that the mind cannot *create* form, it can only *edit* it.... The first suggestion must always come from some existing outside shape.... In the final stage, these figures are so abstract that they are not recognisable as such. In all this process what suggestions of real objects occur, are only as a means of getting the mind going ... In themselves they are of no importance, the controlling interest all the time being the selection and production of abstract form.[83]

Bomberg's foreword to the Chenil Gallery catalogue reflects Hulme's vacillation between the necessity of abstracting from a natural source whilst proclaiming the necessity for aesthetic form to be autonomous. On the one hand Bomberg proclaims that he is constructing 'Pure Form', on the other that he is stripping 'Naturalistic Form of all irrelevant matter'.[84]

The tension between form and content was crucial to Vorticism (as was Hulme's notion of anti-Humanism), and its resolution in the work of Lewis and Wadsworth point out the gulf that existed between this and the more obviously figurative abstraction found in Bomberg that was praised by Hulme. Lewis's Vorticist works were always bound to a specific philosophical grammar; his 'Wild Body' had suggested how aesthetic narratives could be contained alongside harder philosophical imperatives and, even if this might sometimes lead to pictorial contradiction, it offered a depth of reference that was inspirational to the other Vorticists.

Apart from the work exhibited, finally, in the 1915 Doré Galleries exhibition of Vorticism, the nature of a Vorticist aesthetic is locked primarily within the pages of the two issues of *Blast*: in the writing of Pound and Lewis, and the accompanying illustrations. So far, apart from Hulme's theorizing, I have largely described Vorticism in negative terms by what it attacked – the Victorian age which was Blasted in its totality,[85] Italian Futurism, French Cubism, Renaissance Humanism and the Bloomsbury aesthetic labelled as Post-Impressionism. For Pound and Lewis

Vorticism promised much more than this. Pound's vision of Vorticism as providing a unifying theory that might hold good for painting, sculpture, literature, poetry and theatre finds it origin by 1912 in his creation of a poetic 'Imagism' that might be 'austere, direct, free from emotional slither',[86] and its realization in Pound's promotion of the College of Arts[87] in which 'the arts should be gathered together for the purpose of inter-enlightenment'.[88] Pound, with Richard Aldington and Hilda Doolittle, described Imagism's birth by an adherence to three basic principles that would deliver absolute clarity: a direct treatment of the poetic subject; a rejection of any word that was inessential or superfluous to the project of capturing a poetic image; and the allowance of a natural musical rhythm to predominate rather than being led by the strict rhythm of a metronome. With 'In a Station of the Metro', a poem often cited as typical of Imagism, and motivated by the example of Japanese *haiku*, Pound would reduce its original thirty lines to two lines of visual and emotional power. For Pound 'energy' and 'emotion' were interchangeable, and in a 1915 text on Imagism he outlines how emotion not only forms the '"pattern-unit" and the "arrangement of forms", it creates also the image.... The image is more than an idea. It is a vortex or cluster of fused ideas and is endowed with energy.'[89] By this equation energy or emotion is produced out of itself and is delivered up with no diminution in a way that is applicable to all the arts. The Vortex, then, 'is the point of maximum energy'[90] captured, rather than its external pictorialization.

This was far removed from the Futurist rhetoric of speeding motor-cars and aeroplanes and the dynamic rush of the rioting, unthinking crowd. In explaining Vorticism in this way Pound also elaborated on that tension, found in Hulme, between form and content. What was significant to Pound was the 'image' as pure form, emotion and energy, 'the primary pigment'[91] – 'that which presents an intellectual and emotional complex in an instant of time'[92] – not whether something looked or did not look like something else. Pound here seems more concerned to discuss Vorticism's pure form in terms of an emotionally driven concept rather than Hulme's presentation of Vorticism as the mechanical appearance of its painted or sculpted forms. Lewis once described Vorticism in similar terms as a 'whirlpool.... At the heart of the whirlpool is a great silent place where all the energy is concentrated. And there, at the point of concentration, is the Vorticist,'[93] and this conception of Vorticism is defined ultimately by a Nietzschean position of the artist in relation to his art, as much as to his subject and audience: 'You may think of man as that toward which perception moves. You may think of him as the TOY of circumstance, as the plastic substance RECEIVING impressions. OR you may think of him as DIRECTING a certain fluid force against circumstance, as CONCEIVING instead of merely observing and reflecting.'[94]

20　Edward Wadsworth, *A Short Flight*, 1914–15

Pound, like Lewis, saw the role of the artist as existing far beyond the confines of the studio, a role that was summed up in Lewis's belief that Vorticism described 'more than just picture-making: one was manufacturing fresh eyes for people, and fresh souls to go with the eyes'.[95] It was in this respect, and no other, that Vorticism signalled 'The Improvement of Life'.[96]

Given his dismissal of Bergson's 'plunge into life', Lewis was careful in distancing Vorticism from an identification with life itself. Art and life were quite separate entities. Hulme's anti-humanist stance emphasized just this. The removal from life and opposition to nature formed the theme of Lewis's play *Enemy of the Stars*, published in *Blast*, in which Lewis presents us with an image of 'the human mind in its traditional role of the enemy of life'.[97] This distance is clarified elsewhere in *Blast*, where Lewis declares that 'With our Vortex the Present is the only active thing. Life is the Past and the Future. The Present is Art.'[98] Aesthetic reality – something for which Vorticism strived – could not be identified with that naturalistic Life that Lewis equated with the march of life found in the twin poles of Bergsonian duration: a history of tradition and an unknowable future.

21　Edward Wadsworth, *Composition*, 1915, gouache

When Lewis makes the apparently contradictory statement a few lines later that 'There is no Present – there is Past and Future, and there is Art',[99] he is stressing his abhorrence of Bergsonian duration and Futurist dynamism that could also be found in the 'Present' state. Vorticist art, as defined by Lewis, did not exist in time but was held stable in space, distant from life, its representation of energy stilled within the emotion of pure form. Lewis summed up the Vorticist relation to life such that, 'We must have the Past and the Future, Life simple, that is, to discharge ourselves in, and keep us pure for non-life, that is, Art'.[100]

Of the seven artists who made up the Vorticist group[101] that exhibited at the Doré Galleries in 1915, giving, with *Blast*, the only coherent vision of Vorticism as a group, it is Lewis and Wadsworth who come closest to these Vorticist tenets, and they exhibited more work than any of the other artists. No oil paintings by Wadsworth from his Vorticist period have survived, although photographs of paintings such as *A Short Flight* (fig.20), *Composition* (fig.21) and *Combat*, 1915, betray his affinity with Lewis. In *A Short Flight* the aeroplane's gleaming mechanical surfaces intersect with the distant views of the rigorously patchworked landscape below, while the unstable composition of *Combat* recalls Hulme's dismissive (yet accurate) description of Lewis's working practice in which 'His sense of form seems to me to be sequent rather than integral, by which I mean that one form probably springs out of the preceding one as he works, instead of being conceived as part of a whole'.[102] However, *Composition*, in which coloured strips like a piano keyboard are enclosed within hard and long diagonal lines that stretch across the canvas surface, directing the jostling 'keyboards' to the lower right-hand corner of the painting, is much more coherently structured. Writing about Wadsworth in the second issue of *Blast*, Lewis suggested that his painting encapsulated the hard formal realities of the modern city. What was essential for the Vorticist artist was 'to synthesize this quality of LIFE with the significance or spiritual weight that is the mark of all the greatest art.... In Vorticism, the direct and hot impressions of life are mated with Abstraction, or the combinations of the Will.'[103]

Lewis stressed that although Wadsworth's source might be found, in some paintings, within an impression of gaudy seaside architecture, this was powerfully synthesized and held in check by those distanced abstract 'combinations of the will', or what Pound would have termed the dualities of emotion and energy found in the stability of pure form.

Wadsworth's contribution to the Vorticist aesthetic can now only be calculated through the series of woodcuts that he executed after 1914. For Pound these woodcuts are defined by their 'cleanliness, efficiency, precision',[104] and in the prints such as *Mytholmroyd* (plate XXI) he distils the external/internal viewpoint found in *A Short Flight* to a more grounded vision of the industrial landscape. Always from afar, as it were through a window,[105] he provides what Etchells described as 'an interesting simplification of planes', and he continued, 'the closely knitted composition of roofs and chimney stacks seems to me a complete abstract of a modern industrial town'.[106] The energy of modern life is here purified into the hard lines of modern form. In the face of the dynamic subject-matter of the machine age, Vorticism aimed at its transformation through the presentation of such spare austerity as is found in Wadsworth's small, compressed and uncompromising woodcuts. *Illustration (Typhoon)* (fig.22) epitomizes his approach. Taking as his cue a Joseph Conrad short story, 'Typhoon', he places us in that still place within the Vortex as the forces of nature and machine, the internal and the external, battle against each other. When *Illustration (Typhoon)* was exhibited in 1919 a quotation from Conrad's story was printed in the catalogue: 'the iron walls of the engine room. Painted white, they rose high into the dusk of the skylight, sloping like a roof: and the whole resembled the interior of a monument, divided by floors of iron grating, with lights flickering in the middle, within the columnar stir of machinery.'[107] The combination of observation and experience in the passage sums up Wadsworth's creation of an abstract image in his Vorticist work that, although not abstracted from a single figurative source, echoes Hulme's and Lewis's belief that pure form could be suggested only through a detached vision of reality. The reality of a boat caught in a typhoon – its form, its energy, the emotion it projects – could be realized effectively only in an image that was classically stable and hard such as this.

Images such as *Illustration (Typhoon)* by Wadsworth or *Workshop* (plate VII) by Lewis stand as the highpoint of

22 Edward Wadsworth, *Illustration (Typhoon)*, 1914–15, woodcut on paper, 280 x 255 mm (11 x 10 in)

Vorticism. Despite Lewis's editorial in the second issue of *Blast* that 'We will not stop talking about Culture when the War ends!',[108] the Doré Galleries exhibition[109] and this last issue of *Blast* constitute the end of Vorticism as an aesthetic movement and as a group of artists. The war killed or dispersed them. Both Gaudier-Brzeska and T.E. Hulme were killed. Wadsworth was invalided out of the Royal Navy Volunteer Reserve in 1917 to compose 'dazzle' camouflage for ships which formed the subject for some of his best-known woodcuts, such as *Dry Docked for Scaling and Painting* (fig.23). Lewis, Roberts, Bomberg and Nevinson all served at the Front and towards the end of the war gained commissions as Official War Artists, all, except Nevinson, for the Canadian War Memorials Fund. Only Etchells wholly escaped the fighting, having been stricken by tuberculosis at the start of the war; when he, too, was commissioned by the Canadian Fund, he produced a painting of the armistice. The only works that stood apart from this development were the 1917 Vortographs of Alvin Langdon Coburn. These abstract photographs resulted from the construction of a three-sided prism from Pound's broken shaving mirror that, when photographed through, split the image into a series of fragments that approximated to the look of Vorticism. The earliest Vortographs, dating from late 1916, are portraits of Pound which show his face repeated and framed by the prism (fig.24). Moving away from such a pictorial conceit that was

23 Edward Wadsworth, *Dry Docked for Scaling and Painting*, 1918,
    woodcut on paper, 224 x 208 mm (8½ x 8 in)

24 Alvin Langdon Coburn, *Vortograph of Ezra Pound*, 1917
    (printed *c.*1950), photograph, 207 x 158 mm (8 x 6¼ in).
    Courtesy George Eastman House

perhaps too close to Futurism, Coburn then started to take
photographs of crystals, pieces of wood and other ordinary
objects on top of a glass table. The resulting images are
tangibly hard and unremitting, yet also spatially ambiguous
and as difficult to identify as the best Vorticist painting (figs
25, 26). Nevertheless, his wish to place photography on an
equal footing with contemporary developments in painting
and sculpture did not entail making a photographic
transcription of the new art, but instead was the result of his
re-enaction of their break from the old aesthetics. Although
promoted by Ezra Pound as evidence of the continuing
vitality of Vorticism, Coburn's experiment was short lived,
and he abandoned the process soon after the Vortographs'
only exhibition, in London in February 1917 at the Camera
Club.

Lewis's repudiation of Vorticism after the war echoed
Nevinson's rejection of Futurism. In his war paintings,
however, Lewis retained a concern for the primacy of content
and form that looks back to the Wild Body and forwards to
his more satirical Tyro figures of the 1920s (plate XXII). In this
respect, in the foreword to the catalogue of his first solo
exhibition, *Guns*, Lewis contrasts Uccello's painting which
'does not borrow from the fact of War any emotion, any
disturbing or dislocating violence, terror or compassion – any
of the psychology that is proper to the events of War', with

Goya's *The Disasters of War* as an 'alternately sneering,
blazing, always furious satire directed against Fate, against the
French, against every folly that culminates in this jagged
horror'.[110]

It is not only that these artists had been transported from
the urban industrial landscape of pre-war London to the
killing-fields and devastated wasteland of the Western Front.
To an extent the hard mechanical forms of Vorticism were
held to be symbolically complicit in the slaughter of the war,
and even Lewis declared in 1921 that, 'No time has ever been
more carefully demarcated from the one it succeeds than the
time we have entered on has been by the Great War of
1914–18. It is built solidly behind us. All the conflicts and
changes of the last ten years, intellectual and other, are
terribly symbolised by it.'[111] The paintings of Nevinson, such
as *Column on the March* (plate XXIII) or *Searchlights*, *c.*1916,
were similarly described by one critic:

His cubist method does express, in the most direct way, his
sense that in war man behaves like a machine or part of a
machine, that war is a process in which man is not treated as
a human being but as an item in a great instrument of

25 Alvin Langdon Coburn, *Vortograph*, 1917 (printed *c*.1950), photograph, 158 x 207 mm (6¼ x 8 in). Courtesy George Eastman House

26 Alvin Langdon Coburn, *Vortograph*, 1917 (printed *c*.1950), photograph, 207 x 158 mm (8 x 6¼ in). Courtesy George Eastman House

destruction, in which he ceases to be a person and gets lost in a process.[112]

Nevertheless in providing an image, as War Artists, of this 'great instrument of destruction', all the one-time Vorticists compromised their previously held beliefs to the illustrational demands of the various commissions they received. After the war Lewis attempted to form a new group with Wadsworth, Etchells, Roberts, Dismorr and Hamilton, and four other artists, Frank Dobson, John Turnbull, McKnight Kauffer and Charles Ginner. 'Group X' held one exhibition and then it too broke up.[113] The artists had renounced, for one reason or another, not only the Vorticist style but also its critical and theoretical underpinning. The individuals were moving away from each other in separate directions. Roberts's angular figurations became rather bald stylistic formalizations instead of embodying a process of a particular transformation of reality. Similarly, Wadsworth's contribution to the 'Group X' exhibition, industrial landscapes of 'The Black Country', carry the formalized vestiges, but no more, of a Vorticist angularity, and these slag heaps were described as 'metallic-looking boulders hurled out into a desolation that yet teems

with the energy that made and discarded them'.[114] As Andrew Causey has explained, pictures such as *Ladle Slag*, 1919, or the more desolate and forbidding landscape of *Tarmac 1* (plate xxiv), 'emphasise the detritus of civilisation rather than its possible positive social implications'.[115] The Vorticist ideal of 'The Improvement of Life' had been decisively pushed to one side.

Looking back on the events of 1914 and 1915 Lewis later asserted that Vorticism had been, to all intents and purposes, a one-man band to which other people had danced: 'Vorticism, in fact, was what I, personally, did, and said, at a certain period'.[116] To David Bomberg, who had always refused to be enlisted as a Vorticist, Lewis's statement was deeply offensive, and William Roberts was driven to publish a series of pamphlets that attacked its premise. Nevertheless, within each gang of individuals there has to be a leader, and perhaps it is Pound's assessment of the situation that offers a clearer picture: 'As an active and informal association it might be said that Lewis supplied the volcanic force, Brzeska the animal energy, and perhaps that I had contributed a certain Confucian calm and reserve. There would have been no movement without Lewis.'[117]

Vorticism and Sculpture

RICHARD CORK

Both the sculptors who became involved with the Vorticist movement only decided to settle in London after growing up abroad: Jacob Epstein in the USA, and Henri Gaudier-Brzeska in France. Their vantage as outsiders, at a remove from British culture, may have encouraged them to develop a rebellious attitude towards prevailing sculptural conventions in their adopted country.

When Gaudier first visited Epstein in 1911, the latter was working on his monumental *Tomb of Oscar Wilde* for Père Lachaise cemetery in Paris – a carving that would prompt one critic of the period to describe him as a 'Sculptor in Revolt, who is in deadly conflict with the ideas of current sculpture.'[1] Gaudier warmed to Epstein's insistence on extreme renewal, his departure from classical precedent and determination to let the particular character of his material play a vital role in shaping the identity of the work he produced. But Epstein was eleven years older than Gaudier, and armed with far greater experience. When Epstein asked his young visitor 'if he carved direct', Gaudier was 'afraid to acknowledge that he hadn't.' As a result, 'he hurried home and immediately started a carving.'[2] The incident amused Epstein, who recalled that his 'relations with Gaudier were very friendly. We were interested in each other's work. In the French fashion of the younger to the older artist he wrote to me and addressed me as Cher Maître.'[3]

The difference in age between the two men helps to account for their contrasting reactions to the advent of Vorticism. When *Blast* made its initial, rumbustious appearance in the summer of 1914, Epstein and Gaudier were both represented by full-page illustrations of their work.[4] Epstein's involvement with the magazine was, however, limited: his name was markedly absent from the list of artists who signed *Blast*'s opening manifesto. He doubtless felt unwilling to become an official member of a movement dominated by the restless promotional energies of Wyndham Lewis. Throughout his life, Epstein remained fiercely proud of his independence as an artist. He preferred to stand alone, whereas Gaudier had no decisive qualms about adding his name to the manifesto and publishing, in the same issue of the magazine, a militant credo called 'Vortex'. The opening sentences proclaimed the extent of his ambition and a stern insistence on the formal basis of his explorations:

Sculptural energy is the mountain.
Sculptural feeling is the appreciation of masses in relation.
Sculptural ability is the defining of these masses by planes.[5]

When precisely did Gaudier arrive at the position summarized with such precocious authority in his 'Vortex' essay? Since he spent so much of his life in London mastering a whole range of styles, with fantastic dexterity, it is difficult to be precise about his adoption of a viewpoint compatible with the other Vorticists. 'I notice how everything differs, mingles with and knocks up against everything else', he wrote in October 1912,

I am never sure that what I think is true, still less that what I have thought or said is true; and I can't bring myself to sacrifice new ideas, quite different from those I had yesterday, just because the old ones happened to have the honour of passing through my head and I advocated them ferociously.[6]

In part, such sentiments reflect the fact that Gaudier was astonishingly young: he was only twenty-one at the time, and bound to be uncertain about his future direction. All the same, there was even then a detached quality about his hurried experiments, jumping within months from an exotic *Ornamental Mask* to a frankly classical marble torso carved with beguiling dexterity. Gaudier stood outside the styles he borrowed so freely; and while he indulged his talent for entering into the spirit of diverse cultures he was simultaneously appraising them all, asking himself what formal lessons they could teach him. The fundamental constituents of sculpture were kept firmly in view the whole time, for even in 1911 he had listed some basic precepts which anticipated his later interest in more abstract ways of working. 'The great thing is: that sculpture consists in placing planes according to a rhythm', he wrote; 'that painting consists in placing colours according to a rhythm.'[7] The statement would have been approved by Lewis as well as the British Fauves with whom Gaudier came into contact soon after settling in London. But he only started exploring planar austerity in earnest during the first half of 1913, embarking on a bust of his friend Horace Brodzky in which he announced new priorities (plate xxv). Brodzky recalled that the bust, 'to use [Gaudier's] own words, was "cubic".'[8] Although hints of more naturalistic modelling can still be discerned in the construction of this arresting head, it nevertheless shows Gaudier attempting to split up the sections of the face, hair and shoulders into the angular, faceted planes introduced to sculpture four years earlier in Picasso's *Head of a Woman*. The Brodzky bust almost teeters into caricature, but its exaggeration does not spring from a desire to amuse. Rather does it reflect Gaudier's own frantic energy, wilfully imposing itself on the cadaverous forms of his sitter's features and even incising the lines of a gesturing male nude on Brodzky's chest.

The *Bust* was put on display in July 1913 at the Allied Artists' salon, along with five other works by Gaudier. It was his début in the world of London's public exhibitions, but the critics accused him of sensationalism. Their hostility did not deter the young sculptor. By January 1914 he was able to display, at the Grafton Group's Alpine Gallery show, a carving which amounted to a far more extreme statement of intent. One of the preparatory studies for *Red Stone Dancer* reveals, with admirable *élan*, that Gaudier now wanted to inject a more dynamic apprehension of movement into his work (fig.27).[9] Three alternative figures blend into one burgeoning image, their heads, arms and legs jostling with each other to present a paradigm of Futurist simultaneity. The Italian group's experiments obviously helped Gaudier to incorporate so many successive stages of motion in a single sketch, but it would be unwise to limit such a wide-ranging artist to the inspiration of Futurism alone. In one excitable letter to his partner, Sophie Brzeska, he mentioned that during 'a short visit to the British Museum' his omnivorous appetite prompted him to take 'particular notice of all the primitive

27 Henri Gaudier-Brzeska, *Study for 'Red Stone Dancer'*, 1913–14, indian ink on paper, 385 x 250 mm (15¼ x 9¾ in)

statues, negro, yellow, red and white races, Gothic and Greek'.[10] Indeed, it would hardly be fanciful to suggest that the abandon of a multi-limbed Indian dancer also lies behind Gaudier's drawing.

The final carving, however, rejects any Boccioni-like ideas about aping a sequence of movement in sculpture (fig.28). Now it is the geometrical extremism that commands attention, for Gaudier has dispensed with facial features and imposed a large triangle on the empty oval of the dancer's head, complementing it with a circle on the right breast and a rectangle on the left in place of nipples. If these motifs sound in theory dangerously dogmatic, they are given plastic life by the rest of the figure as it unfolds in a remarkable series of intertwining arabesques. The spiral of movement initiated by the round plinth, and the turning of the left foot towards its neighbour, is continued and accelerated as the torso comes to rest at right angles to the pelvis. Then the wildly elongated

28   Henri Gaudier-Brzeska, *Red Stone Dancer*, 1914, red Mansfield
      stone, 430 x 220 x 220 mm (17 x 8¾ x 8¾ in)

Stone Dancer possesses plenty of spontaneity and organic life, it looks almost as if it were constructed according to a theory of art that Gaudier wanted to proclaim as brazenly as possible. Ezra Pound noticed this, and chose to expatiate upon the sculpture in one of his most closely argued passages of criticism. 'This … is almost a thesis of [Gaudier's] ideas upon the use of pure form', he wrote.

> We have the triangle and the circle asserted, *labled* [*sic*] almost, upon the face and right breast. Into these so-called 'abstractions' life flows, the circle moves and elongates into the oval, it increases and takes volume in the sphere or hemisphere of the breast. The triangle moves toward organism, it becomes a spherical triangle (the central life-form common to both Brzeska and Lewis). These two developed motifs work as themes in a fugue. We have the whole series of spherical triangles, as in the arm over the head, all combining and culminating in the great sweep of the back of the shoulders, as fine as any surface in all sculpture. The 'abstract' or mathematical bareness of the triangle and circle are fully incarnate, made flesh, full of vitality and of energy. The whole form-series ends, passes into stasis with the circular base or platform.[11]

Although Pound's interpretation is altogether too neat and conceptual to serve as an accurate summary of Gaudier's intentions, it can stand as compelling evidence of the sculptor's willingness to adhere to the principles of a new avant-garde group. The way was now clear for him to throw in his lot with the Rebel Art Centre, and he supported its activities with enormous enthusiasm when its headquarters opened at Great Ormond Street in the spring of 1914. His effervescent personality, no less than his extraordinary precocity as a sculptor, ensured that he rapidly became one of

right arm takes up the spiral with renewed force, wrapping itself right round the impossibly tilted head in an extended serpentine curve which only comes to rest when it meets the top of the left breast. Gaudier takes astonishing liberties with anatomy, moulding it like rubber to fit in with the abstract rhythms of the sculpture. Viewed in its totality, the result is both tortuous and lyrical, labyrinthine and disarmingly simple.

Red Stone Dancer marks a decisive moment in Gaudier's career. Here he puts eclecticism on one side and embraces the new geometrical art propounded by T.E. Hulme in his Quest Society lecture, 'Modern Art and its Philosophy', delivered at a time when Gaudier's carving was still on view at the Alpine Gallery. Hulme's theories may well have impressed Gaudier at the philosopher's regular salons in Soho. Although *Red*

29   Henri Gaudier-Brzeska, *Portrait of Ezra Pound*, 1913, indian ink
      on paper, 260 x 380 mm (10¼ x 15 in)

30 Gaudier-Brzeska carving *Hieratic Head of Ezra Pound*, 1914

31 Henri Gaudier-Brzeska, *Hieratic Head of Ezra Pound*, 1914,
marble, 915 x 483 x 420 mm (36 x 19 x 16½ in)

the leading adherents to the rebel cause. His callow stylistic
fireworks became far less apparent, and he settled down to
pursue a more consistent course of action. Meeting other
artists in sympathy with emergent Vorticist theories helped
him to fortify his resolve, put imitation behind him and strike
out on his own as one of the most forward-looking sculptors
in Europe.

A fruitful result of Gaudier's involvement with the Rebel
Art Centre was the close friendship he developed with Pound
(fig.29), whose poems the sculptor liked to compare with *Red
Stone Dancer*. They had first come across each other at the
1913 Allied Artists' exhibition; and Pound, with characteristic
generosity, helped his young friend in the most practical way
he could. Short of money himself, he nevertheless spent some
of the £40 given to him as a prize by W. B. Yeats on two small
sculptures by Gaudier. Describing him as '*the* coming
sculptor', Pound told William Carlos Williams that 'I like him
very much. He is the only person with whom I can really be
"Altaforte".… We are getting our little gang after five years of
waiting.'[12] Writing about 'The New Sculpture' in February
1914, Pound equated carvings like *Red Stone Dancer* with the
power of witch doctors, and considered that their magical

qualities would enable the modern artist to rule the world
as firmly as he did in primitive times. 'The aristocracy of
entail and of title is decayed, the aristocracy of commerce
is decaying, the aristocracy of the arts is ready again for its
service,' he cried rhetorically, 'and we who are the heirs of the
witch-doctor and the voodoo, we artists who have been so
long the despised are about to take over control.'[13]

Gaudier agreed with him. In a letter to *The Egoist*, the
magazine in which Pound's article had been published, he
declared that 'the modern sculptor is a man who works with
instinct as his inspiring force.' Showing himself in sympathy
with Pound's ideas about the need for a return to the
'primitive' subconscious, he insisted that the sculptor's 'work
is emotional … what he feels he does so intensely and his
work is nothing more nor less than the abstraction of this
intense feeling.' Just as Pound had referred to the power of
the voodoo, so Gaudier announced that 'this sculpture … is
continuing the tradition of the barbaric peoples of the earth
(for whom we have sympathy and admiration).'[14] By the time
he sat down to compose the *Egoist* letter, Gaudier was
engaged on a monumental portrait of Pound that put these
theories into compelling form (figs 30, 31).

Having purchased the stone block for the impoverished sculptor, Pound posed in the studio. But Gaudier warned him that 'it will not look like you … it will be the expression of certain emotions which I get from your character.'[15] Like Epstein before him, he went to the British Museum's 'primitive' collections for inspiration. In particular, Gaudier seems to have been inspired by a mesmeric carved figure from the Easter Island cult village of Orongo. Ever since entering the museum in 1869 it had reigned over the Polynesian collections, a towering testimony to humanity's ability to create potent symbols of magical beliefs. If particular similarities between this carving and Gaudier's portrait of Pound centre on the area of eyes and mouth, it appears likely that he was impressed above all by the whole vertical identity of the Orongo figure, thrusting its way upwards in one compact cubic mass of stone. Just as the Easter Island head is wedged on to its torso without much regard for the intervening neck, so Pound's face rests on a wide base to ensure that the outlines of the sculpture travel up in one consistent form towards the wider block of hair at the top. The overall silhouette thereby suggests a circumcised penis, and Epstein – who visited his friend while he was at work on the carving – recalled that 'Pound had asked him to make it virile and this Gaudier was endeavouring to do, explaining to me the general biological significance.'[16]

Although Lewis described the finished sculpture as 'Ezra in the form of a marble phallus',[17] there is nothing self-indulgent about the carving. Pound, with his almost sacred belief in the importance of artistic discipline, would have been the first to complain if his portrait had become merely immoderate, a dirty joke done for a snigger. Gaudier, likewise, would not have been prepared to expend so much time on a mere caprice, and the carving itself bears out the seriousness of his intentions. Compared with the eerie blend of realism and stylization employed in the Easter Island figure, his sculpture appears tight and schematic, certainly. But the simplifications are subtle, even devious. No single part of the face has been placed at the same angle as that of its companions; they are all tilted slightly off-balance, so that a palpable tension results. Each separate feature, carefully isolated from the others by a generous expanse of bare marble so that it can enjoy the greatest possible impact, is at odds with its neighbours. Gaudier, despising conventional regularity, has opted for a series of slight disparities in order to keep the massive block of stone alive with uneasy rhythms. Nor has he overstepped himself in his desire for formal contrasts: in the final stages of the carving he deliberately cut out much of its dramatic swagger, fearing no doubt that he had gone too far in his desire for a grand theatrical statement.

Despite initial reservations, Pound was eventually satisfied with the results of Gaudier's last-minute alterations. 'There is in the final condition of the stone a great calm',[18] he wrote, as if in recognition of the fact that Gaudier had seen him as a Buddha in at least one of the preliminary sketches. When the carving was put on display in May 1914, as part of the Whitechapel Art Gallery's ambitious survey 'Twentieth Century Art', it must have signified Gaudier's definitive adherence to Rebel Art Centre aesthetics. But its brusque simplifications could not have looked at their best in the crowded gallery of a mixed exhibition. The Pound bust is a public image, and the features chiselled so boldly on its surface were clearly meant to be admired from a distance. Gaudier, who was fundamentally a maker of small, intimate sculpture, wanted just once to produce something larger than life, to prove that his admiration for the 'barbaric peoples' could be translated into a carving that would not pale in comparison with its 'primitive' predecessors. He justified the phallic metaphor of his carving by describing, in *Blast*, how the Oceanic races, falling 'into contemplation before their sex: the site of their great energy: THEIR CONVEX MATURITY… pulled the sphere lengthways and made the cylinder.'[19] His carving is, therefore, as much a tribute to cylindrical power as it is a symbol of virility, and in that sense its 'primitivism' leads directly on to the mechanistic geometry of Gaudier's Vorticist sculpture.

Towards the end of his credo-like essay in *Blast*'s first issue, he compared his own generation of sculptors with the African and Oceanic races. Gaudier concluded that, just as these primitives had found 'the soil was hard, material difficult to win from nature, storms frequent, as also fevers and other epidemics', so 'WE the moderns: Epstein, Brancusi, Archipenko, Dunikowski, Modigliani, and myself, through the incessant struggle in the complex city, have likewise to spend much energy.'[20] Apart from providing a useful check-list of Gaudier's sculptural heroes, the passage shows how closely he now identified with the other Vorticists' response to twentieth-century urban life. If Lewis likened the capital to a 'modern Jungle', Gaudier's love of archaic art made him take the image further and equate the tom-toms of tribal dances with the roar of contemporary mechanisms.

But when the young sculptor turned away from pictorial activities and addressed himself to his central concern with carving, he eschewed mechanical themes and tried instead to infuse their formal lessons into images of animals and birds. He had been fascinated by wildlife ever since he drew a golden eagle's wing on a trip to Bristol City Museum in 1908; and by 1912 he had begun to pay regular calls on London Zoo to define the essential outlines of monkeys, wolves, tigers and elephants. The obsession remained with him while his drawing style changed from curvilinear to angular, fired by the same priorities which made Lewis declare that 'in Vorticism the direct and hot impressions of life are mated with Abstraction, or the combinations of the Will' (figs 32, 33).[21] But when he set about carving *Duck* from a small

32 Henri Gaudier-Brzeska, *Cock*, *c*.1914, chalk on paper,
505 x 382 mm (20 x 15 in)

33 Henri Gaudier-Brzeska, *Cubist Cock*, *c*.1914, pencil on paper,
234 x 151 mm (9¼ x 6 in)

34 Henri Gaudier-Brzeska, *Stags*, 1914, red-veined alabaster,
355 x 340 mm (14 x 13½ in)

block of marble, the creature lost all its feathery delicacy and
became a functional tool (plate XXVI). The duck's head has
been transformed into the head of a hammer, while its tail
looks as hard as prehistoric flint. The only markings Gaudier
now permits himself to make are strictly geometrical: an eye
is summarized in a cursory circle, scratched out roughly in
the surface of the marble. It seeks to stress the framework
of fundamental units underlying all things, just as the tiny
triangle incised in the tip of the tail echoes the larger triangle
formed by the duck's hindquarters. The whole body is
divided into self-sufficient sections of form.

Gaudier soon felt confident enough to tackle related
subjects on a larger and more ambitious scale. He carved a
lump of pink, veined alabaster into a group of stags (fig.34),
where bellies, legs and antlers are all treated as the swollen
parts of an ambiguous whole. They burgeon mysteriously out
of a decentralized composition which avoids any fixed focal

35 Henri Gaudier-Brzeska, *Study for 'Bird Swallowing Fish'*, 1914,
pencil on paper, 170 x 500 mm (6¾ x 19¾ in)

point. The eye is forced to travel round the entire mass,
searching for clues with which to interpret the meaning of
these huddled forms. The veins streaking their way across the
surface of the sculpture call attention to the nature of the
medium, and this built-in linear camouflage foils any attempt
at a straightforward representational reading. When *Stags* was
illustrated in the first issue of *Blast*, it was carefully photographed from an angle where the animals' fecund proportions
take on the menacing power of boulders.

For the most dynamic of his 1914 sculptures, though,
Gaudier turned away from carving. He probably took as his
cue a small cut-brass *Fish* which he presented to his friend
Mrs Kibblewhite 'as a gift to thank her for all that she had
done for him', telling her with a characteristically puckish
sense of humour that it was 'a little toy to keep in her
handbag.'[22] This diminutive object, with its sharp, pointed
beak and armour-plated flanks, may have encouraged Gaudier
to cast around for a combative motif that would justify the
warlike appearance of his new breed of mechanical creatures.
Whether he actually witnessed the dramatic incident he finally
chose, perhaps during a walk in one of London's parks, is
unknown: he may simply have decided to transpose the
viciousness of *Fish* to a more extended tableau in the privacy
of his studio, relying on memories or a friend's description of
the theme. The preliminary study for *Bird Swallowing Fish*
(fig.35) does not solve the question of the sculpture's origin;
for although its swift delineation of the main sculptural idea
possesses the spontaneity of a sketch from life, Gaudier has
already extracted the essence of the subject and distorted
natural forms to suit his own ends. At this stage details like
the end of the fish's tail and the bird's beak, which would
assume greater importance as the idea developed, are entirely
subservient to the summary of an abrupt physical action –
in itself a vivid paradigm of Vorticism's insistence on the
'maximum point of energy'.[23]

When Gaudier set to work on the plaster, he produced a
masterpiece of Vorticist sculpture (plate XXVII). It formalizes
the anatomical properties of its two protagonists with such
rigidity that most of their recognizable features have
completely disappeared. The fish slots into the bird like a key
that can only fit one particular lock, and they are wedged
together as a single dynamic entity. It is hard, at first, to

realize that two separate creatures are presented rather than a
macabre amalgam containing the characteristics of both: they
seem indistinguishable from each other, as if the fish were a
sinister malignance growing out of the bird's extended beak.
This ambivalence extends to the meaning of the act Gaudier
has chosen to dramatize. The whole eerie operation has been
frozen and held up for inspection, so that the most complicated overtones are given full rein. It is no longer a simple
matter of one creature consuming another. On the contrary,
the fish is not really being devoured at all; rather it is ramming
itself into the bird's open mouth with all the force at its
disposal. The predator's eyes seem to be straining in their
sockets, which swell with the effort involved in finding room
for this awkward visitor. Instead of swallowing, the bird
could actually be choking, gorged with the outsize
dimensions of a prey he was unwise to chase.

An examination of the sculpture from a lower angle shows
how equally matched the two combatants are in reality. The
fish may be the smaller of the pair, but there is nothing slight
about its structure. Its tail sticks up into space like the butt of
a weapon, more than balancing the bird's back that thrusts
itself into an ample triangle at the other end. Both sides shoot
down with comparable strength towards the middle, where all
the force of the sculpture is concentrated inside the bird's
gullet. There the two meet, hidden from view, in a moment of
contact that conveys more than a little sexual frisson. Violence
and lust are never wholly separable impulses, and Gaudier has
exploited this truth in the core of his invention. He has
selected the moment of deadlock, when each party is still
struggling for survival, and the outcome of this stalemate is
still undecided. But despite the tension, there is no hint of a
hectic struggle. The dispassionate dictates of Vorticist art
ensure that bird and fish have a detached air about them: no
emotive expressions, whether of fear, greed or hate, are
permitted to disturb the unruffled impersonality of the
performance. What would normally be a trivial incident, a
callous fact of nature, has been metamorphosed into an
intractable ritual. And the belligerence of the formal language
found its match in the materials employed: although Gaudier
modelled the work in plaster, it was then cast in gunmetal.[24]
Nothing could be more appropriate for a sculpture which
shows above all how Gaudier managed to reconcile his dual
involvement with nature and the machine.

But it was in another cut brass sculpture, the *Ornament/
Toy* (fig.36) which Hulme purchased for £2 and carried
around in his pocket, that Gaudier came closest of all to the
cold militancy of the Vorticist ideal. According to Pound, it
was 'the first experiment and the best of the three' brass
carvings, and he described it as a 'Toy'.[25] Yet Gaudier himself
listed the work more appropriately as an *'ornement
torpille!'*[26] – in other words, a type of flat torpedo fish
capable of giving an electric shock. It was a metaphor after

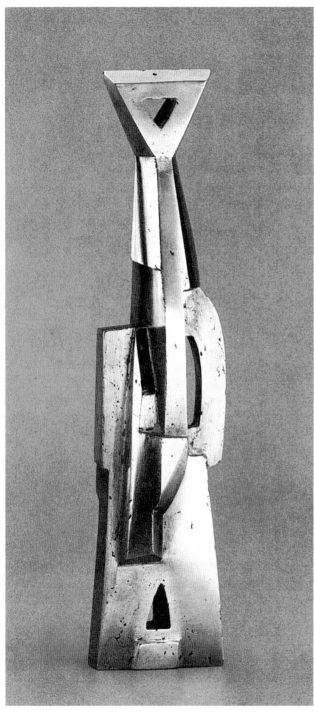

36 Henri Gaudier-Brzeska, *Ornament/Toy (Torpedo Fish)*, 1914, brass, 156 x 36 x 29 mm (6 x 1½ x 1 in)

Lewis's own heart, for this little piece of metal can also be seen as a standing sentinel, as harsh and combative as the 'Primitive Mercenaries in the Modern World'[27] whose birth was announced in the *Blast* manifestos. Like Lewis's mechanized figures, *Ornament/Toy* would be perfectly capable of leading the rebel attack against the forces of reaction: it stands stiff and erect, as if lined up for battle, and its sharp edges seem ready to tear their way through any struggle. Indeed, it is easy to imagine the pugnacious Hulme using it as a weapon. A previous owner, whose father was given the sculpture by Mrs Kibblewhite as a 'personal memento' after Hulme's death, maintained that although it was essentially 'an abstract object for the philosopher to fidget with while his meditations were maturing, Hulme's character was such that he may well have playfully threatened to brain someone with it.'[28]

Despite its miniature scale, the figure is heroic in implications, both as a warrior and a milestone in the evolution of twentieth-century sculpture. For *Ornament/Toy* is one of the very first examples of a completely penetrated carving: later, perhaps, than Archipenko's pioneering experiments in the same field, but innovatory none the less. Gaudier has pierced the brass completely, from front to back, in three places. Viewed from behind, these holes register with just as much effect as they do from the opposite side, even if the lowest triangle is no longer stressed by the larger triangle of metal surrounding it at the front. And the back reinforces the image of a human body, possessing a spine motif that runs down from the top into a knot of more organic forms towards the base. Gaudier often liked to play around with ambiguity: an alabaster *Imp*, carved in the same year, presents an abstract surface on one side and a figurative one on the other (fig.37). In *Ornament/Toy*, however, high spirits are not allowed to interfere with the essential severity of a hieratic presence. It could almost be a three-dimensional statement of Vorticism's most warlike impulses, and might easily have prompted the enthusiasm of Lewis's comments on Gaudier in the second issue of *Blast*, where he praises the 'suave, thick, quite PERSONAL character' of his work and explains how 'it is this, that makes his sculpture what we would principally turn to in England to show the new forces and future of this art.'[29]

One of the most impressive manifestations of Gaudier's new maturity is the limestone carving *Birds Erect* (fig.38). Casting aside the mechanistic rigidity of *Bird Swallowing Fish*, he turned back here to the more organic vocabulary employed in *Stags*; but this time, he allowed no doubt to linger about the anti-realistic nature of his latest enterprise. These freestanding forms are indeed 'erect', like a group of birds thrusting out of a nest in readiness for the arrival of food. But there the connection with identifiable reality is cut short. Gaudier wanted to construct an autonomous equivalent rather than trying to reproduce an episode from natural life.

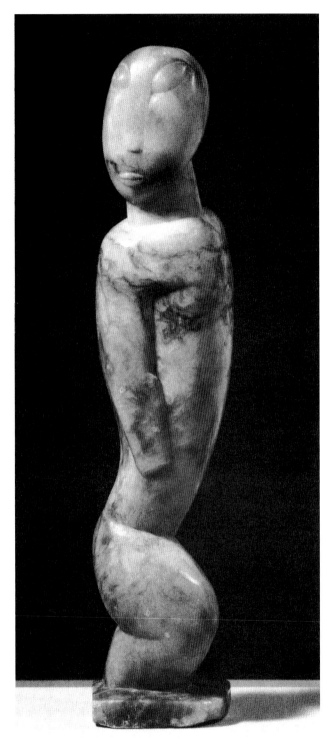

38 Henri Gaudier-Brzeska, *Birds Erect*, 1914, limestone,
667 x 260 x 314 mm (26¼ x 10¼ x 12¼ in)

37 Henri Gaudier-Brzeska, *Imp*, c.1914, alabaster,
406 x 89 x 83 mm (16 x 3½ x 3¼ in)

These crisply articulated segments are grouped together in an ensemble that bristles with vitality. Gaudier has set them down on a tall base shaped into four main planes. These help to punctuate the continuous movement of the sculpture above and, more importantly, provide an uneven sloping surface for the work to rest on. Viewed from one angle, the birds seem to crowd in on each other as if to save themselves from falling off the edge of a precipice. The instability creates a feeling of tightrope tension: Gaudier is pushing asymmetry as far as he can, in the knowledge that the most exciting composition of 'masses in relation' invariably springs from a willingness to take risks, to shock and surprise. So he drives his chisel deep into the fabric of the stone, undercutting in layers, carving violent Vorticist diagonals and zigzags into each swaying upright in order to set the whole structure jerking with syncopated motion. The rhythms created by the work as the eye traverses its convoluted, ever-shifting surfaces are harsh and jarring. The abruptness is intimately related to the essential impact of a Vorticist picture, and yet it is not the same: these hewn fragments have an organic warmth that belongs to Gaudier alone, and goes some way towards counteracting the unrest of the sculpture. The stones appear to be unfolding and expanding outwards from their base, and the continuously changing surfaces they present when the work is walked around seem to reflect this process of growth.

Abstraction gave Gaudier the chance to inject several layers of meaning into one carving, and *Birds Erect* is full of associations with plant life. 'He had several small cacti in his studio', recalled Brodzky, who maintained that the sculpture was directly inspired by their shapes. 'These he liked because they suggested new ideas. All the time, he was going to nature for his forms.'[30] Just as Lewis had always insisted, Gaudier never lost sight of his response to the outside world, even though *Birds Erect* makes plain his desire to erect an alternative realm of his own ordering. 'This is one of the most important pieces', declared Pound, placing the work in a symbolic position at the end of his catalogue of Gaudier's *œuvre*. He made his admiration evident by roundly asserting that 'as a composition of masses I do not think I have seen any modern sculpture to match it.'[31] *Birds Erect* is without doubt among the most defiant and extreme sculptures to have been produced in Europe by 1914. Gaudier enjoys the intrinsic character of the limestone, making its porous texture an integral part of the cool, bleached mood conveyed by the sculpture as a whole. He adjusted his working methods to suit the specific demands which his respect for the sculptor's material imposed on him. What really counted was the use to which the sculptor put the various materials that came his way, enhancing their individual properties rather than hiding them in an attempt to pretend that he only ever employed marble or bronze. 'The sculpture I admire is the work of master craftsmen', Gaudier wrote proudly in *The Egoist*.

'Every inch of the surface is won at the point of the chisel – every stroke of the hammer is a physical and mental effort. No more arbitrary translations of a design in any material. They are fully aware of the different qualities and possibilities of woods, stones, and metals.' He went on to acknowledge the source of his convictions by explaining how 'Epstein, whom I consider the foremost in the small number of good sculptors in Europe, lays particular stress on this. Brancusi's greatest pride is his consciousness of being an accomplished workman.'[32]

Gaudier was right to draw a connection between Epstein and Brancusi. The two men had befriended each other in 1912, when Epstein stayed in Paris for several months while his *Tomb of Oscar Wilde* was installed in Père Lachaise cemetery. Although Epstein became particularly close to Modigliani, whose 'long heads … suggested by African masks'[33] made a forcible impression on him, Brancusi provided an inspiring example as well. Epstein visited his studio, with its neat rows of 'bottles of milk "maturing" … in the passage', and took careful note of the Rumanian's opinions. 'African sculpture, no doubt, influenced Brancusi,' Epstein recalled, 'but to me he exclaimed against its influence. One must not imitate Africans, he often said.'[34] Such a stricture implied a criticism of Modigliani's carvings, and may have temporarily confused Epstein. 'For one reason or another I did little work, and in the end got very exasperated with Paris,' he wrote, 'and determined to go back to England – if possible get into some solitary place to work.'[35]

Epstein urgently needed isolation in order to collect his thoughts and embark on a series of works more audacious than anything he had produced before. Possibly his involvement with the decorations at the Cave of the Golden Calf, a controversial cabaret club founded in 1912 by the former wife of August Strindberg,[36] helped to strengthen his desire for experiment. While Lewis painted 'somewhat abstract hieroglyphics' around the walls, Epstein surrounded 'two massive iron pillars' with sculpture in relief, proceeding directly in plaster and making 'a very elaborate decoration which I painted in brilliant colours.'[37] Epstein must have admired Lewis's work, for Pound wrote in 1916 that

> years ago, three I suppose it is, or four, I said to Epstein (not having seen these things of Lewis, or indeed more than a few things he had then exhibited), 'The sculpture seems to be so much more interesting … than the painting'. Jacob said, 'But Lewis's drawing has the qualities of sculpture' … that set me off looking at Lewis.[38]

But if Epstein was being partially drawn into Lewis's magnetic orbit, he resisted the possibility of an open alliance by retreating from London in 1913 and renting 'a bungalow on the Sussex coast at a solitary place called Pett Level, where

39 Jacob Epstein, *Flenite Relief*, 1913, serpentine,
305 x 280 mm (12 x 11 in)

I could look out to sea and carve away to my heart's
content.'[39] Here, in congenial surroundings where he
embarked on 'a period of intense activity' and became 'very
happy',[40] Epstein produced a group of carvings which placed
him at the forefront of the European avant garde. Although
it is difficult and perhaps unnecessary to establish a firmly
chronological sequence of events, he seems first to have
acquired some pieces of serpentine stone – which he nick-
named 'flenite' – and decided to explore its possibilities.

In *Flenite Relief* (fig.39) the figure of an archaistic baby
appears to have emerged from its mother's bent and straining
body. The forms of woman and child are scored so brusquely
as to constitute a rejection of conventional sculptural skill. It
is as if Epstein wanted to start all over again, forgetting the
technical sophistication he had tried so hard to acquire during
the previous decade, in order to return to the fundamental
principles of sculpture. It must have been a necessary and
refreshing exercise for him, tired as he was of stale recipes and
traditional solutions. Sequestered in a remote part of southern
England, he could afford to dismiss the towering achieve-
ments of the European past and enter into the spirit of his
most distant forerunners, who would have hacked out hieratic
images as cult-objects to fear or worship. If the *Flenite Relief*
now seems rather self-conscious in its attempt to identify
with the beginnings of sculpture – the very choice of the
word 'flenite' indicates how much he wanted to stress the
primitive origins of his inspiration – it did enable Epstein
to clear the ground, establishing his true priorities so that

40 Epstein carving *Mother and Child*, c.1913–15, granite

he could move on to more complex and ambitious carvings.

Turning to another lump of the same material, he
proceeded to fashion a *Female Figure in Flenite* (plate XXVIII)
which exchanged the irregular surfaces of the *Relief* for a
smoother, more highly polished finish. Two robust legs rise
up like leaning columns from the feet's rectangular slabs.
Their slightly diagonal emphasis lends a subtle rhythm to the
carving: the angle of the legs tilts up towards the vital focus of
the belly, and the upper half of the figure sways back before
curving over the pregnant stomach in a sweeping semicircle of
protective movement. Every element in the mother's body is
concentrated on her womb, which she holds with far more
compassion than her successor. In place of the harsh
transitions and deliberate primitivism so evident in the *Relief*,
Epstein has injected his own psychological insight into
Female Figure, so that its archaic qualities are married to the
sculptor's own knowledge of the condition of motherhood.
Possibly remembering Brancusi's counsel not to 'imitate
Africans', he realized that a revival of 'primitive' art for its
own sake was not enough. *Female Figure in Flenite* is
affecting because of its poised interplay between contrasting
rhythms, all conspiring to emanate a feeling of human
tenderness and warmth.

Epstein finally decided to exhibit this outstanding carving
in the 1913 Allied Artists' salon. But he was also at work on
a monumental version of the themes explored by the flenite
images: a granite *Mother and Child*. The final appearance of
this imposing sculpture, which brought together the child of
Flenite Relief and, perhaps, the mother of *Female Figure in
Flenite* in one grand union, is unknown.[41] The only surviving
photograph shows Epstein standing proudly beside the half-
finished block (fig.40). But enough of its structure is visible
to indicate that he proposed to dispense with the pregnancy
theme and show the mother holding the child in front of her.
It must have been one of his most commanding images. The
outlines of the child, firmer and more rigid than the near-
silhouette hewn out of the side of the *Relief*, suggest that the
group would have been more hieratic and geometrically
defined than the flenite carving.

The series of dove carvings (fig.41) move further away from
'primitive' art towards an emulation of the work Epstein
would have seen in Brancusi's Paris studio. One particular
carving, the Rumanian's 1912 *Three Penguins*, seems to have
guided Epstein in his search for even greater simplification.
Its translucent white marble medium, no less than its bare
equation of minimal forms, affected the way he approached
the Tate Gallery's *Doves* in particular. Unlike the first *Doves*
carving, where the male has alighted on his partner's back and
contemplates the next move, this version openly represents
intercourse. The male has now settled in comfortably along
the entire length of his partner, and the new pose works with
conspicuous success. The feeling of extreme stasis conveyed
by the rigidly defined components of the birds' bodies is
echoed in the serenity of their pose, slotted together in a
single compact mass of interlocking forms. Epstein has
calculated his carving so carefully that each element fits into
its neighbour with a satisfying sense of inevitability. The
female's tail, for example, stretches out from the base of the
group to provide a ledge for the downward thrust of her
mate's tail, while her wings curve up at their ends to carry the
rhythm in a circular motion towards the sloping rump of the
male's wings. The contours of both doves are treated as one
coherent whole, whereas the two birds in the first version had
remained separate entities, awkward and disunited.

Taken together, the flenite and dove carvings reinforced
Pound's admiration. 'Epstein is a great sculptor', he
announced categorically to Isabel Pound in November 1913.
'I wish he would wash, but I believe Michel Angelo *never* did,
so I suppose it is part of the tradition.'[42] It seems, in fact, to
have been Epstein rather than Lewis who gradually awakened
Pound to a new, polemical involvement with modern English
art during that year. A little later he declared that, 'so far as I
am concerned, Jacob Epstein was the first person who came
talking about "form, not the *form of anything*"',[43] and Pound
initially showed more enthusiasm for the sculptor's work than

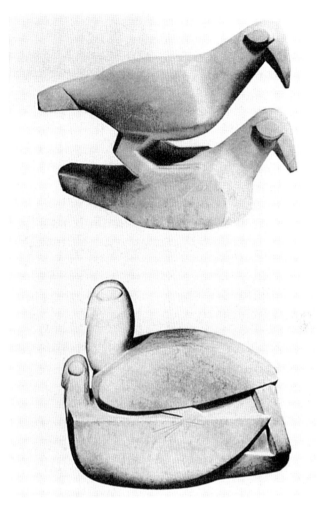

41 Jacob Epstein, *Doves*. 1st version, 1913, marble,
     350 x 495 x 184 mm (13¾ x 19½ x 7¼ in). 2nd version,
     1914–15, marble, 650 x 240 x 710 mm (25½ x 9½ x 28 in)

for Lewis's. He especially admired a fourth dove carving, *Bird
Pluming Itself*, of which no trace now remains. Pound likened
it to 'a cloud bent back upon itself – not a woolly cloud, but
one of those clouds that are blown smooth by the wind. It is
gracious and aerial.'[44] Such appreciation would have been a
huge comfort to Epstein, bedevilled by admirers of his earlier
work who were now retracting their support.

Hostility did not, however, prevent him from realizing his
ambitions to produce sculpture on the most monumental
scale. The three-year period at Pett Level gave Epstein the
necessary solitude to tackle superhuman tasks, and he soon
set about carving two large marble *Venus* figures (fig.43) that
would bring together his twin obsessions with pregnancy and
copulating doves in a monolithic résumé. All the Pett Level
works seem to have grown out of each other, suggesting
variations to the sculptor as he executed them. One of
Epstein's illustrations in the first issue of *Blast*, a lost drawing

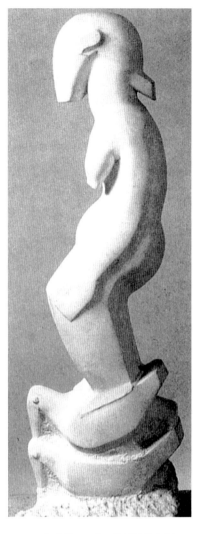

of a pregnant mother enclosed in a mesh of whirling lines that
form a cave-like protection around her (fig.42), stands as a
bridge connecting the preoccupations of the Flenite carvings
with the Venuses. The central figure is no longer a rounded,
essentially archaic creature as she was in *Female Figure in
Flenite*: the head has now taken on the stiff angularity of a
geometrical helmet, and the tensely summarized surroundings
refer as much to a twentieth-century environment as they
do to a primitive jungle. It may well have been one of the
drawings exhibited in Epstein's first one-man show at the
Twenty-One Gallery, for Hulme seized on them as exemplars
of his new theories about art in his Quest Society lecture.
'The tendency to abstraction, the desire to turn the organic
into something hard and durable, is here at work, not on
something simple, such as you get in the more archaic work,
but on something much more complicated', he wrote.
'Abstraction is much greater in the second case, because
generation, which is the very essence of all the qualities which
we have here called organic, has been turned into something

as hard and durable as a geometrical figure itself.'[45] With his
usual perspicacity, Hulme had put his finger on the extraordinary paradox informing both the marble Venuses. For
while they celebrate the wonder of procreation, and become
goddesses of fertility, they are at the same time putting into
practice Epstein's new-found interest in rigidly dehumanized
stylization.

African sculpture, and in particular the great *De Miré
Figure* which later entered Epstein's own collection,[46] still
informs the Venus carvings. But a fascinating sheet of
drawings (plate XXIX) shows how his enthusiasm for
'primitivism' and the power of totemic structures also fuelled
the most mechanistic of all Epstein's major works. Probably
executed in the early months of 1913, the studies on this sheet
reveal the movement of his imagination from tribal art
towards a form-language more redolent of technological
prowess. The central drawing is an arresting angular presence,
in which the hieratic body of a woman is pierced by a man
inverted below her. The phallic tension in this amalgam of

male and female figures is clear enough, and a small sketch of two amorous doves elsewhere on the paper reinforces the theme of copulation. In the rest of the sheet, however, Epstein discloses a determination to explore the possibility of an even more monumental embodiment of masculinity.

On the left, the figure of a man appears, his thrusting and brusquely simplified limbs all embroiled in an activity of intense strain. It is bound up with the 'virility' Epstein had first celebrated in his carving of *Man* for the British Medical Association building five years before,[47] but now the classical anatomy of that early statue has given way to an altogether more schematic alternative. Half human and half automaton, the male figure in this drawing appears to be the harbinger of a different, harsher and more disturbing world. On the right of the paper, Epstein has defined the jagged contours of a rocket-like form which explodes upwards, thereby revealing that he was already beginning to equate phallic power with the driving action of a machine.

Epstein's burgeoning friendship with Hulme helps to account for this new involvement with mechanical metaphor. After all, Hulme had already discovered in the *Tomb of Oscar Wilde* elements which prompted him, as Epstein recalled, to 'put his own construction on my work – turned it into some theory of projectiles.'[48] As Hulme grew more fascinated by the implications of avant-garde art, and Epstein's sculpture in particular, he came to believe that 'the new "tendency towards abstraction" will culminate, not so much in the simple geometrical forms found in archaic art, but in the more complicated ones associated in our minds with the idea of machinery.'[49] Hulme was bound to encourage his new friend to think about moving on from 'archaism' towards a more mechanistic language, and Epstein's passionate concern with sexuality and the procreative force ensured that he would cast around for the mechanical equivalent of a penis. In *Study for Man–Woman* (plate xxx), a drawing of this period, his preoccupation with this theme is strongly apparent, still relying on precedents in primitive sculpture.

The idea of turning a phallus into a drill may have occurred to him during a visit to a stone quarry. Epstein remembered that 'it was in the experimental pre-war days of 1913 that I was fired to do the rock drill',[50] and his choice of the word 'fired' implies that it was a sudden, almost impulsive decision. Perhaps the sight of a drill boring into the rockface with deafening force came as a revelation to him, for there was no doubt about the formidable power of this mechanical tool. Mounted on a tripod, and capable of dislodging impressive quantities of rock in the mines where it was principally employed, the modern drill seemed an implement of prodigious strength and effectiveness.[51] It revolutionized the mining industry, and Epstein decided that his *Rock Drill* (fig.44) would revolutionize twentieth-century sculpture as well.

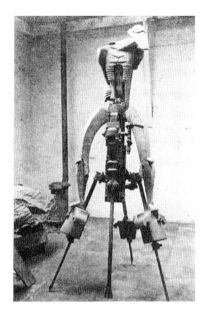

44 Photo of original *Rock Drill*

The first drawings to outline his ideas for the work stress the indomitable character of the machine, and place it in the charge of a driller with equally daunting powers (figs 45, 46). Framed by the gaunt, jutting sides of a cleft which seems to have been created by his mighty weapon, the driller stands on his tripod with legs as straight as pistons. He looks upward, as if to display his supreme confidence, and only in a subsequent back view of the ensemble does his head bend down towards the task in hand. The locale, however, has now become even more awesome. Viewed from behind, the driller rides far above the ground and a cloud floats from the side of the drill as if to emphasize his airborne dimensions.

This cloud also signifies a rush of steam from the machine, proving that it was in motion. As the drawings progressed, and the driller's legs curved into an arch contrasting more strikingly with the pyramidal structure of the tripod, Epstein became intrigued by the possibility of activating the drill. Doubtless aware of the kinetic experiments conducted by some Futurist sculptors, he thought at one stage 'of attaching pneumatic power to my rock drill, and setting it in motion, thus completing every potentiality of form and movement in one single work.'[52] The plan was subsequently abandoned, not so much because it was impractical but because Epstein shared the Vorticists' antipathy towards the blurred motion of Futurist art. Like Wyndham Lewis, who abhorred multiple movement in his work, Epstein preferred to enclose his forms in rigid outlines. His *Rock Drill* drawings show how much reliance he placed on the clean, hard clarity of defining contours, even when he focused on a particularly dynamic study of the drill's head biting into the rock. The lines radiating from the point of impact may represent shattering vibration, but they are handled with a robust lucidity which leaves no room for excitable Futurist confusion. So a machine

45 Jacob Epstein, *Study for 'Rock Drill'*, c.1913,
       charcoal on paper, 641 x 533 mm (25½ x 21 in)

shuddering with movement was ultimately incompatible with
Epstein's own stern imperatives as an artist.

He did, however, go ahead with the plan to incorporate a
real machine in this extraordinary sculpture. With a boldness
which still seems astonishing today, he arranged 'the purchase
of an actual drill, second-hand, and upon this I made and
mounted a machine-like robot, visored, menacing, and
carrying within itself its progeny, protectively ensconsed.'[53]
This foetal form, whose rounded masses could hardly be
more opposed to the schematic harshness of the driller's
torso, is the successor to the embryonic baby lodged within
the rock carried by *Matter* on the British Medical Association
façade.[54] There, on the Strand frontage of Holden's building,
it was exposed to view in the care of an ancient sage. Now, by
contrast, it is securely embedded in a cavity guarded by the
armoured severity of the driller's rib-cage. But its presence in
this strange assemblage still conveys a sense of apprehensive-
ness. Turning the handle to operate the machine, the driller is
unavoidably conscious of his responsibility towards the new
life of the future. Epstein attached great importance to
symbolism, even during this most innovative period when he
came nearer to formal purism than at any other time in his
career. He seems to be asking whether the organic shape of
the foetus will be transformed, with the advent of maturity,
into a robot as dehumanized as the driller himself.

46 Jacob Epstein, *Study for 'Rock Drill'*, c.1913, charcoal on paper,
       425 x 675 mm (16½ x 26½ in)

When he was at work on the first, full-length version of
Rock Drill, Epstein's self-confessed 'ardour for machinery'[55]
probably prevented him from pondering too deeply on its
more sinister implications. His admiration for the drill was,
after all, great enough to convince him that it deserved to
become an integral and, indeed, dominant part of a major
sculpture. When the completed work was put on view in the
March 1915 London Group exhibition, its audacity astounded
most of the viewers who examined it (fig.47). For Epstein had
gone almost as far towards the ultimate aesthetic heresy as
Duchamp, who in 1913 nominated a *Bicycle Wheel* as a work
of art. The ready-made drill was, admittedly, augmented by
the man-made figure of a driller, cast in white plaster to
distinguish it still more dramatically from the black, shining
drill supported by the tripod. But Epstein was still
challenging his audience to accept that a real machine could
be recognized as a legitimate part of a sculpture.

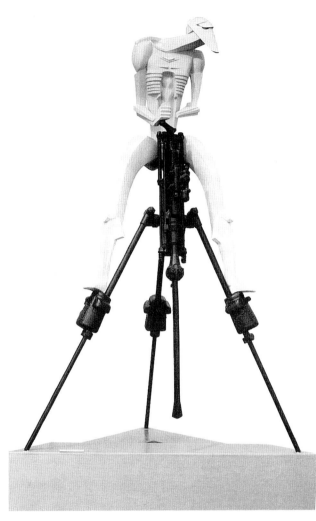

47 Jacob Epstein, *Rock Drill*, 1913–15 (reconstruction 1974), plaster and drill, height 2050 mm (80¾ in)

Most of the critics who wrote about it responded with predictable hostility, siding with P.J. Konody's declaration in the *Observer* that 'the whole effect is unutterably loathsome. Even leaving aside the nasty suggestiveness of the whole thing, there remains the irreconcilable contradiction between the crude realism of real machinery (of American make) combined with an abstractly treated figure.'[56] Only one newspaper reviewer, the *Manchester Guardian*'s correspondent, understood why Epstein had been tempted to place the machine itself on view. His excited reaction vividly conveys the astonishment with which *Rock Drill* must have been greeted by the London Group's visitors. 'He has accepted it all, the actual rock drill is here in this art gallery', wrote the stunned *Guardian* critic.

Mr Epstein has accepted the rock drill, and says frankly that if he could have invented anything better he would have done it.

But he could not. One can see how it fascinated him; the three long strong legs, the compact assembly of cylinder, screws and valve, with its control handles decoratively at one side, and especially the long, straight cutting drill like a proboscis – it all seems the naked expression of a definite force.

Although the reviewer acknowledged that Epstein had 'found in a rock-drill machine the ideal of all that is expressive in mobile, penetrating, shattering force', he finally decided that the inclusion of a ready-made machine was too raw, clashing to an uncomfortable extent with the driller above. 'Even if the figure is to be cast in iron,' he concluded, 'the incongruity between an engine with every detail insistent and a synthetic man is too difficult for the mind to grasp.'[57]

The criticism was understandable enough, for nothing like *Rock Drill* had ever been exhibited as sculpture in a British gallery before. Its reviewers failed to understand why Epstein had not taken as many liberties with the drill as he did with the driller, whose entire body was metamorphosed into a creature of the sculptor's own imagination. The visored helmet, attached to a neck as straight and sharp-edged as the shaft of some mighty engine, leads down towards a torso angular and faceted enough to suggest mechanical components fit for inclusion in a rock drill itself. The gothic arch described by the legs, as they sprout so surprisingly from the driller's narrow waist, introduces a more expansive note. But even here the sense of dehumanization remains as strong as ever, reflecting Epstein's belief that the machine age was transforming humanity into a race of armoured and rigidly constructed figures.

Why, then, had he not subjected the drill to the same schematic treatment? The most convincing reason was voiced by his friend Gaudier, who told Pound in 1914 that 'machinery itself has used up so many of the fine combinations of three-dimensional inorganic forms that there is very little use in experimenting with them in sculpture.'[58] How, Epstein must have thought, could he possibly improve on the magnificence of the real rock drill? There was no point; and besides, he doubtless wanted to make people appreciate the innate qualities of the machine. Pound insisted in 1916 that 'the forms of automobiles and engines … where they are truly expressive of various modes of efficiency, can be and often are very beautiful in themselves and in their combinations, though the fact of this beauty is in itself offensive to the school of sentimental aesthetics.'[59] Epstein would have agreed with this argument when he installed the first version of *Rock Drill* on its triangular plinth[60] at the London Group exhibition, where the implement and its tripod challenged 'sentimentalists' to deny that machinery deserved the respectful attention they normally reserved for more conventional works of art.

It was a brazenly provocative act. Even Wyndham Lewis,

whose own figure drawings had helped Epstein to develop the analogical language employed in the driller's body, could not accept *Rock Drill* without voicing some reservations. 'The combination of the white figure and the rock-drill is rather unfortunate and ghost-like', he wrote in the second issue of *Blast*, before going on to concede that 'its lack of logic has an effectiveness of its own. I feel that a logical co-ordination was not intended. It should be taken rather as a monumental, bustling, and very personal whim.' Lewis was right to argue that Epstein had deliberately created an irrational apparition in *Rock Drill*. The dream-like amalgam of machine and worker certainly had the power to haunt the imagination, and Lewis concluded that it was 'one of the best things Epstein has done. The nerve-like figure perched on the machinery, with its straining to one purpose, is a vivid illustration of the greatest function of life.'[61]

When *Rock Drill* was first placed on view, few writers linked it with the First World War. Epstein had conceived the sculpture long before hostilities were declared, and only later did David Bomberg realize that the assemblage he had first seen in Epstein's studio around December 1913 contained 'a Prophetic Symbol … of the impending war.'[62] As the carnage increased, however, and Britain began to understand just how many lives were being sacrificed in a struggle which showed no sign of ending, so it affected Epstein's attitude towards the sculpture he had made. Looking back on the work many years afterwards, he maintained that *Rock Drill* possessed 'no humanity, only the terrible Frankenstein's monster we have made ourselves into.'[63] But this verdict was delivered with the benefit of hindsight, and bore little relation to the vision which had inspired the superhuman heroism of the original drawings. Only in the latter half of 1915, when Epstein and everyone else left at home began to appreciate just how senselessly destructive the struggle in the trenches had become, did his attitude towards the machine age really alter.

The Great War was the first industrialized conflict suffered by the world, and it claimed an obscene number of victims with the help of inventions like the rapid-fire machine gun. Once the devastating power of such weapons became widely understood, it was no longer possible to regard an object like the rock drill in a straightforwardly positive light. The menacing character of this aggressive implement grew impossible to avoid, and Epstein came to the conclusion that it should be excluded from his sculpture. His widow Kathleen remembered him explaining, decades later, 'that he abandoned the drill because he hadn't made it himself, it was just a machine',[64] and so Epstein may have been impelled as well by misgivings about the controversial status of a ready-made in his own art. By 1916 he was beginning to reconsider the extremism of his work and contemplate returning to a more figurative approach. A growing preference for traditional materials and methods precluded any further dalliance with

Duchampian experiments, and he decided that only the man-made part of his *Rock Drill* should be retained and cast in metal. All the same, an examination of the final version of the sculpture, exhibited in the London Group show of summer 1916 under the title *Torso in Metal from 'The Rock Drill'* (plate XXXI), proves that the discarding of the drill was not prompted simply by objections to the validity of a ready-made. For the truncated upper part of the driller is far removed in meaning from the indomitable man who had once straddled his machine with such imperious confidence. The hand that previously held the drill's controls has been lopped off, too, along with the forearm and elbow. Although the other arm is left unchanged, it likewise lacks a hand and thrusts outwards only to hang uselessly in space. The driller's mask-like head takes on a more defensive and even hesitant air, peering forward as if to search for signs of imminent danger. But his amputated limbs hold out no hope of warding off an assault, and the embryonic form still nestling in his rib-cage appears far more vulnerable than it ever did when positioned above the drill.

Seen from behind, the driller's body looks frail rather than impregnable. His back is riven by a crooked fissure extending from the shoulders to the base of the spine. The left arm is similarly split by a gash savage enough to resemble a wound. In retrospect, Epstein declared that *Rock Drill* was 'a thing prophetic of much of the great war and as such within the experience of nearly all.'[65] He did not explain precisely what he meant, but his shattered *Torso* possesses the melancholy, stooping pathos of a soldier returning from the Front as a helpless invalid. This body will never recover from the damage inflicted on it by the horror of war; and it will certainly be unable to remount the drill and resume the triumphant battle against the primal rock-face. The struggle has been lost.

Epstein hated war, and this final tragic version of *Rock Drill* shows how determined he was to resist the propagandist view of the conflict still promoted by a government anxious to sustain the troops' flagging morale.[66] But the *Torso* also goes a long way towards explaining why he would never again explore machine imagery in his sculpture. Two of his most valued friends, Gaudier and Hulme, were killed during the war, and Epstein himself would suffer a 'complete breakdown'[67] after his enlistment in 1918. He could never, in all conscience, return to the unqualified optimism which had produced his early *Rock Drill* drawings. In the successive stages of one sculpture, Epstein at once defined the central tenets of Vorticism and then eroded them by introducing an element of tragic vulnerability. *Rock Drill* is therefore a pivotal work, summarizing the English movement's funda-mental standpoint even as it ushers in the disenchantment with the machine age that led to the Vorticists' downfall.

Gaudier's death, in a battle at Neuville-Saint-Vaast on

5 June 1915, was an especially grievous blow. His obituary notice in the second issue of *Blast*, printed within a black border under the heading 'MORT POUR LA PATRIE',[68] cast a shadow over the entire periodical. The loss of so promising an artist, at such a young age, made the occasional outbursts of high spirits emitted by other contributors to the magazine seem misplaced. To the end, his work was eclectic enough to resist any attempt to place it all neatly within the orbit of Vorticism. The fact that his departure for the war in France meant 'all the art-feuds of young London were at truce for half an hour'[69] shows how he succeeded in attracting the admiration of a wide cross-section of bitterly opposed factions. The one thing everyone agreed about was Gaudier's talent, his immense promise, and the normally unsentimental Lewis gave way to sadness when he recalled the final farewell on the railway platform. 'I remember him in the carriage window of the boat-train, with his excited eyes', Lewis wrote.

> We left the platform, a depressed, almost a guilty, group. It is easy to laugh at the exaggerated estimate 'the artist' puts upon his precious life. But when it is really an artist – and there are very few – it is at the death of something terribly alive that you are assisting. And this little figure was so preternaturally alive.[70]

Only a few months were left to Gaudier from the time of his final enlistment to death at the age of twenty-three. It would be idle to search for any significant development in his thinking about art among the miscellaneous assortment of letters, postcards and hasty sketches which he sent back to his friends in London from the Front, were it not that he told Pound in October 1914 about his decision to compose 'a short essay on sculpture for the *Blast* Christmas No.'[71] The article arrived at the beginning of December, and it reassured his Vorticist friends by affirming that 'MY VIEWS ON SCULPTURE REMAIN ABSOLUTELY THE SAME. IT IS THE VORTEX OF WILL, OF DECISION, THAT BEGINS.' Dramatically entitled 'VORTEX GAUDIER-BRZESKA (Written from the Trenches)', the essay set out to prove that his ideas had not changed since he wrote the first three lines of his 'Vortex' credo in the first issue of *Blast.* The horror and bloodshed of war had done nothing to make him retract his previous emphasis on the supreme importance of formal rigour. There was plenty of time for thought and observation in the trenches, and he reported that his new experiences had simply strengthened his earlier convictions. 'Just as this hill where the Germans are solidly entrenched, gives me a nasty feeling, solely because its gentle slopes are broken up by earth-works, which throw long shadows at sunset,' he wrote, 'just so shall I get feeling, of whatsoever definition, from a statue ACCORDING TO ITS SLOPES, varied to infinity.' Chance configurations of the landscape affected him far more

than the prospect of death, and so he concluded that his future work would be controlled by the same emphasis on abstract design as it had done hitherto. 'I SHALL DERIVE MY EMOTIONS SOLELY FROM THE ARRANGEMENT OF SURFACES', he declared; 'I shall present my emotions by the ARRANGEMENT OF MY SURFACES, THE PLANES AND LINES BY WHICH THEY ARE DEFINED.'

The extremism was, if anything, even more absolute than it ever had been: now his very emotions would be 'derived' from the structure of a surface itself. As a practical manifestation of his renewed radicalism, a substitute for the sculptures he would have executed had the war not prevented him from doing so, he told his rebel friends that 'I have made an experiment. Two days ago I pinched from an enemy a mauser rifle. Its heavy unwieldy shape swamped me with a powerful IMAGE of brutality.' He had been moved by the shape of the rifle, not by the fact that it was a weapon of destruction. And so, discovering that 'I did not like it', he decided to counteract the 'brutality' with an alternative shape of his own. 'I broke the butt off and with my knife I carved in it a design, through which I tried to express a gentler order of feeling, which I preferred', he wrote. 'BUT I WILL EMPHASIZE that MY DESIGN got its effect (just as the gun had) FROM A VERY SIMPLE COMPOSITION OF LINES AND PLANES.'[72]

The carving has since been lost, and along with it any indication of what Gaudier's last sculpture looked like. If he had not 'gone out through a little hole in the high forehead',[73] as Ford Madox Ford lamented in his obituary article, he might of course have followed his colleagues and reverted to a more representational way of working. Even Pound admitted that 'for the second number of *Blast*, Gaudier had planned an essay on "The Need of Organic Forms in Sculpture"'. Indeed, Pound reported the substance of 'almost [my] last long talk' with Gaudier, in which the sculptor said that 'his conclusion, after these months of thought and experiment, was that combinations of abstract or inorganic forms exclusively, were more suitable for painting than for sculpture.'[74] The practical application of these thoughts can already be seen in the pronounced organic leanings of *Birds Erect*, and Gaudier might well have gone on to achieve a more complete synthesis of the natural and the mechanical had he survived.

The only reliable answer to the question of Gaudier's future development lies in the last works themselves, a brace of hasty, crumpled pencil sketches which he sent back from Craonne for exhibition at the second London Group show. One of them, *A Mitrailleuse in Action* (fig.48), shows how closely allied Gaudier still was with the concerns of the other Vorticists: the soldier bending over his firing gun is as mechanical as the weapon he holds. Indeed, his whole body is defined with such confident precision that it merges with the

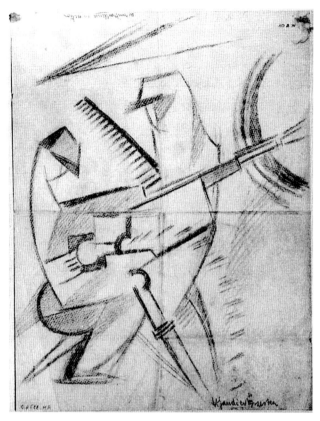

49 Henri Gaudier-Brzeska, *One of Our Shells Exploding*, 1915,
pencil on paper, 220 x 285 mm (8¾ x 11¼ in)

48 Henri Gaudier-Brzeska, *A Mitrailleuse in Action*, 1915, pencil on
paper, 285 x 220 mm (11¼ x 8¾ in)

harsh lines of the gun in a compact mass of aggressive energy.
The drawing, with its swift definition of essential form, would
not have looked out of place in *Blast*'s 'War Number', next to
an illustration like Roberts's *Machine Gunners*, c.1914–15.

Gaudier set his *Mitrailleuse* down with true Vorticist
detachment, just as he calmly traced the exploding arcs of
a shell that could easily have destroyed him in the other
drawing from the trenches, *One of Our Shells Exploding*
(fig.49). His reckless courage became proverbial at the Front –
he was promoted for gallantry twice, becoming a corporal and
then a sergeant. Moreover, he accounted for the analytical
coolness of this remarkable sketch by explaining in his final
Blast essay that 'THE BURSTING SHELLS, the volleys, wire
entanglements, projectors, motors, the chaos of battle DO
NOT ALTER IN THE LEAST, the outlines of the hill we are
besieging.'[75] Those 'outlines' represented the permanent
values in Gaudier's imagination: the fuss and noise were as
unimportant as the hysterics of the Futurists had been to him
in pre-war London. Hence the shell drawing's spare arrangement of lines, which he had successfully extracted from the

blurred confusion of a real explosion without losing sight of
its underlying power.

The 'direct and hot impressions of life' had indeed been
'mated with Abstraction', exactly as Lewis recommended. So
it was entirely understandable that the editor of *Blast* should
have reserved special praise in his magazine for this particular
sketch. 'His beautiful drawing from the trenches of a bursting
shell is not only a fine design, but a curiosity', Lewis wrote.

It is surely a pretty satisfactory answer to those who would kill
us with Prussian bullets: who say, in short, that Germany, in
attacking Europe, has killed spiritually all the Cubists,
Vorticists and Futurists in the world. Here is one, a great artist,
who makes drawings of those shells as they come towards him,
and which, thank God, have not killed or changed him yet.[76]

Soon after these words were written, Gaudier died during an
infantry charge; but if the missiles which he drew finally
destroyed him, this battered sketch survives to prove that war
had not destroyed his belief in Vorticism as well.

Reconceptualizing Vorticism: Women, Modernity, Modernism[1]

JANE BECKETT AND DEBORAH CHERRY

In *Vorticism and Abstract Art in the First Machine Age* Richard Cork advanced three major propositions: that Vorticism was born of a historical moment of turmoil and disruption; that it proposed a radical and avant-garde engagement with contemporary society; and that its rigorous rationalization of pictorial and sculptural form drew inspiration from machinery. Written between 1968 and 1974, Cork's two volumes remain invaluable and the foundation for any study of Vorticism. Yet in the twenty years and more between Cork's account and David Peters Corbett's *The Modernity of English Art* much has changed.[2] As concepts of modernity, modernism and the avant garde have been subjected to sustained investigation, so emphases have shifted and histories been reconfigured. In *English Art and Modernism* (first published in 1981 and in a revised edition in 1994) Charles Harrison traced the development of a formal aesthetic of autonomy from the later nineteenth-century paintings of Whistler through the paintings of Sickert and the Camden Town Group, Bloomsbury and Post-Impressionism to Cubism, Futurism and Vorticism, and beyond into the 1920s and 1930s. If Harrison was disinclined to open up the category of modernism to critical enquiry, he was, as he admitted, equally disinclined 'to offer any radical revision of the history as it has been received',[3] a move which was calculated, as Peters Corbett points out, 'to assert the difference of the English domestic tradition from continental modernism'.[4] Determined to break with persistent narratives of the failure of English art to engage with European modernism, Peters Corbett investigated 'the relationship between modernism in painting and the modernity of English culture', arguing that modernism was only one of many visual responses to modernity and modernity was not dependent on modernism 'for its realisation in the cultural sphere'.[5]

In their accounts of Vorticism, none of these writers has resisted a mesmerizing fascination with Wyndham Lewis, an artist who, through his own efforts as much as those of later supporters, has been the subject of a persistent and increasing literature. There is it seems no escaping Lewis's assertion that 'Vorticism, in fact, was what I, personally, did, and said, at a certain period'.[6] Peters Corbett's opening chapter was almost exclusively concerned with Lewis. For Cork Vorticism's story is that of Lewis; hailed as the 'progenitor' of the movement, his temperament ('often painfully shy'[7] in his early years), interests and friendships were woven through an account as much preoccupied with artists, their fractions and fractiousness, as with the art they produced. While Harrison's stage was filled with larger-than-life masculine egos engaged in combative struggles over definitions of the 'modern', Cork at least acknowledged 'the female members of the movement' although his conceptual framework, on his own admission 'male chauvinist', foreclosed serious attention. Considering many of Helen Saunders's works to be marred by 'female waywardness', 'hurried and ill-considered' composition and a 'careless handling of line', and judging Dismorr's art to be 'oddly feeble-minded', 'wilfully crude' and 'dangerously rudimentary', Cork asserted that both women, spell-bound by Lewis's 'personal charisma', produced art which was by and large derivative. 'Could it be,' he concluded, 'that a feminine temperament was congenitally incapable of sustaining the amount of aggression needed to create a convincing Vorticist work of art?'[8] Ten years later he declined to include them in an essay for the catalogue of an exhibition which largely excluded women artists from its account of modern art in Britain.[9]

50 Dorothy Shakespear, cover design for Ezra Pound, *Catholic Anthology*, c.1915, ink on paper, 283 x 197 mm (11 x 7¾ in)

It was women historians who began the serious reconsideration and recontextualization of the work of Jessica Dismorr, Kate Lechmere, Helen Saunders and Dorothy Shakespear.[10] Dismorr and Saunders signed the manifesto in *Blast* no. 1 of 1914 and both contributed to *Blast* no. 2 of 1915, the 'War Number', Saunders also sharing responsibility for the magazine's distribution.[11] These two contributed to the Vorticist exhibitions in London in 1915 and in New York in 1917, and work by Saunders was included in the 'Cubist Room' of the exhibition 'Twentieth Century Art' held at the Whitechapel Art Gallery in 1914. Designs by Dorothy Shakespear were reproduced in *Blast* no. 2[12] and commissioned for covers of Ezra Pound's publications (fig. 50). Lechmere and Saunders were important creators of Vorticist spaces at the Rebel Art Centre and the Tour Eiffel restaurant respectively. The destruction of both these decorative schemes highlights some of the difficulties confronting the study of Vorticism, hampered as Cork

discovered by 'the loss of about half the movement's most important products'.[13] Discussion and interpretation of works by women artists must necessarily come to terms with the disappearance of much of their work, and a paucity of documentation, in part ameliorated by the recent cataloguing of surviving work by Helen Saunders and Dorothy Shakespear. While watercolours, designs and drawings remain, many major paintings and projects have been destroyed or lost. By 1956 Saunders could no longer locate 'the only pre-1916 work that she had thought worth preserving (a non-figurative oil painting, *c.* 20 x 24 inches)'.[14]

Feminist studies have challenged, contested, revised and resisted the canonical narratives of modernism, as much for their genealogies as for their myths of masculine creativity. Modernism has been analyzed as a 'selective tradition', and as a 'discursive and historical field' with specific formations of sexual and racial difference, and identifiable institutional structures operating in specific arenas of power/knowledge. Attention has been given to the discursive tactics which have marginalized and excluded not only female practitioners but the feminine, the domestic and the decorative.[15] Modernist discourses and institutions have claimed and been ascribed authorizing power to legitimate the modern and to constitute its canon. While there has been pressure on the margins, as new contenders are proposed and debated, the core of artists and movements mapped in Alfred Barr's flow-chart, with its racial and sexual asymmetries, has remained relatively stable.[16] Researching women artists and assessing their uneasy and highly variable relations to definitions of modernism and the changing conditions of modernity remains critically important to feminism, for as Bridget Elliott and Jo-Ann Wallace have explained, what is at issue here is the 'continuing struggle for certain kinds of symbolic power'.[17]

The period 1880 to 1920 has been perceived as one of crisis in which organized movements of women and labour claimed political and social representation, and the 'age of empire' was challenged by anti-imperialism, nationalist campaigns and bids for independence launched in the colonies and the metropole.[18] Modernity in Britain was forged in the tensions and at times violent collisions between the forces of imperialism, colonialism and their oppositions and resistances; it was decisively shaped by the pressures of socialism, class and what Rebecca West called 'sex-antagonism'.[19] While this reconceptualization allows for modernity to be structured less in terms of linear progress and more in terms of unevenness and contradiction, it also assists in displacing the emphasis given to technological modernization and the 'machine aesthetic'.[20]

Like other European avant-garde formations, Vorticism was a metropolitan phenomenon.[21] Early twentieth-century London was perceived by its visitors and inhabitants as changing from city to sprawling metropolis; a centre not only for work and production, the British capital was equally an arena for leisure, spectacle, tourism and consumerism. The name of the movement, which was formed during the years of major rebuilding in the city, seems to have had London resonances, Pound writing in December 1913 of the British capital as 'the Vortex'.[22] And when, two years later, he defined Vorticism as initiating 'new and swift perceptions' which transformed 'a dull row of houses' into 'a magazine of forms', the poet declared that these visual stimuli had struck him 'in going from my home to Piccadilly' in the West End.[23] *Blast* proclaimed in 1914 'LONDON IS <u>NOT</u> A PROVINCIAL TOWN.... We do not want the GLOOMY VICTORIAN CIRCUS in Piccadilly Circus', and the manifesto hailed 'the great art vortex sprung up in the centre of this town'.[24] The second issue included Dismorr's 'London Notes' and 'June Night', along with Etchells's *Hyde Park* (c.1915) and Lewis's 'The Crowd Master', set in London in July 1914. For women artists Vorticism's appeal undoubtedly lay in its visual and literary engagement with metropolitan culture. If rethinking Vorticism demands a break with the grand narratives of modernism which chart its inception in mid-nineteenth-century Paris to its closure in New York in the 1950s, it also requires attention to the sexually differentiated mappings of space and subjectivity in the contested terrain of London at the moment at which suffrage militancy was at its height and which was from August 1914 a capital at war.[25]

Sexualities and Space

City streets and urban spaces were the stage for the performances of and contestations over modern subjectivities and sexualities. Elizabeth Grosz has proposed that bodies and spaces are not discrete entities but mutually defining, contending that the body is a site of inscription for specific modes of subjectivity and sexuality which are shaped in and by the urban environment. In turn, the city is 'one of the crucial factors in the social production of (sexed) corporeality … the condition and milieu in which corporeality is socially, sexually and discursively produced'.[26] Grosz therefore argues that sexualities were not only located in time, as historians have readily admitted,[27] but that they were figured in and by specific locations. Taking up Elizabeth Grosz's analysis in relation to early twentieth-century London enables an exploration of the connections and slippages between sexualities, subjectivities and space.

Artistic subjectivities were formed through the encounters, interactions and experiences which took place within a changing urban environment. Equally the new spaces of modern London shaped social relations and cultural definitions. After 1900, the British capital was the subject of an increasing number of social inquiries, guidebooks and route maps,[28] publications which were simultaneously preoccupied with investigating and categorizing modern sexualities. But just as 'volatile bodies' and 'polymorphous sexualities'[29] proliferated in excess of relentless classification, so too the modern metropolis and its heterogeneous spaces glided beyond the reach of cartography and text.

The most highly contested construction in femininity at the beginning of the twentieth century was that of the modern woman, a formation developed from the 'new woman' of the 1890s. Defined by the historian Lucy Bland as 'a young woman from the upper or middle class concerned to reject many of the conventions of femininity and live and work on free and equal terms with the opposite sex', the distinctive characteristics of the 'new woman' were personal freedom, individualism and independence.[30] Jessica Dismorr, remembered by a friend as a 'new woman', Helen Saunders and Kate Lechmere were among the numerous middle-class women who left home to lead independent lives, to work, socialize unchaperoned in mixed company, and rent rooms.[31] Lechmere studied and worked in France, and attending the Académie de La Palette in Paris, whose teachers included Jacques-Emile Blanche, Metzinger, Segonzac and J.D.Fergusson, she is known to have exhibited at the Allied Artists' Association (AAA) in 1913 (fig.51).[32] Dismorr initially attended the Slade (1902–3); moving to France, she studied with Max Bohm in Etaples (c.1905–8) and at La Palette (1910–13). In Paris she became a member of the 'British-American Fauves', contributing several designs to the group's magazine *Rhythm* and to the London showing of their work, 'Exhibition of Pictures by J.D.Fergusson, A.E.Rice and Others' of 1912; she also exhibited at the Paris Salon d'Automne in 1913 and in London at the AAA from 1912 to 1914.[33] Helen Saunders, having trained at the Slade (1906–7) and the Central Schools of Art, in 1912 sent work to the Friday Club, the broadly based exhibiting group set up in London by Vanessa Bell in 1905. A contributor to Roger Fry's 'Quelques Indépéndents Anglais', she sent work to the AAA in 1912, 1913 and 1914.[34] By contrast, Dorothy Shakespear remained at home, mixing in literary and artistic circles with her mother, a novelist; with lessons but no formal training, she painted watercolours which were not exhibited.[35]

The project of modernity for women was highly contested, not only between women and men but between women. Suffrage supporters focused on inclusion in the democratic state.[36] For Nina Hamnett, to be modern was to pursue an independent working life with all its economic hardships and sexual conflicts in the city spaces of London and Paris.[37] Vanessa Bell and Dora Carrington by contrast redefined modernity in the register of the every day, and in the making of a (rural) life which refashioned the codes of domesticity, sexual partnership and artistic endeavour.[38] Although Duncan Grant contributed a winning design to a suffrage poster competition in 1909, as Elliott and Wallace have noted, 'women associated with various avant-gardes publicly and privately distanced themselves from any sort of political engagement, particularly feminism'.[39] The inclusion of a painting and a drawing by Jessica Dismorr in a women's suffrage exhibition of 1914 may indicate a deeper interest which remains undocumented or a rare instance of support.[40]

Helen Saunders, through her friendship with Harriet Shaw Weaver, may well have come in contact with a group of 'new moralists' associated with three radical journals: the *Freewoman*, launched by Dora Marsden and Mary Gawthorpe as a weekly paper in November 1911 and published up to October 1912; the *New Freewoman*, which succeeded it in June 1913 with the financial help of Shaw Weaver; and *The Egoist: An Individualist Review*, its successor, relaunched in January 1914 initially with Weaver as editor and Dora Marsden as a contributing editor.[41] Gawthorpe and Marsden had been active members of the Women's Social and Political Union, a suffrage organization committed to civil disobedience but, as Helen McNeil has indicated, Marsden 'privileged discourse over politics or aesthetics', dismissing collective action and political intervention.[42] Proclaiming a new version of women's modernity, the 'freewoman' was to be differentiated from the 'bond-woman' by her unfettered individualism and her self-declared freedom. Marsden contended that '[a] very limited number of women have been emphasising … that they are individuals',[43] and she argued for a self which was 'genderless, solitary and unique', a concept which by 1915 she had refined to an impersonal subjectivity shared by all humans. Wrenching feminism away from the 'Woman movement' she reactivated feminist claims for access to bourgeois individualism in a reformulation which, as McNeil traces, owed much to Theosophy and to (contemporary popularizations of) Nietzsche.[44] Refuting categorical oppositions of masculine/feminine, man/woman, Marsden anticipated a future in which the freewoman would 'consider her sex as incidental as men do'.[45] The 'new moralists' dismissed the 'womanly woman', a model of femininity advocated by many suffragists, and the 'old morality' of marriage, denouncing it as the condition of the 'bond-woman', legalized breeding and prostitution. In its place they advocated 'free unions', monogamous relationships freely entered and left. Nevertheless heated disputes took place over the 'free woman': was she free to enjoy sexual activity, rebut undesired advances and/or enjoy celibacy? As Rebecca West, a contributor to both the *Freewoman* and the *New Freewoman* recalled, these papers 'mentioned sex loudly and clearly and repeatedly'.[46] While this frankness was welcomed by many correspondents, both papers met vigorous opposition: Millicent Fawcett, President of the National Union of Women's Suffrage Societies, 'tore [a copy of the *Freewoman*] up into small pieces', and Olive Schreiner

considered its tone to be that of 'the brutal self-indulgent selfish male'.[47]

The concept of an ungendered individuality may well have appealed to women artists by offering to spring the trap of binary opposition which locates them within the category of the feminine and defines the feminine as not-masculine. In Paris Dismorr, then a member of the 'Rhythm' circle, probably encountered Henri Bergson's cultural dichotomy, in which masculinity was linked to culture, (pro)creativity and *élan* or vitality, and femininity with nature's fecundity.[48] While women's difference could be figured into feminist arguments for enfranchisement, writings on art and philosophy, as well as the new 'sciences' of sexology and eugenics, in emphasizing fundamental distinctions between the sexes frequently associated only masculinity with artistic creativity. A strong challenge to such sexual binarism may well have been welcome. The publication in the first issue of *Blast* of Rebecca West's 'Indissoluble Matrimony', the inclusion of art reviews in *The Egoist*, and a shared enthusiasm for individualism by 'new moralists' and vanguard artists indicates some of the links across radical circles before the 1914–18 war.[49]

Urban mobility, central to modern women's independence, was also a key factor in their participation in the avant garde. Metropolitan life and a developed travel network facilitated restless and continual movement – across the city, overground and underground, to work, to study, to shop and eat, to meet and talk, to make, exhibit and sell work. Artistic alliances flourished in the new urban spaces of cafés, cabarets and restaurants as much as in studios and salons. The sexual geographies of the avant garde can be mapped on to the districts of central London. In neighbourhoods with cheap rents and a wide variety of meeting places artists and writers lived and worked in proximity, generating intellectual and artistic communities by organizing studio showings and exhibitions, holding salons, staging performances, giving lectures and issuing publications. From the 1880s onwards women strategically claimed an urban presence.[50] Yet there remained distinct spaces out of reach, as for example meetings of male artists to which they were not invited or locations in which their safety could not be guaranteed. Moreover, questions of propriety (held by men or women) may well have shaped the conduct of middle-class women in 'unconventional' locations: Helen Saunders recalled that Harriet Shaw Weaver 'was silent in "company" as I was myself'.[51]

Any reconstruction of city encounters and urban behaviour in this period remains highly speculative. Much of what is now known about Vorticist meetings is drawn from recollections and memoirs. Speaking of the Saturday afternoon gatherings at the Rebel Art Centre, similar to those initiated by Sickert at Fitzroy Street where invitations were issued to view works displayed on easels and selected from stacks, Kate Lechmere recalled, 'I had to do the honours because Lewis insisted that the organising of tea parties was a job for women, not artists'. Of the launch party for *Blast* no. 1 Douglas Goldring wrote, 'Jessica Dismorr, an advanced painter and poetess … was ordered by the Master, after a counting of heads, to get tea for us. She obeyed with … promptitude.'[52] Several years earlier Sickert had written to Ethel Sands that she and Nan Hudson, the only two women showing work at 19 Fitzroy Street, were to act as hostesses.[53] Yet if these two wealthy and socially well-connected women offered a touch of class for buyers who frequented Sickert's studio, what might not have been offered by Lechmere or Dismorr dispensing tea at Great Ormond Street? To conclude, however, that pouring tea comprised women's contribution to Vorticist meetings would be to leave in the historical archive only these unreliable fragments of reminiscence and to propose them as the truth.[54] As Michel Foucault so often cautioned, historical 'truth' is produced in and by power.

There is no doubt that there were occasions when men acted against women in the formation of art groups by excluding women entirely, as did the Camden Town painters in 1911, and by limiting their number. It is equally the case, as Tickner suggests, that before 1914 contests between rival art groups were played out in terms of conflicting masculinities, although it is worth remembering that in Lewis's infamous denunciation of the Omega Workshops as 'This party of strayed and Dissenting Aesthetes' the provocation was barbed with an allusion to Fry's Quaker family background.[55] Masculinity and particularly Lewis have been extravagantly mythologized in the literature on Vorticism; recollections of aggressive conduct have been repeated uncritically rather than deconstructed or historicized in recent scholarly accounts. As Judith Walkowitz has pointed out, narratives of sexual danger have acted to police the activity, bearing and mobility of women in the modern city. The conduct of male Vorticists may be located within a spectrum of masculine behaviours which included street violence, sexual harassment (crystallized in the figures of the 'hooligan' and 'male pests') and the routine attacks on suffrage demonstrators.[56] Dismissing any view that events at Llanystumdwy in 1912 were 'a mere bit of rowdyism', Rebecca West conjured for the readers of the *Clarion* reactions to women's calls for the vote at Lloyd George's birthday celebrations. Incisively inverting the popular stereotype of hysterical women, she wrote:

Think of a mob of screaming, shrieking men, convulsed with liberalism, throwing themselves on single-handed women, beating them with sticks and stones, tearing out their hair in handfuls, and stripping them down to the waist! Think of them dragging the bleeding bodies of their captives towards the village pump, pitching them over hedges, and trying unsuccessfully to dip them in the river.[57]

Little is known of women's responses to the conduct of their male colleagues in the Vorticist group, apart from Lechmere's scornful riposte to Lewis. When he lost his temper over the Rebel Art Centre and the distribution of *Blast*, she tartly rebuked him for 'loosing [*sic*] your self command & using such ugly insulting language & again letting that extravagant imagination of yours run away with you'.[58]

In the years before the 1914–18 war, art coteries and fractions in London were constantly in the process of re-forming and regrouping. Like the constantly changing fabric of London, alliances were temporary; names were taken from particular areas – as for example the Fitzroy Street Group or the Camden Town Group – or from the metropolis itself, as in the case of the London Group. At the height of this rivalry, there was a contest over territory in central London. The Rebel Art Centre, set up to stage Vorticism, opened in spring 1914 at 38 Great Ormond Street, Queen Square, not far from the Omega Workshops showroom (established in May 1913) in Fitzroy Square and Sickert's studio showings at 19 Fitzroy Street. All were sited near the cafés, clubs, cabarets and restaurants frequented by artists and not infrequently decorated by them. At the Tour Eiffel restaurant, decorated by Saunders and Lewis in 1915, as at the earlier Cabaret Theatre Club at the Cave of the Golden Calf opened by Mme Strindberg in 1912, artists exhibited their work outside a gallery or studio setting to a self-conscious metropolitan audience. Café and cabaret culture was occasionally portrayed by Vorticist artists, from Lawrence Atkinson's *Café Tables,* c.1914–18, to the numerous images of dancers by male artists. Helen Saunders's drawing *Cabaret* (probably executed in 1913–14) shows her interest in metropolitan entertainment; irregularly squared up, it may be a preparatory study for a decorative scheme.[59]

The Rebel Art Centre was funded and largely organized by Kate Lechmere, co-director with Wyndham Lewis.[60] It is uncertain how, or from whom, this venue, registered as The Cubist Art Centre Ltd, acquired its name.[61] The word 'rebel' was already in currency in claims for modernity, the art critic Frank Rutter dedicating his defence of Post-Impressionism in 1910, *Revolution in Art*, to 'Rebels *of either sex* all the world over who in any way are fighting for freedom of any kind' (our italics).[62] As the building is now demolished, the Centre, its layout and decoration can only be partially reconstructed. Lechmere took premises on the first floor and arranged for building works to create the space comprising a large room, to be used for showing works, holding meetings and lectures, a smaller room used as a picture store, and an office. In July she wrote to Lewis that 'the large Studio at the end of the corridor is large enough for anything that you will require &

51 Kate Lechmere with her painting *Buntem Vogel* at the Rebel Art
    Centre, 1914

hold[s] 40 people or more for lectures.'[63] She organized and
presumably paid for the interior decoration.[64] The *Daily
News* reported doors of 'lawless scarlet' and 'decorous carpets
of dreamy blue'. The walls were painted lemon yellow.
Lechmere painted a large divan red and covered it with red,
blue and white striped fabric from Liberty. With another
woman, as yet unidentified, she made curtains apparently
designed by Atkinson or Hamilton. The *Daily News*
commented on 'Curtains of crocus gold falling in long
laughing lines' and on a white curtain hung across the room,
to divide the space, on which 'points of purple and cubes of
green and yellow, intermingling with splashes of deep rose-
red, formed themselves … into fantastic human figures'.[65]
Although the prospectus claimed that 'Ormond Street is
being decorated by several artists … with a series of large
mural paintings and friezes', only one, by Lewis, is known.[66]
Existing accounts give little indication that women artists
painted wall decorations or exhibited work at the Centre, but
this may be as much to do with the reporting of women
artists in the press as with the extensive disappearance or
destruction of Vorticist work. Only one of the contemporary
photographs taken at the Centre, that of Lechmere with her
painting *Buntem Vogel* (exhibited at the AAA in 1913), shows
work securely identified by a woman artist (fig.51).[67] On 19
May 1914 Lechmere requested contributions towards the
payment of the rent from some of the artists then showing
work at the Centre, namely Lewis, Wadsworth, Nevinson and
Atkinson.[68] This may suggest that she, Dismorr and Saunders
did not show or store work there, or that Lechmere had
already received the women's contributions, or that she was
somewhat desperate to get economic assistance from the
confrères whose artistic masculinity shied away from
collective or financial responsibility.

At the Rebel Art Centre there were schemes for the
production of decorative arts, and some items (including
'fans, scarves, boxes and a table')[69] were displayed at the
group stand at the Allied Artists' Association exhibition of
1914. Like Bloomsbury painting and perhaps to rival Omega,
Vorticist art was forged around redefinitions of modern
interior space. Lechmere had trained at La Palette in Paris,
and the plan for an art school run along the lines of a French
atelier to impart training in the principles of 'Cubist, Futurist
and Expressionist' art, with Lewis acting as visiting professor,
may have been hers. It failed however to attract pupils, and by
July Lechmere remarked that 'the fate of the School rather
hangs in the balance'.[70] Despite wide press coverage and
lectures by Pound, Marinetti and Ford Madox Ford, the
Rebel Art Centre foundered after four months on quarrels
between the co-directors, squabbles over the distribution of
the first issue of *Blast* and difficulties over its funding.[71]

The Tour Eiffel restaurant in Percy Street was a popular
meeting-place for Vorticists. A first-floor dining-room was
decorated by Helen Saunders and Wyndham Lewis in the
latter half of 1915. This complex decorative interior
comprised, it would appear, wall panels, light fittings and
table decorations, all completed in some six months.
Contemporary and later reports remarked on the colour and
the effects of a Vorticist formal syntax. Not long after the
interior was opened for viewing in January 1916, *Colour
Magazine* reported that 'gay Vorticist designs cover the walls
and call from the tablecloth'; also noted were the effects of
giddiness, doubtless induced by Vorticist spatial structures as
well as jarring colour contrasts. Another visitor considered
that 'the appeal of the colour is undeniable', concluding that
'provocative and arresting power is also to be felt when
confronting the storied walls'.[72] Long demolished, the scheme
can only be glimpsed from contemporary reports, the 1938
sale catalogue and reminiscences, and it is now extremely
difficult to ascertain the contributions of either artist.
Although the decorations have been attributed to Lewis, the
possibility of more direct and equal collaboration should not
be ruled out. Saunders's acquisition in late 1915 of two
watercolour and pen drawings by Lewis – *Composition in
Blue* and *Composition in Red and Purple* – tantalizingly
suggests that these might be associated with the Tour Eiffel
wall panels, being schematic cartoons and/or gifts to Saunders
following their joint work. William Roberts recalled that
there were three abstract panels: if these two watercolours by
Lewis can be linked to the decorative scheme could a third
panel have been by Saunders? This can only remain specu-
lation. Harry Jonas recollected that the predominant colours
were 'bright red and green' and 'very raw' yet 'low-toned'.[73]
Certainly Lewis's two watercolours are built up from
modulated low-toned red/purple and blue respectively; the
purple can be tied to a recollection that the floors of the

decorated room were stained purple.[74] If Saunders did contribute a panel, several works executed at about this date, including *Vorticist Composition with Figure in Blue and Yellow* (plate XXXII), *Vorticist Composition in Blue and Green* (plate XXXIII), or *Vorticist Design (Man and Dog)* (plate XXXIV),[75] are possible contenders, demonstrating the range of her work as a daring and effective colourist, prepared to take risks.

The Rebel Art Centre, Vorticist decorative schemes and *Blast* all enjoyed spectacular and prolific news coverage. General arts coverage in the period ranged from broadsheet newspapers and illustrated papers to specialist magazines. Whereas specialist papers offered interpretative readings, conjuring a community of well-informed London readers, photo-stories in the illustrated papers presented the antics of modern artists as strange, bizarre and baffling. Vorticists performed for the press and exploited the relatively new techniques and technologies of photo-journalism. Publicity was also generated in *Hello!*-style coverage of the aristocracy, many of whom patronized 'modern' art.[76] As John Rodker reported in *Dial Monthly*, 'the leaders of the new movement, be it in painting, music or literature are photographed daily, their eccentricities detailed and their photographs scattered broadcast'.[77] A photo-story on the 'Centre for Revolutionary Art: Cubist Pictures and Cubist Curtains' which appeared in the *Daily Mirror* of 30 March 1914 included a photograph of Lewis at work on an unfinished mural, another with Hamilton (?), Wadsworth, Nevinson and Lewis hanging Wadsworth's painting *Caprice*, and a third featuring Kate Lechmere standing by the curtains (figs 52, 53).[78] Underneath was the caption, 'With these revolutionary "works" however it is not always possible to tell "t'other from which" and until the average man can learn to penetrate their meaning he will probably pin his faith on the old schools.' Artistic identities were carefully staged. On this occasion Lewis and his male companions appeared with neat, clipped hair and attired in the dark suits favoured not only by Marinetti and the Futurists but by middle-class businessmen and Camden Town artists. Lewis thoroughly enjoyed dressing up, early on presenting himself as a bohemian, complete with sweeping cloak and broad-brimmed hat; somewhat later, but before October 1913, posing with an oversized cloth cap in front of a mirror at the Omega Workshops; and not long after this appearing at a fashionable dinner-party in informal day wear.[79] Business suits differentiated Lewis and his associates from Augustus John's cultivated appearance as a 'gypsy patriarch' as well as Roger Fry's studied informality.[80] A picture-feature titled 'A Post-Impressionist flat: what would the landlord think?' included a snapshot of Roger Fry, his hair unkempt and tousled, captioned 'Mr Fry thinking out some new futurist nightmare'. Fry is caught in a moment of deep concentration, seemingly unaware of his spectators.[81]

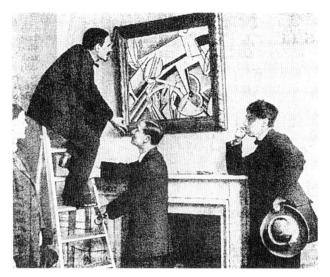

52 Cuthbert Hamilton (?), Edward Wadsworth, C.R.W. Nevinson, and Wyndham Lewis hanging *Caprice* in the Rebel Art Centre

53 Kate Lechmere at the Rebel Art Centre

54 Kate Lechmere, Cuthbert Hamilton (?), Edward Wadsworth and
    Wyndham Lewis at the Rebel Art Centre

In contrast to the action shots of her colleagues, Lechmere
posed beside the Rebel Art Centre curtains, gracefully
fingering them. On another occasion, she was positioned
equally within the group, seated beside Hamilton (?) on the
striped divan, adjacent to a stack of framed work; Wadsworth
and Lewis are standing in front of the curtains (fig. 54).[82]
For newspaper photographs Lechmere wore a gown in a
fashionable tubular shape composed of layers or bands of
different patterned and plain fabrics, its cut, layering and
looseness (there is probably no corseting) comparable to the
'oriental' gowns popularized by Paul Poiret and the Ballets
Russes. In a visual regime in which the artist was not marked
by signs of the trade, Lechmere's apparel registers her as a
woman of advanced artistic taste.[83] Her apparel in a set of
unpublished photographs taken at the Rebel Art Centre could
not be of greater contrast: Lechmere wears a loose white
blouse with a softly tied dark-coloured bow and plain skirt,
the hallmark attire of the modern woman.[84] Enactments
varied, for while Dismorr, Saunders and Shakespear did not
appear in published photographs of the Rebel Art Centre,
Lechmere, who was 'blessed' in Blast no. 1, was not included
in either issue of the Vorticist journal as a signatory, artist or
writer. Moreover, as has been suggested earlier, the performance of modern femininities often took place outside the glare
of publicity: in the Bloomsbury home of the Stephenses, in
the offices of the New Freewoman, in the studios of independent women like Dismorr and Saunders, on a bus or tram
travelling across London. Furthermore, if David Peters
Corbett's arguments are accepted that the spectacular
promotion of Vorticism in the popular press presented a
'radical modernism' to a society 'secure enough to enjoy the
titillation of iconoclasm', then the self-fashionings of

masculine artists may be linked to the play of sexual politics
in fashionable patronage. By commissioning interiors from
Lewis, aristocrats such as Countess Drogheda and West End
residents like Mrs Mary Turner were patronizing, and,
through the contemporary press coverage, being seen to
patronize, smart young men and stylish new art.[85]

Avant-garde positioning also took place on the pages of
national broadsheet newspapers. Women artists neither
initiated this polemicizing nor contributed greatly to it, none
of those in the Vorticist group signing either the published
letter disputing the commission for the Ideal Home
Exhibition, which gave Lewis and his associates their first
opportunity to break with Fry and Omega, or the repudiation
of 'Vital English Art: Futurist Manifesto'. Dismorr lent her
support for the former in a letter to Lewis: 'I wonder how
you are getting on with the Fry campaign. I am really with
you in spite of my apparent want of sympathy.'[86] As a
signatory to the manifesto Helen Saunders's last name was
printed as 'Sanders', as it was in the captions to her graphic
work published in Blast no. 2 of 1915, the announcement of
her inclusion in Blast no. 3, and in the catalogue for the
Vorticist exhibition in London in 1915. Whether this spelling
was a transliteration of the pronunciation, a persistent
typographical error, a careless disregard on the part of the
editor, or in deference to the proprieties of her family, remains
unknown. However, in Gaudier-Brzeska's review of the
Allied Artists' Association exhibition in 1914 and on the
poster for the Vorticist exhibition of 1915 Saunders's name is
given correctly.[87] Shakespear's name was rendered
'Shakespeare' in the caption to Snow Scene in Blast no. 2.
There was at least one occasion elsewhere on which Dismorr
was rendered as 'Dismore'.[88] As uncommon men's names
seem not to have been subject to alteration, the point at issue
may have been the gendering of the artistic name, certainly a
concern for women students at the Slade who in the second
decade preferred to be addressed by their patronymic, as for
example Carrington and Brett.[89]

While women artists were included in the exhibitions in
which definitions of the modern were fought out in Britain,
their names, unlike men's, were not put into repeated
circulation. Position papers, such as Pound's exposition of
Vorticism or Hulme's four lectures and articles on 'Modern
Art', cited no women artists. Across the struggles to find a
language in which to write about modern art and despite a
vehement repudiation of the years 1837 to 1900, the sexual
stereotyping of the previous half century was revitalized.
Reviewing the AAA exhibition of 1914 Gaudier-Brzeska
pronounced sculpture a 'virile art' and 'the new painting' at
the Rebel Art Centre stand 'capable of great strength and
manliness in decoration'. By contrast Renée Finch was 'a
greater talent than I have ever met in a woman artist'. In
tracing movements towards abstraction and 'a new evolution

in painting', Gaudier-Brzeska equivocally remarked, 'People like Miss Dismorr, Miss Saunders and Miss Jones are well worth encouraging in their endeavours towards the new light. With them stops the revolutionary spirit of the exhibition.'[90] Gaudier-Brzeska's review appeared in *The Egoist*, the successor to the *New Freewoman*. Announced as 'an organ for individualists of both sexes from every department of life', its pages were increasingly filled with contributions by men and reviews of their art and writings. James Joyce's *A Portrait of the Artist as a Young Man*, Pound's eulogy on Lewis ('one of the greatest living masters of design in the occident') and his essay on 'The New Sculpture' proclaiming the artist to be a 'savage' who lives by 'craft and violence' were published in early issues.[91] At first challenged, a feminist ideal of a subjectivity unmarked by sexual difference was finally conceded.

Street Hauntings/Body Scrypts

'June Night', Jessica Dismorr's prose poem in *Blast* no. 2, provides a mapping of pleasure, danger and desire in the spaces of the modern city. Criss-crossing London like the new transport systems, the journey's itinerary is from the suburbs to the centre.

No 43 bus; its advertisements all lit from within, floats towards us like a luminous balloon. We cling to it and climb to the top. Towards the red glare of the illuminated city we race through interminable suburbs. These are the bare wings and corridors that give on to the stage. Swiftness at least is exquisite....

We stop for passengers at Regent's Corner. Here crowds swarm under green electric globes. Now we stop every moment, the little red staircase is besieged. The bus is really too top-heavy. (p. 67)

The text registers many of the key characteristics of modernity, a compression of space and time, the jostling crowd, the excitement of fast movement and sensations of the fragmentary, yet all these are marked with the experience of modern women for whom mechanized transport facilitated access to urban space. As the modern metropolis was transformed into a theatre of consumption, spectacle and leisure, modern women were contradictorily placed: viewers and viewed, they were both among the 'new social actors' and targets of that vision so necessary to the navigation of this environment. Refusing, however, to take a place on the 'stage', the narrator of 'June Night' gets off the bus. Occupying neither of the masculine subject positions in relation to the crowd – distant observer or active participant – the pro-

tagonist is held in tension with this surging mass, moving away and yet returning. And if this is a June night in 1915, this must be a crowd reconfigured by the mobilization of soldiers and shuttling to and from the Front by men and women.

Tempted at first by 'spacious streets of pale houses' and taking 'refuge in mews and by-ways', the protagonist wanders alone, but the silence of uninhabited streets and her echoing footsteps trigger 'widening circles of alarm' which are only dispelled by returning 'to the life of the thoroughfares to which I belong'.[92] A similar fear is conjured in Dismorr's 'Promenade' (also printed in *Blast* no. 2): 'It is possible that we are being led by different ways into the same prohibited and doubtful neighbourhood.'[93] This spatial anxiety may be compared to that attributed to Miriam Henderson in early volumes of Dorothy Richardson's *Pilgrimage*, begun in 1917, in which the female narrator moves alone through London, at times with security, at times with an acute sense of danger of the risks to a corporeal presence marked as feminine.[94]

'June Night' is a richly multivalent piece of writing; an interest in formations in modern sexuality and 'free unions' as well as the tension between differing kinds of visual representation and plastic values collide in the narrative of a street adventure.[95] The protagonist dispenses with her escort, bored by his romantic fever and accelerated pulse, preferring a solitary ramble on an independent route to reach the richly ambivalent conclusion: should she sight her companion again she will acknowledge him. 'But I am not returning that way'. Interrupting the planned itinerary and 'walking in the city' she makes her own way. In *The Practice of Everyday Life*, Michel de Certeau differentiated between the organized routes of the planned city seen from above (from a tall building or in a map) and the intertwined pathways of pedestrians wandering, window-shopping, walking in the city.[96] Taking up his propositions and moving beyond his inattention to difference, it is possible to propose a gendered reading of urban space in which modern women refused the itineraries planned for them for a cross-hatching of inscriptions, individual and collective, on the spaces of the city. De Certeau indicates that 'the ordinary practitioners of the city live ... below the thresholds at which visibility begins', making 'use of spaces that cannot be seen outside historical record' and thus 'Escaping the imaginary totalizations produced by the eye'. Similarly, much of women's use of the modern metropolis lies beyond the historical archives or, in Dismorr's words in 'London Notes', 'beyond the lines of sight'.

The narrator of 'June Night' characterizes herself as 'a strayed bohemian, a villa resident, a native of conditions, half-sordid, half-fantastic', a creature who is neither of the centre nor the outskirts, but volatile, unfixed, provisional. In wandering, this figure becomes temporarily 'an outcast, a shadow that clings to walls'. This unfixing of identity in women's city narrative may be compared to Virginia Woolf's concept of 'street haunting', devised in an essay of 1930. In this discourse on women and the legibility or illegibility of the city, the wanderer leaves behind 'the straight lines of personality' and slips out of the familiar self left at home to stroll the streets devising itineraries and spinning stories. Complexly resonant, 'street haunting' conjures both haunts as often frequented places – the spaces visited and enjoyed by women which for Woolf include shops (the piece takes as its ostensible purpose the purchase of a pencil, necessary for the writer's craft) – and haunting as an elliptical and, to some, imperceptible, even invisible, form of presence which includes walking, looking and making art. Along the walk of the essay are fragmentary glimpses of hidden lives, partial observations of half-concealed sights, glances at incidents occluded from view. The evening light fragments the city's surfaces into 'islands of light' and 'long groves of darkness'.[97] 'Street haunting' provides a metaphor for, a way or route for thinking through, Vorticist women's representations of architectural spaces, of bodies in cities and their presence on the London streets.

From the later nineteenth century the urban fabric of London underwent constant redevelopment; new buildings, especially department stores, hotels, offices and theatres, were erected, the infrastructures of transport, water and waste were extended and wide avenues were projected through congested older areas.[98] London was full of holes, caverns and spaces: the tunnels of the Underground, crypts and sewers, basement areas, building sites, and from 1915 bombed craters. Lacking a central plan or centralized finance or plenary image, redevelopment progressed piecemeal.

Dismorr's prose poem, 'London Notes' (published in *Blast* no. 2 in 1915), provides a series of disconnected, fragmentary perceptions of the British capital.[99]

> Towers of scaffolding draw their criss-cross pattern of bars upon the sky, a monstrous tartan.

> Delicate fingers of cranes describe beneficent motions in space.

> Glazed cases contain curious human specimens.

> …

> Precious slips of houses, packed like books on a shelf, are littered all over with signs and letters.

> A dark, agitated stream struggles turbulently along the channel bottom; clouds race overhead.

> Curiously exciting are so many perspective lines, withdrawing, converging; they indicate evidently something of importance beyond the limits of sight. (p.66)

55 Helen Saunders, *Vorticist Composition (Study for 'Cannon'?)*, c.1915, pen and watercolour on paper, 380 x 300 mm (15 x 11¾ in)

For Dismorr, London is a city in collapse; houses fall like books on a shelf. Cranes tower overhead, their movements like aerial tracery – a comparison which has none of Lewis's relish for the crane's strength: 'It is a pity that there are not men so strong that they can lift a house and fling it across a river.'[100] Rebuilding, along with the pits, fissures and destruction created by the bombing raids, brought to visibility inner, underground and hidden spaces, equally the subject of new technologies of vision. One of the concerns of the increasing number of publications on London from the 1880s to the 1920s was a mapping of these 'holey' spaces, a will to know, to prise into the seemingly unknown, dark and hidden spaces of the modern city. At the same time, visual technologies, which shared the metaphor of 'bringing to light', enabled photography of these hidden architectural spaces and brought new perceptions, through the invention of X-ray, of the interior of the body. Bodies and cities were turned inside out.

56 Jessica Dismorr, *Landscape: Edinburgh Castle (?)*, *c.*1914–15, pen and watercolour on paper, 240 x 190 mm (9½ x 7½ in)

57 Helen Saunders, *Vorticist Composition with Figures in Black and White*, *c.*1915, indian ink and pencil on paper, 255 x 175 mm (10 x 6¾ in)

In a brilliant and witty analysis of architecture and the text, architecture as text, Jennifer Bloomer has proposed, in contrast to conventional architectural drawing in which line delimits space, *scrypt*. She defines this as 'a writing that is other than transparent, a writing that is illegible in the conventional sense', continuing, 'this writing of something that is empty space, where something secret and sacred – something unspeakable or unrepresentable – is kept, a holey space'.[101] To read Saunders's drawings and watercolours as *scrypts* is to perceive line not simply as drawing round space, colour as filling it in, but to attend to the inscription of line, line as cutting into the paper, cutting out and into space. In Saunders's dazzling displays of vertiginous perspectives are deep recesses, unplumbed depths, uncertain reaches. Dizzying heights plunge to uncharted depths in *Vorticist Composition: Black and Khaki (?)* (plate XXXIV); ascent risks a fall into a void over which, in *Vorticist Composition (Study for Cannon)* (fig.55), swings a hook, outlined in eye-catching blue.[102] For

Bloomer, *scrypt* doubles upon *crypt*, a cavernous void hewn into solid material. Crypts and caves are brought into view in an early 'Vorticist' drawing by Jessica Dismorr, *Landscape: Edinburgh Castle (?)*, *c.*1914–15,[103] in which architectural forms hewn into and fashioned from rock are sliced through (fig.56), and Saunders's *Untitled Drawing*, *c.*1913, in which figures and cavities are mutually defining.[104] Internal depths come into view in Saunders's *Vorticist Composition with Figures in Black and White* (fig.57); space is indeterminate in Dismorr's *Abstract Composition* (plate XXXVI), both behind and between the forms which float across, and are suspended upon, a sombre ground. Voids seen and unseen are uncertain: as the cave is hollowed out, so the cavity may cave in, jeopardizing solidities of form and securities of movement.

More than any other work by a Vorticist artist, *Atlantic City*,[105] reproduced in *Blast* No. 2 of 1915 (fig.58), provides an image of the fragmentation, dispersal and non-unitary perception of the modern city, exceeding that hinted at by

58 Helen Saunders, *Atlantic City*, illustration in *Blast* No. 2

Lewis or Wadsworth. Sight lines converge and depart; sights and sites collide. Richard Cork has remarked upon the lack of internal coherence of Saunders's compositions, which indeed seem to lack the logical variation of those by her contemporaries.[106] In *Atlantic City* the image seems to explode outwards from the centre. Broken shards of urban architecture are lit by arrows of brilliant light. As in *Vorticist Composition in Blue and Green* (plate XXXIII), the glare of electric light (so unlike the soft diffusions of gaslight) breaks up surfaces, incises the façades of buildings, gleams from illuminated windows and borders deep caverns. In common with other Vorticist artists, Saunders breaks with two representational strategies devised in the nineteenth century and retained in some modern images of the city: the framing of a view from the threshold of a window, and the depiction of urban interiors.[107] In *Atlantic City* the view is everywhere and nowhere; it is not fixed at any point which can be granted to the spectator who is precipitated into its unhomely/ *unheimlich* spaces.[108]

Helen Saunders experimented with new perspectival paradigms developed in the years immediately before 1914 in which, through an interrogation of one-point perspective, the subject was fractured and displaced. Vorticist artists took up the spatial propositions of analytic Cubism and Futurism (both however marginalized in *Blast* no. 1). Jane Beckett has explored elsewhere the experimentation by the European avant garde with analytic geometries and new mathematical projections of space and the significance in the British context of military ordnance, aerial cartography, aeroplane travel and an interest in experimental perspective developed by Slade students, including Saunders's close friend, Rosa Waugh.[109] For Ezra Pound the new mathematics provided paradigmatic exemplars of the interrelatedness of knowledge and representational forms, and in his account of Vorticism he drew attention to analytic geometries of space.[110] A glance at Lewis's overmantel for Countess Drogheda's dining-room, designed 1913–14, confirms these interests.[111] The framing of the central mirror with narrow black bands projects orthogonal lines converging as if to a central vanishing point; these are however left unresolved in the mirror surface, which reflects ambiguous spatial relationships through chance perception. Lewis here seems to employ a form of axonometric projection in which receding parallel lines remain in a fixed relation without resolution in the vanishing point. The result is both a flat plane and an infinite space (in both cases the mirror), unsettling the spectator and putting into play the vertigo often referred to in contemporary accounts of Vorticist spaces, as in the decorated room at the Tour Eiffel. A similar effect is achieved in *Atlantic City*.

If *Atlantic City* is centrifugal, *War Scare, July 1914*, by Dorothy Shakespear, maps a vortex simultaneously imploding and exploding (fig.59). Inscribed 'Not to be shown to anyone done when the Stock Exchange shut, before war was declared', it hints at the chaos which will be produced by the war and the collapse signalled in Dismorr's 'London Notes'. Arcing and angular forms converge. Shared by another contemporary watercolour, this restless movement, oscillating from concave to convex, contrasts strongly to the poise of Shakespear's *Abstract Compositions* of *c.*1914–15 (fig.60; plate XXXVII) in which the formal architecture of the composition is carefully balanced by the use of colour.[112]

Many of Saunders's watercolours, such as *Gulliver in Lilliput* (plate XXXVIII),[113] portray bodily forms without the registration of masculine or feminine. This intimation of a corporeal politics beyond the absolutes of sexual difference may be linked to the writings of the 'new moralists' who, as has been argued, strongly challenged sexual binarism. In others, as in images by Dismorr (fig.56; plate XXXVI), traces or 'hauntings' of bodily forms may be perceived, often indistinguishable from architectural or mechanical shapes. That this irresolution comes with the processes of abstraction

59 Dorothy Shakespear, *War Scare, July 1914*, 1914, watercolour on paper, 255 x 355 mm (10 x 14 in)

60 Dorothy Shakespear, *Abstract Composition*, c.1914–15, watercolour on paper, 133 x 209 mm (5¼ x 8¼ in)

61 Helen Saunders, *Vorticist Composition with Bending Figure*, c.1914, watercolour and pencil on paper, 250 x 350 mm (9¾ x 13¾ in)

is suggested by the relation between Saunders's *Vorticist Composition with Bending Figure* of c.1913–14 (fig.61) and her *Abstract Multicoloured Design* of c.1915–16 (plate XXXIX).[114] In the first a bending figure, almost ovoid in shape, leans forward, hands gesturing with three strings or staves.[115] Linking it to William Blake's *Newton*, Cork has interpreted this figure as 'involved in a measuring, mathematical task'.[116] Traces from *Vorticist Composition with Bending Figure*, notably the converging lines, semicircular and serpentine shapes and a hand, are also to be seen in the multicoloured design. With its sharp and at times close contrasts of colour, *Abstract Multicoloured Design* may be read in terms of an interplay between interiors and exteriors of bodies and cities, as a representation in which architectural forms pierce and fragment the body and in which the body reshapes architectural space.

In this 'undecidability' where images slip between site and body, slide across delineations of interior and exterior, hover between two and three dimensions, marked distinctions of sexual difference are evaded. The internal conduits of buildings and the body are precipitated into visibility in Saunders's *Vorticist Composition: Black and Khaki (?)* (plate XXXIV). The interlocking shapes, lines and colour fields simultaneously conjure images of architecture (perhaps a stairwell) and the form of a gigantic head, an artistic project undertaken by several Vorticists.[117] Dismorr's *Edinburgh Castle* (fig.56) and Saunders's *Vorticist Composition with Figures in Black and White* (fig.57) are characterized by this spatial and corporeal interplay. The chaotic colliding shapes, angularity and jarring colours of Saunders's *Vorticist Design (Man and Dog)* (plate XXXV) suggest an interplay of architectural, bodily and canine forms. Saunders's *Vorticist Composition with Figure in Blue and Yellow* (plate XXXII) may depict a figure ascending upwards along the constructional diagonal, a massive head facing left, and/or intersecting shapes. These oscillations of form and dimension are intensified by the colour movements of yellow and blue, pushing planes into recession and thrusting them forward, and the use of the varying media and textures of crayon and watercolour with collage. Her *Vorticist Composition (Study for 'Cannon' ?)* (fig.55) may well portray, as Brigid Peppin has suggested, 'an angular figure … represented simultaneously as gunfire and victim'.[118] Yet it may also, if interpreted as an interplay of fins, register a preoccupation shared by Vorticist artists for an elision between the human and the mechanical, to be found not only in Epstein's *Rock Drill*, but also in Saunders's watercolour of *The Rock Driller* (fig.62) and Dismorr's 'Monologue' (published in *Blast* in 1915) spoken by a figure with 'arrogant spiked tresses' and 'new machinery that wields the chain of muscles fitted beneath my close coat of skin'.[119] Dismorr's fascination with technology and an interest in the representation of motion may have

62 Helen Saunders, *The Rock Driller*, c.1913, ink and watercolour on paper, 95 x 125 mm (3¾ x 5 in)

63 Jessica Dismorr, *The Engine*, illustration in *Blast* no.2

underpinned both this artist's work and her titling of it: to the Vorticist exhibition of 1915 she contributed *Shapes, Interior, Movement* and *Design* as well as providing the rationale for *The Engine* (fig.63) and *Design*, her visual contributions to *Blast* no.2. The shapes in Dismorr's *Abstract Composition* (plate XXXVI) are highly ambivalent, at first glance possibly derived from architectural and mechanical forms but, by comparison to Bomberg's contemporary works, perhaps reworkings of the body. Their movement is suggested as much by their interaction as by the uncomfortable but not dissonant colour contrasts.

Women artists participated in and contributed to the Vorticist movement in a variety of ways and by no means all shared a common aesthetic. Vorticism offered not only an art which engaged with metropolitan modernity, but a visual economy not founded on the trade in woman as sign, and in which bodily forms were not necessarily coded for sexual difference. In this it differed from the modern sexualities depicted in the Bloomsbury painting, the highly corporeal imagery of Camden Town artists, and contemporary beliefs that the vices and virtues were 'written on the body'. In the hands of women artists, Vorticism's visual language of abstraction could shift the ground away from an engagement with 'sex-antagonism' and sexual difference for an art which could play with and over (and in this it contrasted to the abstraction of the Bloomsbury painters Vanessa Bell and Duncan Grant)[120] the fragmented forms of the modern city, the scattered/shattered perceptions of modern urban environment and new visions of the body. The work of the four women artists associated with Vorticism – in painting, drawing, design, poetry and prose – powerfully and heterogeneously addressed the project of modernity, and the intersections between sexuality, subjectivity and space.

1 Wyndham Lewis, *Sunset among the Michelangelos*, c.1912, pencil, ink and gouache on paper, 325 x 480 mm (12¾ x 19 in)

11 Wyndham Lewis, *Timon of Athens: The Thebaid*, 1913, photomechanical print, 387 x 272 mm (15¼ x 10¾ in)

III Wyndham Lewis, *Composition*, 1913, pencil, pen and watercolour on paper, 343 x 267 mm (13½ x 10½ in)

IV Wyndham Lewis, *Timon of Athens*, 1913–14, pen, ink and watercolour on paper, 345 x 265 mm (13½ x 10½ in)

v Wyndham Lewis, *Portrait of an Englishwoman*, 1914, pencil, pen and watercolour on paper, 560 x 380 mm (22 x 15 in)

VI Edward Wadsworth, *(Reflections in Water) Pool with Trees and Punt*, 1913, watercolour on paper, 350 x 482 mm (13¾ x 19 in)

VII Wyndham Lewis, *Workshop*, 1914–15, oil on canvas, 765 x 610 mm (30 x 24 in)

VIII Frederick Etchells, *Gouache: Stilts (?)*, 1914–15, gouache and pencil on paper, 315 x 230 mm (12½ x 9 in)

IX Frederick Etchells, *Progression*, 1914–16, pen and watercolour on paper, 145 x 230 mm (5¾ x 9 in)

x Lawrence Atkinson, *Abstract*, c.1915, oil on wood,
1295 x 508 mm (51 x 20 in)

XI William Roberts, *Study for 'Twostep II'*, *c*.1915, pencil watercolour and gouache on paper, 300 x 230 mm (11¾ x 9 in)

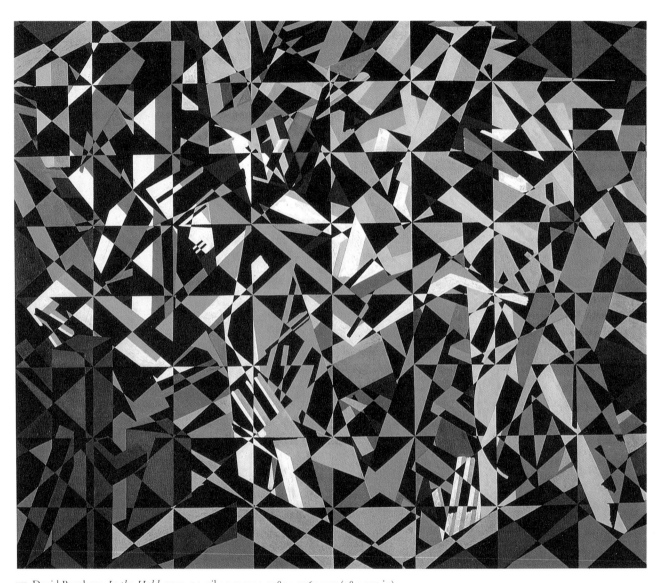

XII David Bomberg, *In the Hold*, 1913–14, oil on canvas, 1980 x 2565 mm (78 x 101 in)

XIII Wyndham Lewis, *Red Duet*, 1914, chalk and gouache on paper, 385 x 560 mm (15¼ x 22 in)

XIV David Bomberg, *Figure Composition*, c.1913, oil on board, 351 x 258 mm (13¾ x 10¼ in)

xv David Bomberg, *Study for 'The Mud Bath'*, *c.*1914, pencil and gouache on paper, 535 x 710 mm (21 x 28 in)

XVI David Bomberg, *The Dancer*, 1913–14, wax crayon and watercolour on paper, 685 x 560 mm (27 x 22 in)

XVII David Bomberg, *Vision of Ezekiel*, oil on canvas, 1143 x 1372 mm (45 x 54 in)

XVIII William Roberts, *Study for a Nativity*, c.1913, charcoal and watercolour on paper, 280 x 355 mm (11 x 14 in)

XIX William Roberts, *The Return of Ulysses*, 1913, oil on canvas, 305 x 455 mm (12 x 18 in)

xx David Bomberg, *The Mud Bath*, 1914, oil on canvas, 1524 x 2242 mm (60 x 88¼ in)

XXI Edward Wadsworth, *Mytholmroyd*, c.1914, woodcut on paper, 215 x 175 mm (8½ x 7 in)

XXII Wyndham Lewis, *A Battery Shelled*, 1919, oil on canvas, 1525 x 3175 mm (60 x 125 in)

xxiii C.R.W. Nevinson, *Column on the March*, 1915, oil on canvas, 638 x 766 mm (25 x 30¼ in)

XXIV Edward Wadsworth, *Tarmac 1*, 1919, pen and watercolour on paper, 317 x 444 mm (12½ x 17½ in)

xxv Henri Gaudier-Brzeska, *Portrait of Horace Brodzky*, 1913 (cast 1932), bronze, 700 x 530 x 370 mm (27½ x 20¼ x 14½ in)

XXVI Henri Gaudier-Brzeska, *Duck*, *c.*1914, marble, 65 x 120 x 40 mm (2½ x 4¾ x 1½ in)

XXVII Henri Gaudier-Brzeska, *Bird Swallowing Fish*, 1914, bronze, 310 x 600 x 290 mm (12¼ x 23¼ x 11½ in)

xxviii Jacob Epstein, *Female Figure in Flenite*, 1913, serpentine, 457 x 950 x 121 mm (18 x 37½ x 4¾ in)

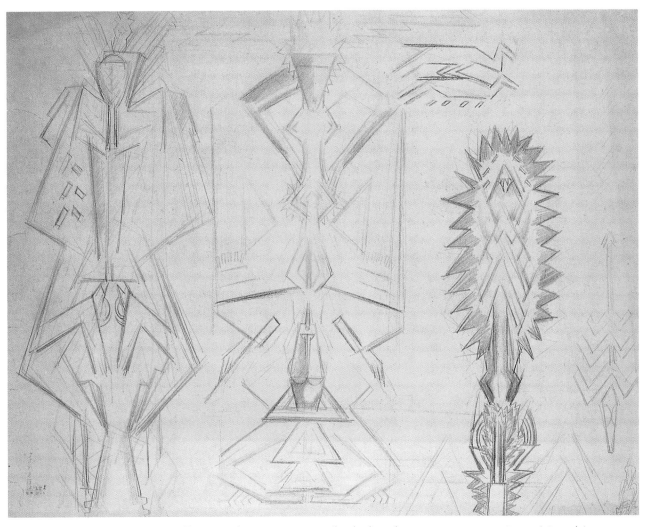

XXIX Jacob Epstein, *Study for 'Rock Drill, Venus and Doves'*, c.1913, pencil and coloured crayon on paper, 455 x 585 mm (18 x 23 in)

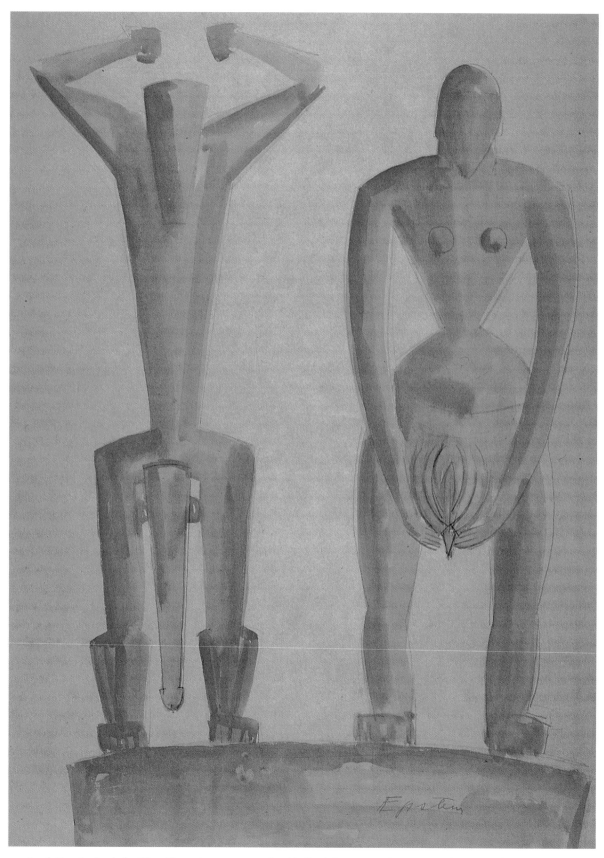

xxx Jacob Epstein, *Study for 'Man–Woman'*, 1913–15, pencil and indian ink on paper, 615 x 415 mm (24¼ x 16¼ in)

XXXI Jacob Epstein, *Torso in Metal from 'Rock Drill'*, 1913–15 (cast 1962), bronze, 710 x 660 x 445 mm (28 x 26 x 17½ in)

XXXII Helen Saunders, *Vorticist Composition with Figure in Blue and Yellow*, *c*.1915,
pencil, chalk, indian ink and collage on paper, 276 x 171 mm (10¾ x 6¾ in)

xxxiii Helen Saunders, *Vorticist Composition in Blue and Green*, *c*.1915, watercolour on paper, 250 x 195 mm (9¾ x 7¾ in)

xxxiv Helen Saunders, *Vorticist Composition: Black and Khaki (?)*, *c*.1915, indian ink and watercolour on paper, 225 x 180 mm (8¼ x 7 in)

xxxv Helen Saunders, *Vorticist Design (Man and Dog)*, c.1915, gouache on paper, 380 x 300 mm (15 x 11¾ in)

XXXVI Jessica Dismorr, *Abstract Composition*, c.1914–15, oil on wood, 413 x 508 mm (16¼ x 20 in)

XXXVII Dorothy Shakespear, *Composition in Blue and Black*, 1914–15, collage and watercolour on paper, 385 x 563 mm (15¼ x 22¼ in)

XXXVIII Helen Saunders, *Gulliver in Lilliput*, *c*.1915–16, gouache on paper, 385 x 305 mm (15¼ x 12 in)

xxxix Helen Saunders, *Abstract Multicoloured Design*, c.1915–16, pencil, watercolour and gouache on paper, 359 x 257 mm (14 x 10 in)

xl Wyndham Lewis, *The Crowd*, 1914–15, oil on canvas, 2005 x 1535 mm (79 x 60½ in)

'You Must Speak with Two Tongues': Wyndham Lewis's Vorticist Aesthetics and Literature

PAUL EDWARDS

By 1914 the Vorticist artists had arrived at a style and aesthetic for their work through various routes, all of them independent of the concept of the vortex itself. For Wyndham Lewis, who along with Pound was the chief theorist of the movement, the concept of the vortex had mainly a rhetorical significance. Typically, he liked its potential for symbolizing contradictory qualities – first, Futurist dynamism, second, the stillness at its centre, the point of 'maximum energy'. Similarly, he liked the contradictory implications in the title of the magazine, *Blast*: simultaneously a destructive explosion and the germ cell from which an organism grows. The *Blast* manifestos were also double-barrelled. The Blast–Bless formula of the opening pages of the magazine was modelled on Apollinaire's 'L'anti-tradition futuriste' and its 'rose à' and 'merde à' format. What is different, and characteristic of Lewisian Vorticism, is that the *Blast* manifestos do not simply line up heroes and villains, for what is blasted on one page may be blessed a few pages later. France, England and Humour all receive this treatment. Self-contradiction is programmatic, self-conscious, playful but aggressive:

> We start from opposite statements of a chosen world. Set up violent structure of adolescent clearness between two extremes.
>
> We discharge ourselves on both sides.
>
> We fight first on one side, then on the other, but always for the SAME cause, which is neither side or both sides and ours.[1]

This is a violent, expressive version of Nietzsche's 'perspectivism'. Perspectivism, or the multiplication of points of view, was Nietzsche's response to a weakening of faith in the coherence of the world and our models of it, a failing confidence in the Romantic idea that behind the world of appearances there lay some authentic absolute, or absolute authenticity. The whole of modernism turns around this crisis, which has its roots in the material history of modernity at least as much as in the philosophy that accompanies, or in Nietzsche's case seems to predict it.

One way of categorizing different types of modernism is to distinguish them on the basis of their attitude towards the primal authenticity that, to today's readers, Nietzsche seems to deny. Such a denial was far from clear to Nietzsche's early readers, however, and he was read, usually alongside Henri Bergson, rather as an exponent of a route to an authenticity transcending the limitations of traditional enlightenment and scientific ways of knowledge.[2] Most modernisms actually do postulate such an authenticity, usually in some region that precedes the sundering of subject from object, and most are concerned to recover that realm to consciousness by signs or other forms of subterfuge – maybe just by driving fast, for example. Even driving fast, though, to be successful, needs to culminate in a crash that flings the occupant back into the 'maternal ditch', reviving for the driver memories of the 'black breast of my Sudanese nurse'. I am referring, of course, to the 'Founding and Manifesto of Futurism', the document (along with other of Marinetti's Futurist literature) that encapsulates most vividly and optimistically a specifically modern version of this fantasy. In England, D. H. Lawrence's *The Rainbow* (1915) is an example of the accommodation of Nietzsche to the project of establishing a new authenticity based on pre-rational and 'natural' forces. Like the Expressionist fantasies on which it is partly modelled, it puts apocalypse forward as the symbolic – and perhaps literal – accomplishment of this.

The kinship with the simultaneously destructive and creative potential punningly encompassed in the name *Blast* should be clear. But within *Blast* no. 1 is a document that calls into question the whole possibility of attaining the post-romantic goal of primal authenticity.

This is Wyndham Lewis's prose-poem or dream-play *Enemy of the Stars*, avowedly placed in *Blast* as an example of what Vorticist literature ought to be. It is an exemplary text in several respects: formally it is as cinematic as it is literary, proceeding almost as a series of discrete 'shots' in the form of isolated paragraphs that by gradual accretion create a narrative. This cinematic model is explicitly evoked in one passage that presents the two main characters at a moment of dialogue:

> Two small black flames, wavering, as their tongues moved, drumming out thought, with low earth-draughts and hard sudden winds dropped like slapping birds from climaxes in the clouds.

> No Morris-lens would have dragged them from the key of vastness. They must be severe midgets, brain specks of the vertiginous, seismic vertebrae, slowly living-lines, of landscape. (p.66)

The images this predominantly phrasal prose evokes are as disruptive of normal reading as the violent shifts in perspective accomplished between paragraphs. The syntactic and metaphoric dislocation is an analogue of Vorticist painting's loosening of the ties between elements of design and their customary representational functions. As Lewis later recognized, language resists abstraction as radical as that which can be achieved in visual art. Nevertheless, in *Enemy of the Stars* the narrative propriety of the realist novel has been abolished, and information that in such a text would function to bolster the 'reality' of what is described is here as incongruous as it might be in the work of a postmodernist writer like Donald Barthelme:

> They lay in a pool of bleak brown shadow, disturbed once by a rat's plunging head. It seemed to rattle along, yet slide on oiled planes. Arghol shifted his legs mechanically. It was a hutch with low loft where they slept.

> Beyond the canal, brute-lands, shuttered with stoney clouds, lay in heavy angles of sand. They were squirted in by twenty ragged streams; legions of quails hopped parasitically in the miniature cliffs.

> Arghol's uncle was a wheelwright on the edge of town.

> Two hundred miles to the north the Arctic circle swept. Sinister tramps, its winds came wandering down the high road, fatigued and chill, doors shut against them. (pp.66–7)

In the face of such writing, it is easy to see why Lewis considered the writing of the Imagist poets too '*pompier*' to include in *Blast*. (He included Pound, but with a series of poems that avoided his imagistic aestheticism only by substituting unconvincing aggression and smugness.) *Enemy of the Stars* is recognizably modern also in its self-reflexive awareness of its own fictive status: it is not so much the script of a play as an imaginary performance of a play in

> SOME BLEAK CIRCUS, UNCOVERED, CAREFULLY-CHOSEN, VIVID NIGHT. IT IS PACKED WITH POSTERITY, SILENT AND EXPECTANT. POSTERITY IS SILENT, LIKE THE DEAD, AND MORE PATHETIC.

And it is 'VERY WELL ACTED BY YOU AND ME.' (p.55) If *Enemy of the Stars* is not a well-known modernist literary text, that is at least partly because its affiliations are with Expressionism, and its intellectual lineage, correspondingly, is through Nietzsche, Schopenhauer and Max Stirner. Criticism has been reluctant to recognize such a genealogy for anglophone modernism.[3] Equally, visual Vorticism's connections with Cubism and Futurism have been acknowledged more fully than its no less important connections with Expressionism.[4] Both Edward Wadsworth and Wyndham Lewis had spent some time as students in Munich in around 1906, and the first issue of *Blast* contains Wadsworth's synoptic review of Wassily Kandinsky's *On the Spiritual in Art*, under the title 'Inner necessity'. It contains also Lewis's poetic celebration of an exhibition of German Expressionist woodcuts.

Enemy of the Stars is Expressionist above all as an *agon* of violence that aspires to break through to a realm of primal authenticity. It is violent both in imagery ('a canal at one side, the night pouring into it like blood from a butcher's pail') and action, commencing with a brutal assault on the protagonist, and concluding with his murder and the suicide of his killer.[5] The principle of contradictory dualism that underlies the epistemological and rhetorical approach of *Blast* (and of the Vorticists' aesthetics) is here tested to destruction. It is embodied in the two principal 'characters', Arghol and Hanp. Arghol, obsessed with the Romantic urge to transcendence of the imperfections of material existence, is described as being in 'immense collapse of chronic philosophy'. Philosophy, such as Bergson's, that postulates a 'true' self under the accretions of material and intellectual life (that constitute a false 'extensive' self), has become a 'chronic' disease in him. He wishes to overcome death and find his own original, true identity. He has abandoned the 'art-life' he led in the metropolis to work in his uncle's workshop, hoping thus to escape the false second self that his social commerce in the city has created. Arghol explains his attempts to purge this social excrescence and reach authenticity:

> 'Men have a loathsome deformity called Self; affliction got through indiscriminate rubbing against their fellows: Social excrescence....
>
> Or an immense snuffling or taciturn parasite, become necessary to victim, like abortive poodle, all nerves, vice and dissatisfaction.
>
> I have smashed it against me, but it still writhes, turbulent mess.
>
> I have shrunk it in frosty climates, but it has filtered filth inward through me, dispersed till my deepest solitude is impure.' (p.71)

But his chronic philosophizing continues in the wheelwright's yard, where it has become his daily practice to exercise it upon his fellow-worker, Hanp:

> 'The process and condition of life, without any exception, is a grotesque degradation, and "souillure" [soiling] of the original solitude of the soul. There is no hope for it, since each gesture and word partakes of it, and the child has already covered himself with mire.
>
> 'Anything but yourself is dirt. Anybody that is. I do not feel clean enough to die, or to make it worth while killing myself.' (p.70)

Though he may not feel clean enough to die, another part of his daily routine is the brutal assault he suffers from his uncle, who kicks him nearly to death in the prelude to the main action. This is willed by Arghol as part of his programme of ascetic self-mortification. Though he will not kill himself, he feels that by this means he can 'Accumulate in [himself], day after day, dense concentration of pig life. Nothing spent, stored rather in strong stagnation, till rid at last of evaporation and lightness characteristic of men. So burst Death's membrane through, slog beyond, not float in appalling distances.' (p.68) His workmate, Hanp, is not the type to be troubled by philosophical discontent, but is apparently materially discontented with his meagre lot as a labourer, and values Arghol precisely for his tales of the exciting world of the metropolis. Hanp has 'bourgeois aspirations', fostered at first by Arghol's accounts of the city, then turned bitter and resentful as Arghol recounts his disillusion. Hanp's own resentment enables him to perceive the motivation behind Arghol's apparently disinterested aspiration to another world of authenticity and truth: 'Sour grapes! That's what it's all about! And you let yourself be kicked to death here out of spite.' (p.70)

What Hanp has unwittingly pointed out is that Arghol is one of Nietzsche's 'ascetic priests':

> Here rules resentment without parallel, the resentment of an insatiate instinct and ambition, that would be master, not over some element in life, but over life itself … here is an attempt made to utilise power to dam the sources of power; here does the green eye of jealousy turn even against physiological well-being, beauty, joy; while a sense of pleasure is experienced and *sought* in abortion, in decay, in pain, in misfortune, in ugliness, in voluntary punishment, in the exercising, flagellation, and sacrifice of the self.[6]

The various references in the play to Max Stirner's *The Ego and his Own* suggest that Stirner's similar idea that an obsession with a world of truth beyond the material world is a continuation of Shamanism and asceticism, and the product of a culture of guilt and bad conscience. Arghol conforms to Stirner's and Nietzsche's descriptions when he proclaims, 'Energy has been fixed on me from nowhere – heavy and astonished: resigned. Or is it for remote sin! I will use it, anyway, as prisoner his bowl or sheet for escape: not as means of idle humiliation.' (p.63) This theme of the play will be important for an understanding of Vorticist aesthetics, for it is precisely the aim of the main proponent of abstraction in painting, Wassily Kandinsky, to reveal such a world of spirit, not through asceticism, but through form and colour.

The action of *Enemy of the Stars* amounts to a demonstration that Arghol's quest for the original purity of his spirit 'self' is doomed. Prompted by Hanp's questioning, he realizes that, however much he mortifies himself, the everyday world of desires, appetites and companionship will always have a claim on him and actually be a part of him. Hanp, indeed, now represents for him that rejected and contemptible 'other' which he is incapable of shaking off. Angered at Arghol's scorn, Hanp attacks him, but the hitherto passive Arghol now surprisingly goes against his own self-mortifying principles and fights back: 'Arghol used his fists. To break vows and spoil continuity of instinctive behaviour, lose a prize that would only be a trophy tankard never drunk from, is always fine.' (p.74) Arghol defeats Hanp, then falls asleep; 'Now a dream begins valuing, with its tentative symbols, preceding events'. (p.76) The dream replays Arghol's original rejection of the false art-life of the metropolis, and of the 'Arghol' that has been created in that society. The rejection seems successful: 'He was Arghol once more.... "I am Arghol." He repeated his name – like sinister word invented to launch a new Soap, in gigantic advertisement – toilet-necessity, he, to scrub the soul.' (p.80) But no sooner has this assertion (with its sardonically 'modern' imagery) been made, than he realizes that the 'false' Arghol he imagines he has discarded and left in the city has 'followed him, in

Hanp. Always à deux!' While Arghol sleeps and snores in apparent animal contentment, the resentful Hanp now picks up his knife and slices into the 'impious meat' of the prone body. 'The blood burst out after the knife.' Having killed Arghol, he sinks into despair and throws himself into the canal to drown. For he is part Arghol, just as Arghol is part Hanp ('always à deux').

Enemy of the Stars has a rich, almost esoteric, significance which it is unnecessary to explore fully. What is most important in the present context is that it provides an indirect critique of the transcendental aspirations (Bergsonian, theosophical, technological) embodied in the chief artistic practices of the period leading up to the First World War. Just as the conditions of 'life' prevent any self becoming, unalloyed, the true authentic self towards which it nostalgically aspires, so the condition of painting or any other signifying system prevents the work of art from becoming the direct communication of that self or of any pure, transcendent world of spirit. Even Arghol's aspiration to explain and philosophize in language has to be recognized as 'con-taminated': 'I think it's a physical matter: simply to use one's mouth' (p.73). *Enemy of the Stars* is Lewis's sceptical reply to Nietzsche's 'final question concerning the conditions of life' in section 110 of *The Joyful Wisdom*. This concerns the conflict between a will to truth and a will to illusion, a conflict beside which everything else is a matter of indifference: 'How far is truth susceptible of embodiment?' Lewis's sceptical reply (signalled by Arghol's failure) does not involve a complete rejection of spiritual aspirations for paintings, however, and the presence of Wadsworth's synoptic review of Kandinsky's treatise *On the Spiritual in Art* shows the importance of these aspirations as an ingredient in Vorticist aesthetics.

This was also made clear by Lewis in an interview with a reporter in April 1914. In it he endorses the Futurist ambition to make an art out of the materials of modernity, but more surprisingly at first sight, also announces that he is 'planning a design for a devotional room in a well-known society woman's house'.[7] Only such a room would, in the modern world, be suitable for the art of a painter whose 'soul was too religious for his works to be mere entertainments and drawing room pictures'. The shamanistic ambitions to reach a spirit world, mocked by Stirner and embodied in Arghol, are then endorsed by Lewis in a statement that echoes the short *Blast* essay, 'Fêng Shui and Contemporary Form', which he must have been composing at about the time the interview was given: 'I believe the super-sensible will play a greater part in life and art as time goes on. The spiritual world is the Polar regions of our psychic existence, and useful ghosts will meet us on its borders, even if we do not adventure more.'[8] It is the final clause, suggesting that the artist should not aspire to abandon the real world, which echoes the limiting scepticism

of *Enemy of the Stars* about spiritual aspirations that Lewis would later express explicitly in the second number of *Blast*, where he derides Kandinsky for the easy access to this authentic realm implicitly claimed by his work:

> Kandinsky, docile to the intuitive fluctuations of his soul, and anxious to render his hand and mind elastic and receptive, follows this unreal entity into its cloud world, out of the material and solid universe.…
>
> He allows the rigid chambers of his Brain to become a mystic house haunted by an automatic and puerile Spook, that leaves a delicate trail like a snail.[9]

The implications are, first, that actually the spiritual world as such isn't particularly interesting if it seems to have no bearing on the world we live in, and, second, that the cloud-world inside Kandinsky's brain is solipsistic. In this world we are 'always à deux', never truly our solitary selves, and the 'other' always lays its claims on us: 'Most fine artists cannot keep themselves out of wood and iron, or printed sheets: they leave too much of themselves in their furniture'.[10]

Nevertheless, the principle of 'inner necessity' that Kandinsky proposed is a vital one for explaining what artists do with the external world into which their personalities are in danger of dissolving.

> In a painting certain forms MUST be SO; in the same meticulous, profound manner that your pen or a book must lie on the table at a certain angle, your clothes at night be arranged in a set personal symmetry, certain birds be avoided, a set of railings tapped with your hand as you pass, without missing one.[11]

Writing in 1949, Lewis explained that the force that arranged the blocks and lines of a Vorticist abstraction was 'a mental-emotive impulse', 'subjective intellection, like magic or religion'.[12]

For both Stirner and Nietzsche, the turn towards 'another world' of the spirit represents a rejection of our world of the senses. It was not until T. E. Hulme, who was in Germany from the spring of 1912 to early 1913, brought back to England the ideas of Wilhelm Worringer that such a turn against the sensual world could be given a character in terms of visual form that was not like the 'cloud-like' fluidity of the 'Blavatskyish soul' visible in Kandinsky's paintings.[13] As summarized in Hulme's paraphrase of Worringer's views, the artistic impulse corresponding to a feeling of separation from the sensual world is a tendency to abstract from natural form into something more geometrical, monumental and rigid:

> While a naturalistic art is the result of a happy pantheistic relation between man and the outside world, the tendency to

abstraction, on the contrary, occurs in races whose attitude to the outside world is the exact contrary of this....

Take first, the case of more primitive people. They live in a world whose lack of order and seeming arbitrariness must inspire them with a certain fear.... The fear I mean here is mental.... They are dominated by what Worringer calls a kind of spiritual 'space-shyness' in face of the varied confusion and arbitrariness of existence. In art this state of mind results in a desire to create a certain abstract geometrical shape, which, being durable and permanent shall be a refuge from the flux and impermanence of outside nature.... This leads to rigid lines and dead crystalline forms, for pure geometrical regularity gives a certain pleasure to men troubled by the obscurity of outside appearance. The geometrical line is something absolutely distinct from the messiness, the confusion, and the accidental details of existing things.[14]

Curiously, Hulme felt that abstraction in the work of Vorticist painters (and of David Bomberg), which he understood to be non-representational rather than a stylized representation, was a heretical departure from these ideas. Hulme favoured 'abstraction' as a tidying of nature – for the modern, its representation in forms that suggest the qualities of machinery – rather than as an autonomous language of form or an approach to the 'other world' lying across the border from our own. In his review of the London Group exhibition of March 1914, he singles out Jacob Epstein's carving in flenite as the only work that fulfils his desiderata (plate XXVIII).[15] In keeping with this preference, he reserves what praise he has for Lewis's work for the small drawing *The Enemy of the Stars*, which is a comparatively naturalistic representation of an imaginary object: a carved fetish that we might well imagine Epstein producing. The drawing would later be reproduced in *Blast* no. 1. As a representation of Arghol, who is the 'Enemy of the Stars', it draws attention to an aesthetic consequence of the thought about identity explored in the play: if *Enemy of the Stars* denies the possibility of truth being embodied, it cannot itself be the expression of the truth. If we are inclined to think that the heroic Arghol is a self-portrait of Wyndham Lewis, while Hanp is a representative of the resentful, philistine public that battens on but eventually destroys him – and there is plenty in the text to encourage such identifications – we should realize that they are quite consciously embodiments of something other than such 'truth'. The supposed 'characters' Hanp and Arghol are not authentic, unique individuals, or expressions of Lewis's own true self: rather, they are abstractions from it or (it would be less misleading to say) fetishes or totems, parts of Lewis's personal mythology, produced under the compulsions of an 'inner necessity', products of that superstitious sense that says certain railings have to be tapped as you pass them on the street or that

certain forms in a picture 'must be so'. A short narrative passage in *Enemy of the Stars* seems actually to present Arghol as such a fetish, a relic of one of Worringer's 'primitive' tribes, modelled on the artists of Easter Island, but in this case nomadic and Siberian:

Head of black, eagerly carved, herculean Venus, of iron tribe, hyper barbarous and ascetic. Lofty tents, sonorous with October rains, swarming from vast bright doll-like Asiatic lakes.

Faces following stars in blue rivers, till sea-struck, thundering engine of red water....

Cataclysm of premature decadence.

Extermination of the resounding, sombre, summer tents in a decade, furious mass of images left: no human.

Immense production of barren muscular girl idols, wood verdigris, copper, dull paints, flowers.

Hundred idols to a man, and a race swamped in hurricane of art, falling on big narrow souls of its artists. (pp.67–8)

The Siberian location is not an accident. Lewis called England 'the Siberia of the mind', and welcomed its philistinism as the ideal environment for a new art: 'As the steppes and the rigours of the Russian winter, when the peasant has to lie for weeks in his hut, produces that extraordinary acuity of feeling and intelligence we associate with the Slav; so England is just now the most favourable country for the appearance of great art.'[16] It is not too far-fetched, I think, to see the 'iron tribe' as Lewis's vision of the Vorticists themselves, the 'Primitive Mercenaries in the modern world'.

On 12 June 1914, Wyndham Lewis signed a contract with the publishing firm Max Goschen for a book, 'Our Wild Body', that would collect all his early essays and stories deriving from travel in Brittany and Spain, written largely over the period 1909 to 1912.[17] Lewis wrote a new introduction for it and delivered the complete manuscript to the publisher, probably during the summer of 1915, but certainly some time before he joined the army in March 1916. There it remained until May 1917, when Ezra Pound retrieved it from the publishers' office, the partners in the firm having been killed in France.[18] The introduction, 'Inferior Religions', was published separately through Pound's agency in the small-circulation magazine *The Little Review* in September 1917, and it has never been considered as a document having a bearing on Vorticism, though it was written during the Vorticist period. The essay is concerned more with comedy and laughter than with the tragic dimensions of the relation between art and religion that are the subject of *Enemy of the Stars*. But 'Inferior Religions' reiterates the idea of artistic creations as fetishes or superstitions: 'Sairey Gamp and Falstaff are minute and rich religions. They are illusions hugged and lived in. They are like little dead Totems. Just as all Gods are a repose for humanity, the big religions an immense refuge and rest, so these little grotesque idols are.'[19] These 'inferior' religions, however, like the superstitions that demand that certain railings be tapped, can become restrictive and enclosed – too much of a fetish, in fact. Lewis uses the image of a treadmill to convey such limitation: 'The wheel at Carisbrooke [Castle] imposes a set of movements on the donkey inside it, in drawing water from the well, that it is easy to grasp'. To recognize the limits of our fetishes and routines and seek for ones that are less inferior is an act of ultimate piety: 'All religion has the mechanism of the celestial bodies, has a dance. When we wish to renew our idols, or break up the rhythm of our naïvety, the effort postulates a respect which is the summit of devoutness.'[20]

What this is saying is that the best homage we can make to any inaccessible authentic absolute is to break out of our personal routines and abstractions, lay them open to the assaults of what contradicts them: 'to break vows and spoil continuity of instinctive behaviour, lose a prize that would only be a trophy tankard never drunk from, is always fine', as he put it in *Enemy of the Stars*. Superstitions are a hedge against 'life', so life must be allowed to contradict and reshape them. Another of Lewis's plays of the period, the more conventionally written and conceived *The Ideal Giant*, contains a character who organizes his life and his writing in accordance with certain superstitions that have become a necessity for him. In life, he is always truthful, for example, while in his writing he sticks rigidly to the purely imaginary. To break this fetish he decides deliberately to undertake a programme of lying: 'The Ego's worst enemy is Truth. This gives Truth the slap in the face good for us.'[21] 'Art is never at its best without the assaults of Egotism and of Life', he adds, indicating the need for a similar disruption in art.

So, what exasperated Arghol, and was revealed as, ultimately, a tragic condition – the impossibility of ever giving expression to the transcendent spirit – becomes for the artist the basis of a series of strategic self-disruptions by which the two principles of life and abstraction compete with and enrich each other, producing an art of increasing scope and elusive complexity. Hence the personal manifesto or 'Art Vortex' that Lewis contributed to *Blast* no. 2, 'Be Thyself':

> You must talk with two tongues, if you do not want to cause confusion.
>
> You must also learn, like a Circassian horseman, to change tongues in mid-career without falling to Earth.
>
> You must give the impression of two persuaders, standing each on a different hip – left hip, right hip – with four eyes

vacillating concentrically at different angles upon the object chosen for subjugation.

> There is nothing so impressive as the number TWO.
>
> You must be a duet in everything.
>
> For, the Individual, the single object, and the isolated, is, you will admit, an absurdity.
>
> Why try and give the impression of a consistent and indivisible personality?[22]

In terms of painting, this means that the tendency to abstract formalization in Vorticist works must be quite pro-grammatically pitted against elements of 'life' that contradict it. Vorticist paintings refuse to lie quiet and always contain an internal competitive disruption to prevent any complacent assumption that they have embodied some transcendent truth. 'Art is never at its best without the assaults of Egotism and of Life'. So in a Vorticist painting the conception is usually at war with the execution, and the signifying systems employed are at war with each other, because no signifying system can give sole access to the truth. To simplify: visually, the signifying systems in competition with each other in Vorticist painting are those of Cubism, Expressionism and Futurism. Vorticism competes with these movements, but also makes itself a site where they compete with each other, for no visual element in a Vorticist 'abstraction' has a fixed function, but can be read in accordance successively with a perception of the work as a design, as an unstable 'non-Euclidean' space, or as mechanically stylized representation of figures or buildings. The possibility of such multiple readings, each in tension with another, and none usually dominant, is felt as dynamism within the perceiver's mind. This is the 'essential' movement (rather than the cinematic movement for which they criticized the Futurists) that Vorticists sought to capture.

In parallel to this we can see why, despite the masculinist bravado (amounting at times to crude misogyny) of Lewis and Pound, Vorticism may have been felt by women (and feminist) artists to be on balance a liberatory movement more than an oppressive one. Vorticism's refusal of all unitary, fixed definitions of the self has been traced in this essay to what is virtually a metaphysical critique of a Romantic urge to transcendent authenticity. But that critique is only an expression of the new sense of the self that modern material conditions were themselves making possible. Life and the self are different for the modern town-dweller from what they were for people in earlier types of civilization, as the Futurists perceived. So the 'esoteric' or metaphysical critique of unitary truth is doubled by a more straightforward 'Futurist' recognition that the transformed sense of self is grounded in material change:

the modern town-dweller of our civilization sees everywhere fraternal moulds for his spirit, and interstices of a human world.

He also sees multitude, and infinite variety of means of life, a world and elements he controls.

Impersonality becomes a disease with him.

Socially, in a parallel manner, his egotism takes a different form....

We all to-day (possibly with a coldness reminiscent of the insect-world) are in each other's vitals – overlap, intersect, and are Siamese to any extent.[23]

The 'overlapping' of possible readings of a Vorticist image mirrors this change in the sense of self. In their contribution to the present volume, Jane Beckett and Deborah Cherry show how this sense of multiple identity, exploring the hidden and varied spaces of the city, was felt as a real opportunity by artists like Jessica Dismorr and Helen Saunders. It not only validates a refusal to be limited, but, by its emphasis on the violence of contradictions, validates what must have been at times a painful and aggressively self-contradictory struggle to make new social identities for women. It was certainly not painless either for Saunders or Dismorr. Saunders's *Atlantic City* (fig.58), with its centripetal organization and self-contradictory space, is almost a primer in this new sense of urban identity. Her *Abstract Multicoloured Design* (plate XXXIX) may be read as showing the tension between the new mechanized sense of self and a traditional sense of the body as a site of maternity, a preoccupation also found (in a slightly different way) in Jessica Dismorr's poem 'Monologue', in *Blast* No.2:

Pushing my hard head through the hole of birth
I squeezed about with intact body.
I ache all over, but acrobatic, I undertake the feat of existence.
Details of my equipment delight me.
I admire my arrogant spiked tresses, the disposition of my
    perpetually foreshortened limbs,
Also the new machinery that wields the chains of muscles
    fitted beneath my close coat of skin. (p.65)

In tracing the ideas that underlie a specifically Vorticist literature and, by extension, visual aesthetic, I have so far ignored the Poundian perspective that is usually most prominent in discussions of literary Vorticism. Part of the reason for this is Pound's peripheral status in the actual creation of Vorticist art – even of Vorticist literature. By Pound himself, however, at least in 1914, Vorticist literature was identified as the work of him and his Imagist associates. In his article 'Vorticism', published in September 1914 but

based on a lecture composed in the spring, he does not even mention Lewis as a writer, going so far, indeed, as to link Lewis with Wadsworth and state that they 'are not using words, they are using shape and colour'.[24] But Lewis had a poor opinion of the imagist work of Pound, Aldington and H.D. (Hilda Doolittle), at least in so far as it pretended to 'avant-garde' credentials, and he made sure that the only Imagist represented in *Blast* was Pound himself – not with poems that were readily identifiable as Imagist however. In an exasperated letter written in 1949, Lewis went so far as to state that '*imagism* was a purely literary movement, having no relation to *vorticism*, nor anything in common with it'.[25] Lewis and Pound were great friends, but they did not share many assumptions about writing.[26]

They did share some views, however, or 'Vorticism' would never have been accepted as the name for the new movement. Pound, in 'Vorticism', attempts to define various levels of abstraction from reality, using mathematical examples. The arithmetical examples he gives are simple abstractions from particular facts, while his algebraical expressions operate at a higher level of generalization and therefore cover a wider variety of facts. The type of 'abstraction', however, that Pound is most interested in is exemplified by analytical geometry, where an equation does not merely encode facts but, according to Pound, actually creates them:

Thus, we learn that the equation $(x - a)^2 + (y - b)^2 = r^2$ governs the circle. It is the circle. It is not a particular circle, it is any circle and all circles. It is nothing that is not a circle. It is the circle free of space and time limits. It is the universal, existing in perfection, in freedom from space and time.

Pound goes on to give, like Lewis, a quasi-religious turn to this piece of Platonism: 'The statements of "analytics" are "lords" over fact. They are the thrones and dominations that rule over form and recurrence. And in like manner are great works of art lords over fact, over race-long recurrent moods, and over tomorrow.'[27] The objective of the poem is to embody this level of abstraction, but to do so through the world of sense in revealing 'a sort of permanent metaphor' through content, and through 'absolute rhythm' that corresponds to emotions that are also permanent and re-current.[28] A work of art that does so is, or contains, a 'vortex'. These statements of Pound's are now recognized as setting out the method and rationale of his long poem, *The Cantos*, the last complete section of which, indeed, was entitled 'Thrones' as if to affirm its ambition to lordship over fact and over tomorrow. For Pound in 1914, then, there is a possibility that truth can be embodied (though the artist might in particular cases not be successful in carrying this out).

Pound was therefore shocked when he learned of Lewis's deliberate spurning of the ambition to make the work of art a seamless embodiment of the abstract conception it stands in for, or in some way represents. He attempted in July 1916 to explain to John Quinn Lewis's peculiar attitude to colour and finish in painting as he now understood it. First, he emphasized the deliberate materiality of Lewis's choice of colour and texture: 'I think … that Lewis with his fundamental realism has been trying to show the beauty of the colour one actually sees in a modern brick, iron, sooty, railroad yarded smoked modern city.' And a week later:

> I do know that he is very contemptuous of people who will look at nothing but a *certain sort* of technical ??? excellence ???? or finish.
>
> I was a bit shocked at his first denunciation, and stayed so until I found out what he was driving at. It is part of his general surge toward the restitution of the proper valuation of *conception*, i.e. C O N C E P T I O N then finish.
>
> Whereas the journalistic attitude at present is concerned solely with brush strokes and colour, N E V E R with conception.
>
> That is I dare say a clumsy way of saying it. Still you may get what I mean. *By conception* I mean *conception in form and colour*. I don't mean a desire to paint something expressive of faith hope and charity …[29]

Pound was right to emphasize the importance of the conceptual element in Lewis's work. Lewis himself had done so in a statement in *Blast* no. 1 that gives the rationale for a whole strand of modernism that had not yet come into being: 'At any period an artist should have been able to remain in his studio, imagining form, and provided he could transmit the substance and logic of his inventions to another man, could have, without putting brush to canvas, [been] the best artist of his day.'[30] In Lewis's practice, however, the separation of form and content was more actively emphasized, to the extent of its becoming a competitive relationship that carried out the 'assault' on art desiderated in *The Ideal Giant*.

It was perhaps this competitive aspect of Vorticist art from which Pound learnt most as he became more friendly with the notoriously suspicious Lewis. Pound's most important poetic contribution to *Blast* no. 2 is far closer to the artistic spirit of the movement than any of his poems in the first number. 'Dogmatic Statement on the Game and Play of Chess' envisages chess as a series of Vorticist abstractions figuring a continually renewed contest.[31] *The Cantos* as we have them now emerged out of 'Canto IV' (completed in 1919), which began as a juxtaposition of intransigent and contingent historical material (a stumbling monologue on the wartime experience of an Englishman who liked the Germans but fought against them) with several allusions to, or invocations of, religious practice and communication with a world of spirit.[32] *The Cantos*, though their aim is to bridge the gap between brute historical fact and the abstract, religious dimension of form, or to show the latter somehow emerging

from the former, resist an easy consonance between the two. In Pound's words, they are a 'record of struggle', for only a competitive relationship can prevent an easy relapse into an 'inferior religion'.[33] Thus we always find that, whenever *The Cantos* have apparently reached some plateau of transcendent authenticity (or 'absolute rhythm' as Pound calls it), there is a 'renewal of contest' as another load of chaotic or unsavoury material is suddenly discharged on to the page.

To return, finally, to visual Vorticism. It seems to me that a fuller recognition of the internal disruptiveness and multivalency of the aesthetic developed by Lewis will complicate our readings of Vorticist painting, at least. Wyndham Lewis's *The Crowd* (plate XL), which was also at one time known under the title *Revolution*, is clearly in 'external' competition with Luigi Russolo's *The Revolt*, 1911 (Gemeentemuseum, The Hague). Russolo's revolutionary crowd, helped on by their force-lines, carry all before them and break through, we must assume, to the political equivalent of absolute authenticity. In contrast, Lewis's painting has always been read as deeply conservative and pessimistic. The fretwork of the small red crowd is based on Russolo's figures, but they do not break through the stable and massive structure that seems to determine their possibilities. The fullest, and most politically pessimistic, reading of the painting is Tom Normand's in his *Wyndham Lewis: Holding the Mirror up to Politics*. For Normand it embodies Lewis's opposition to mass-action for social justice and equality.[34] Normand's reading is an extensive and subtle one, and I shall not argue with it as such. But it needs to be pitted in competition with a quite different one. Since cleaning, the colours of *The Crowd* are no longer as drab and oppressive as they used to seem. In particular, the paler spaces in the interstices of the blocks have a glow that contradicts the oppression of the larger structure, for, perceptually, they have the effect of opening out the spaces they represent. To assume that in 1915 Lewis's attitude to this crowd is simply one of reactionary superiority is to misunderstand his attitude to the masses. What the crowd is storming in the top right-hand corner is a set of treadmills, modelled on the 'wheel at Carisbrooke' that Lewis used as an analogy for our confinement within 'inferior religions'. The activity, then, of the Vorticist artist in both constructing and demolishing such structures is actually a parallel to the 'swift anarchist effort' of the revolutionary crowd. As Lewis's spokesman in *The Ideal Giant* says,

> 'The artist is the Ideal Giant or Many. The Crowd at its moments of heroism also is. But Art is never at its best without the assaults of Egotism and of Life.
>
> For the health of the Giant as much as for that of the individual this conflict and its alertes are necessary.
>
> Revolution is the normal state of things.'[35]

Notes

Notes to Introduction, pages 9–13

1 In raking light, traces of geometrical abstractions can be discerned beneath the surfaces of three of Lewis's paintings of the 1920s, *Praxitella* (Leeds City Art Galleries), *Portrait of the Artist as the Painter Raphael* (Manchester City Art Galleries) and *Edith Sitwell* (The Tate Gallery).

2 'Other Vorticists' comprised Lawrence Atkinson (three works), David Bomberg (one work), Jessica Dismorr (three works), Frank Dobson (two works), Frederick Etchells (four works), Henri Gaudier-Brzeska (seven works), Cuthbert Hamilton (one work), Edward McKnight Kauffer (two works), Jacob Kramer (one work), C.R.W. Nevinson (three works), William Roberts (seven works), Helen Saunders (one work) and Edward Wadsworth (five works). Of these artists, Atkinson, Bomberg, Kramer and Nevinson did not consider themselves Vorticists but had been 'invited to show' at the original Vorticist exhibition (though Atkinson had actually been one of the signatories of the Vorticist Manifesto). Dobson and Kauffer were not brought into the circle until after the war, with the formation of Group X. Works exhibited were not confined to those conforming to what we now think of as the 'Vorticist' style of geometric abstraction.

3 Wyndham Lewis, catalogue introduction, *Wyndham Lewis and Vorticism*, London: Tate Gallery, 1956, p.4.

4 Lewis's more tactful expression of his view of Vorticism at this time can be found in his article 'The Vorticists', published in *Vogue* in September 1956, reprinted in *Creatures of Habit and Creatures of Change: Essays on Art, Literature and Society, 1914–1956*, ed. Paul Edwards, Santa Rosa: Black Sparrow Press, 1989, pp.378–83.

5 Anthony d'Offay, catalogue introduction, *Abstract Art in England 1913–1915*, London: d'Offay Couper Gallery, 1969.

6 Richard Cork, *Vorticism and Abstract Art in the First Machine Age*, 2 vols, London: Gordon Fraser, 1976.

7 William C. Wees, *Vorticism and the English Avant-Garde*, Manchester: Manchester University Press, 1972.

8 Hugh Kenner, *The Pound Era: The Age of Ezra Pound, T.S. Eliot, James Joyce and Wyndham Lewis*, London: Faber and Faber, 1972.

9 Reed Way Dasenbrock, *The Literary Vorticism of Ezra Pound and Wyndham Lewis: Towards the Condition of Painting*, Baltimore and London: Johns Hopkins University Press, 1985. Timothy Materer's *Vortex: Pound, Eliot, and Lewis*, Ithaca and London: Cornell University Press, 1979, had already supplemented Kenner's discussion, valuably, but with a less systematic intention than Dasenbrock's.

10 Jane Beckett and Deborah Cherry, 'Women under the Banner

of Vorticism', *ICSAC Cahier 8/9: Vorticism*, December 1988, pp.129–43.

11 The exhibition also comprised Bloomsbury artists, Vanessa Bell, Duncan Grant and Fry himself, and the Camden Town artists Spencer Gore and Charles Ginner.

12 For an invaluable account of the exhibitions through which this assimilation can be traced, see Anna Gruetzner Robins, *Modern Art in Britain 1910–1914*, London: Merrell Holberton in association with Barbican Art Gallery, 1997.

13 English artists in the 'Second Post-Impressionist Exhibition' were Vanessa Bell, Frederick Etchells, Jessica Etchells, Roger Fry, Eric Gill, Spencer Gore, Duncan Grant, Henry Lamb, Wyndham Lewis and Stanley Spencer. The show was extended and rehung in January 1913, and Edward Wadsworth and Cuthbert Hamilton were added.

14 Clive Bell, 'The English Group', 1912; reprinted in J.B. Bullen, ed., *Post-Impressionists in England: The Critical Reception*, London and New York: Routledge, 1988, p.351.

15 Wyndham Lewis to Roger Fry, February–March 1913, *The Letters of Wyndham Lewis*, ed. W.K. Rose, London: Methuen, 1963, pp.46–7. Rose dates the letter August–September, but the Liverpool exhibition took place February–March.

16 Spencer Gore to Roger Fry, 7 October 1913, published in Quentin Bell and Stephen Chaplin, 'The Ideal Home Rumpus', *Apollo*, LXXX, October 1964, p.289. This article contains a full set of correspondence relating to the affair. Fry made his attitude to a shared commission crystal clear in his reply to Gore: 'in no case could the Omega share a job like that' (Fry to Gore, 9 October 1913, ibid). He had earlier explained that 'the Omega produces its work anonymously and would not expect to have the work distributed beforehand by outsiders amongst the various artists' (Fry to Gore, 5 October 1913, ibid); and as far as Fry was concerned, 'Lewis was one of the Omega artists'. In executing the commission, Fry set Lewis to work carving a mantelpiece. The walls were anonymously decorated by Fry, Bell and Grant. Bell and Chaplin produce as evidence in support of Fry a letter dated 20 October from the exhibition secretary, F.G. Bussy, to Vanessa Bell, confirming that the commission was indeed awarded unconditionally to Fry, and that the official who met Fry did not recall Gore and Lewis being mentioned at the meeting. This, they claim (p.291), contradicts Gore's account of the affair. But it was never disputed that Fry acquired the commission for the Omega; in fact it was the chief cause of Gore's and Lewis's complaints.

17 Etchells had a grudge of his own. On his own authority Fry had

falsely informed Frank Rutter that Etchells had no work available for Rutter's 'Post-Impressionist and Futurist' exhibition. After the walk-out, Duncan Grant and Vanessa Bell spent two hours trying to persuade Etchells of the rectitude of Fry's character, but they 'couldn't convince him of anything' (Vanessa Bell to Fry [12 October 1913?], ibid, p.290). A letter that Rutter addressed to Lewis at the Omega, inviting him to contribute to the show, was opened by Fry and not passed on to Lewis until Lewis mentioned the fact in the 'Round Robin'.

18 Recollection of Winifred Gill, recorded in Bell and Chaplin, 'The Ideal Home Rumpus', p.289.

19 The 'Round Robin' [11 October 1913?], *The Letters of Wyndham Lewis*, p.49. According to John Rothenstein, *Modern English Painters*: Vol.1 *Sickert to Grant*, London: Arrow, 1962, the Round Robin was intended to function as a 'trailing of a coat', presumably to induce a libel action (p.292).

20 Wyndham Lewis, 'The Cubist Room', reprinted in *Post-Impressionists in England*, p.468. For a fuller list of the 'Cubist Room' exhibitors, see note 52, p.124 below.

21 Wyndham Lewis, 'A Man of the Week: Marinetti', 30 May 1914; reprinted in Wyndham Lewis, *Creatures of Habit and Creatures of Change*, pp.29–32.

22 F.T.Marinetti and C.R.W.Nevinson, 'Vital English Art', *Observer*, 7 June 1914; reproduced in facsimile in *ICSAC Cahier 8/9: Vorticism*, December 1988, pp.123–4.

23 For a careful analysis of the chronology of events, see Paul O'Keeffe, 'The Troubled Birth of *Blast*: December 1913–June 1914', ibid, pp.43–57.

24 The letter, signed by Richard Aldington (Imagist associate of Pound), Bomberg, Etchells, Pound, Wadsworth, Atkinson, Gaudier-Brzeska, Hamilton, Roberts and Lewis, is reproduced in facsimile, ibid, p.125.

Notes to 'A Laugh Like a Bomb', pages 14–23

1 Manifesto – II, *Blast* no.1, June 1914, p.32.

2 'Vital English Art. Futurist Manifesto' is the title of the manifesto that C.R.W. Nevinson and Filippo Tommaso Marinetti first published in the *Observer*, 7 June 1914, reproduced in facsimile in *ICSAC Cahier 8/9: Vorticism*, December 1988, pp.123–4.

3 Manifesto – II, p.39.

4 In connection with the reception afforded the Futurist exhibition see Milton A. Cohen, 'The Futurist Exhibition of 1912: A Model of Prewar Modernism', *European Studies Journal*, vol.12, no.2, 1995, pp.1–31.

5 Richard Cork, *Vorticism and Abstract Art in the First Machine Age*, London: Gordon Fraser, 1976, vol.1, p.28.

6 'Initial Manifesto of Futurism', *Exhibition of Works by the Italian Futurist Painters*, London, 1912, p.3.

7 ibid.

8 ibid, pp.28–9.

9 Rebel Art Centre prospectus, 1914, cited by Cork, *Vorticism and Abstract Art*, vol.1, p.158.

10 F.T. Marinetti and C.R.W. Nevinson, 'Vital English Art', *Observer*, 7 June 1914; reproduced in facsimile in *ICSAC Cahier 8/9: Vorticism*, December 1988, pp.123–4.

11 Wyndham Lewis, *Blasting and Bombadiering*, revised ed., London: John Calder, 1982, p.35.

12 Ezra Pound, 'Vortex Pound', *Blast* no.1, p.154.

13 Wyndham Lewis, quoted by Violet Hunt. Cited in Cork, *Vorticism and Abstract Art*, vol.1, p.254.

14 Pound, 'Vortex Pound', p.153.

15 R. A. Scott-James, 'Blast', *New Weekly*, 4 July 1914, p.88.

16 Manifesto – II, p.33.

17 ibid, p.35.

18 ibid, p.39.

19 T. E. Hulme, *Speculations: Essays on Humanism and the Philosophy of Art*, ed. Herbert Read, London: Routledge and Kegan Paul, 1924, p.97.

20 *Blast* no.2, July 1915, p.5.

21 See Maria Tippett, *Art at the Service of War*, Toronto and London: University of Toronto Press, 1984, Nigel Viney, *Images of Wartime: British Art and Artists of World War I*, Newton Abbot: David & Charles, 1991, and Paul Edwards, *Wyndham Lewis: Art and War*, London, The Wyndham Lewis Memorial Trust in association with Lund Humphries, 1992.

22 Letter from Ezra Pound to Wyndham Lewis, 24 June 1916, *Pound/Lewis: The Letters of Ezra Pound and Wyndham Lewis*, ed. Timothy Materer, New York: New Directions, 1985, p.39.

23 Letter of 21 August 1916, *The Letters of T.S. Eliot*, ed. Valerie Eliot, London: Faber, 1988, vol.1, p.144.

24 Ezra Pound, 'Wyndham Lewis', *The Egoist*, 15 June 1914, p.234.

25 Henri Gaudier-Brzeska, 'Vortex. Gaudier-Brzeska', *Blast* no.2, p.34.

26 ibid.

27 See Samuel Hynes, *A War Imagined: The First World War and English Culture*, London: Bodley Head, 1990, chapter 5.

28 Lewis, *Blasting and Bombardiering*, p.213.

Notes to Rebels and Vorticists, pages 24–39

1 Ezra Pound had written to William Carlos Williams in December 1913 to the effect that 'We are getting our little gang after five years of waiting'. *The Letters of Ezra Pound, 1907–1941*, ed. D.D. Paige, London: Faber and Faber, 1951, p.27. He refers to those artists, led by Lewis, who had walked out of the Omega Workshops that October.

2 Ezra Pound, 'Edward Wadsworth, Vorticist', *The Egoist*, 15 August 1914, p.306.

3 Wyndham Lewis, 'Long Live The Vortex!', *Blast* no.1, June 1914, p.7.

4 In this field historians are indebted to the exhaustive archaeology on the subject that has been carried out by Richard Cork as

published in his *Vorticism and Abstract Art in the First Machine Age*, 2 vols, London: Gordon Fraser, 1976.

5 'As one that would draw thru the node of things, Back-sweeping to the vortex of the cone ...', Ezra Pound, *A Lume Spento*, Venice: Antonini, 1908, p.44.

6 *The Spectator*, 13 June 1914, p.1015, carries a note to the effect that *Blast* would contain a 'Manifesto of the Vorticists' which had probably been written by the time of the publication of Nevinson and Marinetti's 'Vital English Art' manifesto on 7 June 1914. For a suggested chronology for the contents of *Blast* see Paul O'Keeffe, 'The Troubled Birth of *Blast*: December 1913–June 1914', *ICSAC Cahier 8/9: Vorticism*, December 1988, pp.43–57. The use of the term Vorticism had been suggested by Pound.

7 For the March lecture see F.T. Marinetti, *Teoria e Invenzione Futurista*, ed. L. De Maria, Milan: Mondadori, 1968, p.483; for the April lecture see ibid, pp.240–45, 514–16, and Douglas Goldring, *South Lodge*, London: Constable, 1943, p.64; for the December lecture see Margaret Nevinson, 'Futurism and Woman', *The Vote*, 31 December 1910, p.112.

8 F.T. Marinetti, 'Futurist Venice', *The Tramp: An Open Air Magazine*, August 1910, pp.487–8.

9 The title of a satirical cartoon on Futurism by C. Harrison published in the *Daily Express*, 4 March 1912, p.5.

10 Roger Fry, Introduction, *Manet and the Post-Impressionists*, London: Grafton Galleries, 1910, p.7. The introduction was written by the exhibition's secretary, Desmond MacCarthy, from notes furnished by Fry.

11 ibid, p.9.

12 ibid, pp.11–12.

13 C.J. Holmes, *Notes on the Post-Impressionist Painters. Grafton Galleries 1910–1911*, London: Philip Lee Warner, 1910, p.10.

14 Roger Fry, 'The French Group', *Second Post-Impressionist Exhibition: British, French and Russian Artists*, London: Grafton Galleries, 1913, p.26.

15 ibid.

16 ibid.

17 ibid, p.27.

18 'A Post-Impressionist regards motif as an end in itself, as a significant form related on terms of equality with other significant forms.... Forms and the relation of forms have been ... not means of suggesting emotion but objects of emotion. It is this emotion they have expressed. Their drawing and design have been plastic and not descriptive.' Clive Bell, 'The English Group', ibid, p.22.

19 ibid, p.23. 'If bearing in mind the difference between the treatment of form as an object of emotion and treatment of form as means of description, we turn now, to these pictures an important distinction will become apparent. We shall notice that the art of Mr Wyndham Lewis, whatever else may be said of it, is certainly not descriptive. Hardly at all does it depend for its effect on association or suggestion.' Against this Clive Bell balanced the more obviously descriptive painting of Vanessa Bell, Duncan Grant and Roger Fry.

20 Listed as no.128 in the 1912 edition of the catalogue and as no.154 in the 1913 edition (which included a number of Russian paintings whose arrival had been delayed).

21 F.T. Marinetti, 'Initial Manifesto of Futurism', *The Italian Futurist Painters*, London: Sackville Gallery, 1912, p.3.

22 Umberto Boccioni, Carlo Carrá, Luigi Russolo, Giacomo Balla, Gino Severini, 'Manifesto of the Futurist Painters', ibid, pp.28–9.

23 A letter from Lewis to Sturge Moore that has been ascribed to September 1909 relates how much Lewis wanted to spend that autumn and winter in Paris and then pointedly asks Sturge Moore if he had been able to 'see any Picasso or Matisse paintings in Paris'. Sturge Moore Papers, University of London Library, 'The Sturge Moore Letters', ed. Victor M. Cassidy, *Lewisletter*, no.7, October 1977, pp.10–11.

24 An indication of the huge popularity of these lectures may be found in *La Vie Parisienne*, no.50, 1912, p.509, cited in Mark Antliff, *Inventing Bergson: Cultural Politics and the Parisian Avant-garde*, Princeton, N.J.: Princeton University Press, 1993, p.4.

25 The first of these stories was published in 1909; they were collected and revised by Lewis and republished in 1927 by Chatto and Windus. Both versions of the stories, along with other previously uncollected material, were edited by Bernard Lafourcade as *The Complete Wild Body*, Santa Barbara: Black Sparrow Press, 1982.

26 'The Vorticist is at his maximum point of energy when stillest'. Wyndham Lewis, 'Our Vortex', *Blast* no.1, p.148.

27 Tom Normand, *Wyndham Lewis the Artist: Holding the Mirror up to Politics*, Cambridge: Cambridge University Press, 1992, p.61.

28 Wyndham Lewis, 'Review of Contemporary Art', *Blast* no.2, July 1915, p.43: 'Michelangelo is probably the worst spook in Europe, and haunts English art without respite'. However, Lewis's satirical target was not just Michelangelo but also the arcadian fantasy of Matisse found in his *Danse* of 1909, all mediated by the ritual carnivalesque dance of the 'Wild Body'.

29 Although signed and dated '1909' this drawing has been dated to 1909–12 on stylistic grounds. The dating of Lewis's pre-1912 work is often a matter of guesswork, given the small body of work that has survived.

30 These drawings were intended to accompany an edition of Shakespeare's play. For reasons that are unclear Lewis, under the guise of 'The Cube Press', published the drawings independently in a portfolio and the illustrated edition of the play never appeared.

31 See Richard Cork, 'The Cave of the Golden Calf', *Artforum*, December 1982, pp.56–68.

32 Michael Durman and Alan Munton, 'Wyndham Lewis and the Nature of Vorticism', in Giovanni Cianci, ed., *Wyndham Lewis: Letteratura/Pittura*, Palermo: Sellerio, 1982, p.111. This assessment paraphrases Pound's understanding of the drawings: 'If you ask me what his *Timon* means, I can reply by asking you what the old play means. For me his designs are a creation on the same *motif*. That *motif* is the fury of intelligence baffled and shut in by circumjacent stupidity. It is an emotional *motif*. Mr Lewis's painting is nearly always emotional.' See Ezra Pound, 'Vorticism', *Fortnightly Review*, 1 September 1914, p.470.

33 Wyndham Lewis, *The Lion and the Fox*, London: Grant Richards, 1927, p.254.

34 This drawing was previously in the collection of John Quinn, and in a letter to him of 23 August 1915 Ezra Pound writes that it is 'of the later or second phase of the Timon stuff'. John Quinn Memorial Collection, New York Public Library, cited in Walter

Michel, *Wyndham Lewis: Paintings and Drawings*, London: Thames and Hudson, 1971, p.356.

35 Clive Bell, 'The London Salon at the Royal Albert Hall', *The Athenaeum*, 27 July 1912, pp.98–9. It was at this time that Bell bought a large painting from Lewis for £50, probably *The Laughing Woman*, now lost.

36 Roger Fry, 'The Allied Artists at the Albert Hall', *Nation*, 20 July 1912, p.583.

37 Work by Kandinsky was regularly exhibited in London in the salons of the Allied Artists' Association between 1910 and 1914; Brancusi exhibited *Prométhée* at the 1914 salon and *La Sagesse* and *Tête d'Enfant* at the 1916 salon.

38 On 1 April 1912 Fry had written to Charles Vildrac, concerning his exhibition at the Galerie Barbazanges that included Fry, Grant, Lewis and Etchells among others, that 'Duncan Grant will exhibit and certainly he has genius, perhaps Etchells also'. *The Letters of Roger Fry*, ed. Denys Sutton, London: Chatto and Windus, 1972, p.356.

39 Cork, *Vorticism*, vol.1, p.53.

40 For a detailed discussion of this decorative scheme and of the critical reaction to it see Richard Cork, 'Wyndham Lewis and the Drogheda Dining Room', *Burlington Magazine*, October 1984, pp.610–19.

41 Frank Rutter, Foreword, *Post-Impressionists and Futurists*, Doré Galleries, London, October 1913. Unfortunately work by Hamilton from this period has not survived, although of the three pictures he exhibited at the exhibition, *Portrait* was viciously attacked by Clive Bell for its 'ugliness'. See 'The New Post-Impressionist Show', *Nation*, 25 October 1913, p.173, that suggests that his work had moved close to Lewis.

42 Surprisingly Clive Bell, in his review of the exhibition, still praised Lewis's paintings but with the fundamental reservation that his attachment to literary subject-matter held him back from the elaboration of significant form: 'Kermesse ... has been altered and greatly improved since its last appearance at the London Salon. Lewis promises to become that rare thing, a real academic artist ... he uses a formula of which he is the master and not the slave.... The enemy that dogs him in all his works is an excessive taste for life. He is inclined to modify his forms in the interests of drama and psychology to the detriment of pure design. At times his simplifications and rhythms seem to be determined by a literary rather than a plastic conception.' ibid, p.172. He also suggested that Delaunay's *The Cardiff Football Team* (1913), suffered in comparison with Lewis.

43 Fry, Introduction, *Second Post-Impressionist Exhibition*, p.19.

44 These three paintings were, respectively, numbered 64, 66 and 67 in the catalogue and it is likely that they were hung together. *The Departure of the Train de Luxe* was reproduced by Rutter on the invitation for the exhibition's private view.

45 C.R.W. Nevinson, *Paint and Prejudice*, London: Methuen, 1937, p.47.

46 Marinetti, 'Initial Manifesto of Futurism', p.4.

47 ibid.

48 Nevinson relates how 'Marinetti ... thought of coming to England and told Severini, who wrote to me about him. I asked Severini to persuade him to come.' Nevinson, *Paint and Prejudice*, pp.56–7.

49 ibid, p.57. This poem was later published as *Zang Tumb Tumb:*

Parole in Libertà, Adrianopoli, Ottobre 1912, Milan: Edizioni Futuriste di 'Poesia', 1914.

50 The founding of the London Group is related in some detail by Wendy Baron, *The Camden Town Group*, London: Scolar Press, 1979, pp.54–65.

51 J.B. Manson, 'Introduction, Rooms I.–II.', *Exhibition by The Camden Town Group and Others*, Brighton: Public Art Galleries, 1913, p.8.

52 The 'Cubist Room' contained work by W.B. Adeney, Bomberg, Epstein, Frederick Etchells, Jessica Etchells, Fanny Eveleigh, Hamilton, Lewis, Nevinson and Wadsworth. Adeney was the only artist to exhibit in both the Cubist and the Camden Town–Fitzroy Street group. Eveleigh had married Wadsworth in 1912. In his catalogue introduction Lewis only mentioned Etchells, Hamilton, Wadsworth, Nevinson, Epstein, Bomberg and himself.

53 Wyndham Lewis, 'The Cubist Room', *The Camden Town Group and Others*, p.10.

54 ibid, pp.11–12.

55 ibid, p.9. Lewis suggests that Severini's subject-matter, 'the night resorts of Paris ... is obviously not of the future. But we all foresee, in a century or so, everybody being put to bed at 7 o'clock in the evening by a state nurse. Therefore the Pan Pan at the Monaco will be, for Ginos of the future, an archaistic experience'.

56 ibid. Lewis sarcastically writes that the Futurists outlook is 'flavoured strongly with H.G. Wells' dreams of the dance of monstrous and arrogant machinery, to the frenzied clapping of men's hands'.

57 ibid, pp.10–11.

58 Sickert, enraged by the work in the 'Cubist Room', unleashed a torrent of critical invective in *The New Age* especially against Lewis's painting *Creation*. See Cork, *Vorticism and Abstract Art*, vol.1, pp.144–5.

59 The premises for the Centre (and its financial backing) had been provided by a recent friend of Lewis, Kate Lechmere, who painted in a Cubist style. She also provided £100 so that *Blast* could be published. Lewis was named as 'manager' of the Rebel Art Centre, whilst Etchells, Hamilton, Nevinson and Wadsworth were listed as 'associates'. According to the Centre's prospectus, membership was £1 a year. Only two students enrolled, 'a man who wanted to improve the design of gas brackets, and a lady pornographer'; see Cork, ibid, p.160. The closure of the Centre coincided with Lewis's break with Lechmere as a result of her affair with T.E. Hulme. Lewis also broke with Hulme at the same time, feeling that his leadership of the Rebel Art Centre and the artists who congregated there was threatened by Hulme's attachment to Lechmere and his vocal criticism of Lewis's painting.

60 This event is well described by Henri Gaudier-Brzeska, 'Allied Artists' Association Ltd., Holland Park Hall', *The Egoist*, 15 June 1914, p.228: 'The Rebel stand is in unity. A desire to employ the most vigorous forms of decoration fills it with fans, scarves, boxes and a table, which are the finest of these objects I have seen. The spirit in the [Omega] lounge is one of subtlety ... there is too much prettiness. Happily the Rebel stand shows that the new painting is capable of great strength and manliness in decoration'.

61 The title was Nevinson's idea, see *Paint and Prejudice*, p.60. The idea for the magazine was probably initiated in November or December 1913.

62 Full-page advertisement for *Blast* in *The Egoist*, 1 April 1914, p.140, repeated 15 April, p.160.

63 Advertisement for *Blast* in *Spectator*, 13 June 1914, p.1015.

64 See O'Keeffe, 'The Troubled Birth of *Blast*', for a valuable discussion of *Blast*'s genesis.

65 The manifesto was printed as a pamphlet as well as in *The Times*, *Observer*, *Daily Mail* and *Lacerba*. The Rebel Art Centre replied in a letter that was published in the *Observer*, *The Egoist* and the *New Weekly*; to this Nevinson replied in a letter published in the *New Weekly*. All these documents are reprinted in facsimile in *ICSAC Cahier 8/9: Vorticism*, pp.123–6.

66 In his lecture 'Vital English Art' delivered at the Doré Galleries before the publication of the manifesto, Nevinson described Etchells as a Cubist and Lewis and Wadsworth as Expressionist, before then describing them as 'Vorticists as I believe [they] … now like to be called', in *The New Age*, 18 June 1914, pp.160–2. Nevinson 'was fiercely heckled by Gaudier-Brzeska at this event', *Paint and Prejudice*, p.61.

67 Wyndham Lewis, *Time and Western Man*, 1927; reprinted, ed. P. Edwards, Santa Rosa: Black Sparrow Press, 1993, p.201.

68 For more on this distinction see Sara Sellwood, 'The Dissemination of Ideas about Abstract Art in England and America', *Towards a New Art: Essays on the Background to Abstract Art, 1910–1920*, ed. Michael Compton, London: Tate Gallery, 1980, pp.207–9.

69 Ezra Pound to John Quinn, 19 July 1916, *Ezra Pound and the Visual Arts*, ed. Harriet Zinnes, New York: New Directions, 1980, p.240.

70 Wyndham Lewis, 'The New Egos', *Blast* no.1, p.141.

71 Hulme had immersed himself in Bergson's work to a far greater degree than Lewis ever did. Hulme first read Bergson in 1907. Between 1909 and 1912, through a series of articles and lectures, he became one of the main interpreters of Bergson's ideas in England, culminating with the publication in 1912 of his translation of Bergson's *Introduction à la métaphysique*, as well as the receipt of a letter of recommendation from Bergson when Hulme applied for readmission to St John's College, Cambridge, in the same year. However, interest in the work of the leading thinkers of *L'Action française*, such as Pierre Lasserre (whom Hulme met in 1911) and Charles Maurras, as well as the writing of Georges Sorel (whose *Réflexions sur la violence* he later translated), compelled him to revise his earlier opinion of Bergson in the realization of a confusion in his thought, typical of Romanticism, between biology and theology. Hulme's belief in a new Classicism was confirmed by his discovery of Wilhelm Worringer's writing by 1912 or 1913, the turning point of which was Worringer's lecture, 'Entstehung und Gestaltungsprinzipien in der Ornamentik', given at the 1913 Kongress für Ästhetik und Allgemeine Kunstwissenschaft in Berlin, which Hulme attended. This lecture on the origins and development of abstract ornament in art, already discussed in his 1908 book *Abstraktion und Einfuhlung* (*Abstraction and Empathy*). It was under Worringer's influence, not Bergson's, that Hulme wrote about the Vorticists. For a clear discussion of Hulme's intellectual development, from which this account is drawn, see *The Collected Writings of T. E. Hulme*, ed. Karen Csengeri, Oxford: Clarendon Press, 1994, pp.ix–xxxvi.

72 T. E. Hulme, 'Modern Art and Its Philosophy', ibid, p.269.

73 Hulme's first piece of art criticism was 'Mr Epstein and his Critics', *The New Age*, 25 December 1913, pp.251–3.

74 Hulme, 'Modern Art and Its Philosophy', pp.271–2.

75 ibid, p.279.

76 ibid, p.277.

77 ibid, p.283.

78 Lewis later stated, erroneously, that 'All the best things that Hulme said about the theory of art were said about my art…. We happened to be made for each other, as critic and "creator". What he said should be done, I *did*. Or it would be more exact to say that I did it, and he said it.' Wyndham Lewis, *Blasting and Bombardiering*, London: John Calder, 1982, p.100.

79 Not listed in the catalogue, this painting was shown at 'The Camden Town Group and Others' exhibition. Apparently Lewis attempted to prevent its carriage to Brighton, possibly because he felt threatened by it.

80 Hulme, 'Modern Art and Its Philosophy', p.273.

81 Cork, *Vorticism and Abstract Art*, vol.1, p.80.

82 T. E. Hulme, 'Contemporary Drawings, 2', *The New Age*, 2 April 1914, p.688.

83 T. E. Hulme, 'Modern Art IV: Mr David Bomberg's Show', *The New Age*, 9 July 1914, pp.230–31.

84 David Bomberg, Foreword, *David Bomberg*, London: Chenil Gallery, 1914: 'I APPEAL to a *sense of form*. In some of the work shown in the first room, I completely abandon *Naturalism* and Tradition. I am *searching for an Intenser* expression. In other work in this room, where I use Naturalistic Form, I have *stripped it of all* irrelevant matter. I look upon *Nature*, while I live in a *Steel City*. Where decoration happens, it is accidental. My object is the *construction of Pure Form*. I reject everything in painting that is not Pure Form. I hate the colours of the East, the modern Mediaevalist, and the Fat man of the Renaissance'.

85 'BLAST years 1837 to 1900 … WRING THE NECK OF all sick inventions born in that progressive white wake. BLAST their weeping whiskers – hirsute RHETORIC of EUNUCH and STYLIST', *Blast* no.1, p.18.

86 Ezra Pound, 'Prologomena', *Poetry Review*, February 1912, p.76.

87 'Preliminary Announcement of the College of Arts', *The Egoist*, 2 November 1914, pp.413–14. This encapsulated sculpture, painting, music, letters, photography, crafts and the dance.

88 Letter from Ezra Pound to Harriet Monroe, 10 November 1914, *Ezra Pound and the Visual Arts*, p.275.

89 Ezra Pound, 'Affirmations IV: As For Imagisme', *The New Age*, 28 January 1915, p.349.

90 Ezra Pound, 'Vortex Pound', *Blast* no.1, p.153.

91 ibid.

92 'The Image is the poet's pigment. The painter should use his colour because he sees it or feels it. I don't much care whether he is representative or non-representative. He should *depend*, of course, on the creative, not upon the mimetic or representational part in his work. It is the same in writing poems, the author must use his image because he sees it or feels it, not because he thinks he can use it to back up some creed or some system of belief.' Ezra Pound, 'Vorticism', *Fortnightly Review*, 1 September 1914, p.464. This text was originally given as a lecture at the Rebel Art Centre.

93 Douglas Goldring, *South Lodge*, p. 65. This can be compared to Wyndham Lewis's statement that 'The Vorticist is at his maximum point of energy when stillest', 'Our Vortex', *Blast* no. 1, p.148.

94 Pound, 'Vortex Pound', *Blast* no. 1, p.153.

95 Wyndham Lewis, *Rude Assignment*, London: Hutchinson, 1950, p.125.

96 Wyndham Lewis, 'The Improvement of Life', *Blast* no. 1, p.146.

97 Wyndham Lewis, 'Physics of the Not-Self', *Enemy of the Stars*, London: Desmond Harmsworth, 1932, p.51.

98 Lewis, 'Our Vortex', *Blast* no. 1, p.147.

99 ibid.

100 ibid, p.148.

101 The contributions of Dismorr, Etchells, Gaudier-Brzeska, Lewis, Roberts, Saunders and Wadsworth were augmented by a grouping of artists 'invited to show': Adeney, Atkinson (who had signed the Vorticist Manifesto in *Blast*), Bomberg, Grant, Kramer and Nevinson. Cuthbert Hamilton and the photographer Malcolm Arbuthnot, both of whom had signed the Vorticist Manifesto, did not participate.

102 T. E. Hulme, 'Modern Art III: The London Group', *The New Age*, 26 March 1914, p.661.

103 Wyndham Lewis, 'The London Group (March 1915)', *Blast* no. 2, pp. 77, 78.

104 B. H. Dias (Ezra Pound), 'Art Notes', *The New Age*, 27 March 1919, p.342.

105 Many of the woodcuts have subjects that are viewed from a distance, while one is titled *The Open Window*.

106 Frederick Etchells, 'A Note', *Exhibition of Original Woodcuts and Drawings by Edward Wadsworth*, London: Adelphi Gallery, 1919, reprinted in Frances Carey and Anthony Griffiths, *Avant-Garde British Printmaking 1914–1960*, London: British Museum, 1990, p.31.

107 ibid.

108 Wyndham Lewis, 'Editorial', *Blast* no. 2, p.5.

109 John Quinn organized an exhibition of Vorticism, largely from his own collection, in New York at the Penguin Club in 1917. This was poorly received, and as most of the work had been executed before 1913–14 was hardly representative of Vorticist achievement.

110 Wyndham Lewis, Foreword, *Guns*, London: Goupil Gallery, February 1919.

111 Wyndham Lewis, 'The Children of the New Epoch', *The Tyro* No. 1 [April], 1921, p.3.

112 A. Clutton-Brock, 'Process or Person', *Essays in Art*, London: Methuen, 1919, pp. 98–9.

113 For an account of Group X see Andrew Wilson, 'Demobilisation: The End of Vorticism or Another "Blast"? 1919–1921' in: *ICSAC Cahier 8/9: Vorticism*, pp.205–30.

114 'Press Notices' extracted from the *London Mercury*, Edward Wadsworth, *The Black Country*, London: Ovid Press, 1920. For Wadsworth this landscape also represented his coming inheritance. In his obituary Lewis remembered driving with Wadsworth around Yorkshire in 1920; stopping on a hill above Halifax they gazed 'down into its blackened labyrinth. I could see he was proud of it. "It's like Hell, isn't it?" he said enthusiastically.' *Wyndham Lewis on Art*, ed. C. J. Fox and Walter Michel, London: Thames and Hudson, 1969, p.421.

115 Andrew Causey, 'Wadsworth in the Early Twenties', *A Genius of Industrial England: Edward Wadsworth 1889–1949,* ed. Jeremy Lewison, London: Arkwright Arts Trust, 1990, p.36.

116 Wyndham Lewis, Introduction, *Wyndham Lewis and Vorticism*, London: Tate Gallery, 1956, p.3.

117 Ezra Pound, 'Ezra Pound Files Exceptions', *Reedy's Mirror*, 18 August 1916, *Ezra Pound and the Visual Arts*, p.219.

Notes to Vorticism and Sculpture, pages 40–58

1 *Pall Mall Gazette*, 6 June 1912.

2 Jacob Epstein, *Let There Be Sculpture*, London: Michael Joseph, 1940, p.58.

3 ibid, p.59.

4 Epstein was represented by two *Drawings*, and Gaudier by the *Stags* carving.

5 Henri Gaudier-Brzeska, 'Vortex. Gaudier-Brzeska', *Blast* No. 1, June 1914, p.155.

6 Gaudier to Sophie, October 1912, H. S. Ede, *Savage Messiah: A Life of Gaudier-Brzeska*, London: Heinemann, 1931, p.256.

7 Gaudier to Sophie, inscribed 'Sunday, May 1911', ibid, p.58.

8 Horace Brodzky, *Henri Gaudier-Brzeska, 1891–1915*, London: Faber and Faber, 1933, p.67.

9 The drawing was reproduced by Hulme in *The New Age*, 9 March 1914, as part of his 'Contemporary Drawings' series.

10 Gaudier to Sophie, 28 November 1912, Ede, *Savage Messiah*.

11 Pound, 'Prefatory Note' to the catalogue of *A Memorial Exhibition of the Work of Henri Gaudier-Brzeska*, London: Leicester Galleries, 1918.

12 Pound to Carlos Williams, 19 December 1913, *The Letters of Ezra Pound, 1907–1941*, ed. D. D. Paige, London: Faber and Faber, 1951, p.65.

13 Ezra Pound, 'The New Sculpture', *The Egoist*, 16 February 1914; reprinted in *Ezra Pound and the Visual Arts*, ed. Harriet Zinnes, New York: New Directions, 1980, p.182.

14 Gaudier to *The Egoist*, 16 March 1914.

15 Ezra Pound, *Gaudier-Brzeska: A Memoir*, London: John Lane, 1916, p.50.

16 Epstein, *Let There Be Sculpture*, p.59.

17 Wyndham Lewis, 'Early London Environment', *T. S. Eliot*, ed. Richard March and Tambimuttu, London: Editions Poetry, 1948, p.27.

18 Pound, *Gaudier-Brzeska: A Memoir*, p.52.

19 Gaudier, 'Vortex. Gaudier-Brzeska', p.157.

20 ibid, p.158.

21 Lewis, *Blast* no. 2, July 1915, p.78.

22 Celia Clayton to the author, 15 October 1972. Mrs Clayton is Mrs Kibblewhite's granddaughter, and her information comes from that source.

23 *Blast* no. 1, p.148.

24 According to the catalogue of the Allied Artists' Association salon of 1914.

25 Pound, *Gaudier-Brzeska: A Memoir*, p.160.

26 See Ede, *Savage Messiah*, p.200. The carving was listed as *Ornament* in the catalogue of the 1914 AAA salon.

27 *Blast* no.1, p.30.

28 Grattan Freyer, 'Blast and Counter-blast', *Irish Times*, 12 August 1972.

29 Lewis, *Blast* no.2, p.78.

30 Brodzky, *Henri Gaudier-Brzeska*, p.92.

31 Pound, *Gaudier-Brzeska: A Memoir*, p.161.

32 Gaudier, *The Egoist*, 15 June 1914.

33 Epstein, *Let There Be Sculpture*, p.61.

34 ibid, p.63.

35 ibid, p.64.

36 For a detailed account of the Cave of the Golden Calf and its avant-garde decorations, see Richard Cork, *Art Beyond The Gallery in Early 20th-Century England*, New Haven and London: Yale University Press, 1985, chapter two.

37 Epstein, *Let There Be Sculpture*, p.134.

38 Pound to John Quinn, 10 March 1916, *The Letters of Ezra Pound*, p.122.

39 Epstein, *Let There Be Sculpture*, p.64.

40 ibid.

41 It was exhibited at the Leicester Galleries, London, February–March 1917 as *Carving in Granite. 'Mother and Child'. Unfinished*. According to family legend, Epstein is supposed to have angrily ordered his brother to dump it in the East River after John Quinn had rejected it for his New York collection.

42 Pound to Isabel Pound, November 1913, *The Letters of Ezra Pound*, p.63.

43 Ezra Pound, 'Affirmations III: Jacob Epstein', *The New Age*, 21 January 1915.

44 Pound, *The Egoist*, 16 March 1914.

45 T.E.Hulme, *Speculations: Essays on Humanism and the Philosophy of Art*, ed. Herbert Read, London: Routledge and Kegan Paul, 1924, p.107.

46 For a discussion of the relationship between the Venus carvings and the *De Miré Figure*, see Richard Cork, *Vorticism and Abstract Art in the First Machine Age*, vol.2, London: Gordon Fraser, 1976, pp.457–8.

47 See Cork, *Art Beyond The Gallery*, chapter one, for an examination of Epstein's statues on the British Medical Association building.

48 Epstein, foreword to Hulme's *Speculations*.

49 Hulme, ibid, p.104.

50 Epstein, *Let There Be Sculpture*, p.70.

51 For an account of the rock drill machines of the period, see Cork, *Vorticism and Abstract Art*, vol.II, p.471.

52 Epstein, *Let There Be Sculpture*, p.70.

53 ibid.

54 See Cork, *Art Beyond The Gallery*, chapter one.

55 Epstein, *Let There Be Sculpture*, p.70.

56 *Observer*, 14 March 1915.

57 *Manchester Guardian*, 15 March 1915.

58 Pound, *Gaudier-Brzeska: A Memoir*, p.17.

59 ibid.

60 The plinth is visible in a photograph of *Rock Drill* reproduced in the *Daily Graphic*, 5 March 1915 (illustrated in Cork, *Vorticism and Abstract Art*, vol.II, p.474).

61 Lewis, *Blast* no.2, p.78.

62 Bomberg, draft of unsent letter to William Roberts, 1957 (collection Tate Gallery Archives, London).

63 Epstein, *Let There Be Sculpture*, p.70.

64 Lady Epstein interviewed by Richard Cork (see *Vorticism and Abstract Art*, vol.II, p.479).

65 Epstein, *Let There Be Sculpture*, p.56.

66 For an examination of innovative artists' response to the First World War, see Richard Cork, *A Bitter Truth: Avant-Garde Art and the Great War*, New Haven and London: Yale University Press, 1994.

67 Evelyn Silber, *The Sculpture of Epstein*, London: Phaidon, 1986, p.36.

68 *Blast* no.2, p.34.

69 Wyndham Lewis, *Blasting and Bombardiering*, London: Eyre and Spottiswoode, 1937, p.114.

70 ibid.

71 Gaudier to Pound, 24 October 1914, Pound, *Gaudier-Brzeska: A Memoir*, p.61.

72 Gaudier, *Blast* no.2, p.34.

73 Ford Madox Ford, *The Outlook*, 31 July 1915.

74 Pound, *Gaudier-Brzeska. A Memoir*, pp.16–17.

75 Gaudier, *Blast* no.2, p.33.

76 Lewis, ibid, p.78.

Notes to Reconceptualizing Vorticism, pages 59–72

1 In developing a study of women and Vorticism and in the preparation of a third article on this subject, the authors would like to extend their warmest thanks to Helen Peppin, Brigid Peppin and Omar Pound for discussing the lives and works discussed here. In developing a new analysis of the relations between avant-garde and feminist circles *c.*1914–15, we drew on Helen McNeil's essay 'Vortex Marsden', kindly sent before publication. Deborah Cherry would also like to thank her students on her course *Modernism and Its Texts* (1999) for discussion of some of these issues.

2 Richard Cork, *Vorticism and Abstract Art in the First Machine Age*, 2 vols, London: Gordon Fraser, 1976; David Peters Corbett, *The Modernity of English Art*, Manchester: Manchester University Press, 1997.

3 Charles Harrison, *English Art and Modernism*, London: Allen Lane, 1981, p.6.

4 Peters Corbett, *The Modernity of English Art*, p.5.

5 ibid, pp.5, 14.

6 Wyndham Lewis, Introduction, *Wyndham Lewis and Vorticism*, London: Tate Gallery, 1956, p.3.

7 Cork, *Vorticism and Abstract Art*, vol.1, p.8.

8 ibid, vol.2, pp.414–27.

9   Richard Cork, 'The Vorticist Circle, Bomberg and the First World
    War', *British Art in the Early Twentieth Century*, London: Royal
    Academy, 1987.

10 Jane Beckett, *'A Terrific Thing': British Art 1910–1916*, Norwich:
    Norwich Castle Museum, 1976; Margot Speight, 'The Women in
    the Picture', *Enemy News*, no.9, 1978, pp.7–11. It is of interest to
    consider why Jessica Etchells (1893–1933), associated with
    modern art circles before 1914, did not join the Vorticist group;
    see Jane Beckett and Deborah Cherry, 'Women under the Banner
    of Vorticism', *ICSAC Cahier 8/9: Vorticism*, 1988, pp.129–43.

11 Saunders's address at 4 Phené Street, Chelsea, is given in *Blast*
    no.2. In addition Shakespear (p.47) and Saunders (p.16)
    contributed endpieces to this issue. *Blast* no.3, announced but
    never produced, was to have included 'Poems and Vortices' by
    Dismorr and reproductions of work by Dismorr and Saunders.

12 *Ripostes*, 1915, and *Catholic Anthology*, c.1915, reproduced in
    Blast: Vortizismus – Die Erste Avant-Garde in England, 1914–18,
    ed. Karin Orchard, Berlin: Ars Nicolai, 1996, pp.194,196–7.

13 Cork, *Vorticism and Abstract Art*, vol.1, p.xxiii.

14 Brigid Peppin, *Helen Saunders, 1885–1963*, Oxford: Ashmolean
    Museum, 1996, p.41.

15 Bridget Elliott and Jo-Ann Wallace, *Women Artists and Writers:
    Modernist (Im)positionings*, London and New York: Routledge,
    1994, pp.1–30; Katy Deepwell, *Women Artists and Modernism*,
    Manchester: Manchester University Press, 1998, pp.1–10; Griselda
    Pollock, *Vision and Difference: Feminism, Femininities and the
    Histories of Art*, London and New York: Routledge, 1988,
    pp.50–52. See also Christopher Reed, ed., *Not at Home: The
    Suppression of Domesticity in Modern Art and Architecture*,
    London: Thames and Hudson, 1996, and Andreas Huyssen, 'Mass
    Culture as Woman. Modernism's Other', *After the Great Divide:
    Modernism, Mass Culture, Post-Modernism*, Bloomington:
    Indiana University Press, 1986.

16 Alfred Barr, *Cubism and Abstract Art*, New York: Museum of
    Modern Art, 1936, cover, reproduced in Elliott and Wallace,
    Women Artists and Writers, p.152.

17 Elliott and Wallace, op.cit., p.1.

18 Mary Langhan and Bill Schwarz, eds, *Crises in the British State,
    1880–1920*, London: Hutchinson, 1985. Although it is often
    argued, following Virginia Woolf, that 'in or about December
    1910 human character changed', it should be noted that this
    pronouncement was made in an essay written in 1924 (first
    presented as a lecture) in which Woolf was plotting a break
    between the Victorians and the Georgians; see 'Mr Bennett and
    Mrs Brown', 1924, *Collected Essays of Virginia Woolf*, vol.1,
    London: Hogarth Press, 1966, pp.319–37, quotation p.320.

19 Rebecca West, 'An orgy of disorder and cruelty: the beginnings of
    sex antagonism', *Clarion*, 27 September 1912, reprinted in Jane
    Marcus, ed., *The Young Rebecca West*, London: Macmillan/
    Virago, 1982, pp.97–101, quotation p.98. For a more recent
    argument see Sandra Gilbert and Susan Gubar, *No Man's Land:
    The Woman Writer in the Twentieth Century*, London and New
    Haven: Yale University Press, 1994.

20 For a critique of linear technocentric accounts of modernism see
    David Harvey, *The Condition of Post-Modernity*, Oxford:
    Blackwell, 1989, p.35.

21 The term 'avant garde' has been subject to considerable definition,

see R. Poggioli, *The Theory of the Avant-Garde*, Cambridge,
    Mass.: Harvard University Press, [1962] 1968; Peter Bürger,
    Theory of the Avant-Garde, Minneapolis: University of
    Minnesota Press, [1974] 1984; Rosalind Krauss, *The Originality of
    the Avant-Garde and Other Modernist Myths*, Cambridge, Mass.:
    MIT Press, 1985. It is used here in the historical specificity argued
    for by Susan R. Suleiman, *Subversive Intent: Gender, Politics and
    the Avant-Garde*, Cambridge, Mass.: Harvard University Press,
    1990. The involvement of women in the modern movement in
    Russia is well documented. In Britain none of the other modernist
    groups issued manifestos.

22 *The Letters of Ezra Pound, 1907–1941*, ed. D.D. Paige, London:
    Faber and Faber, 1950, p.28.

23 Ezra Pound, 'Affirmations II: Vorticism', *The New Age*, 14
    January 1915, quoted in Cork, *Vorticism and Abstract Art*, vol.1,
    p.xxi.

24 *Blast* no.1, June 1914, pp.19,11.

25 For a more detailed study of the implications of war see Jane
    Beckett, 'I(s)land Narratives: Englishness, Visuality and Vanguard
    Culture 1914–18', in *Modernities and Identities in English Art*,
    ed. David Peters Corbett, Manchester: Manchester University
    Press, forthcoming.

26 Elizabeth Grosz, 'Bodies/Cities', in *Sexuality and Space*, ed.
    Beatriz Colomina, Princeton, N.J.: Princeton Architectural Press,
    1992, pp.242–3.

27 For example, J. Weeks, *Sex, Politics and Society*, London:
    Longmans, 1981, and Lucy Bland, *Banishing the Beast: English
    Feminism and Sexual Morality, 1880–1914*, Harmondsworth:
    Penguin, 1995. Michel Foucault however wrote of the locations
    and institutions shaping discursive formations of sexuality and
    the body, see *History of Sexuality: Vol.1 The Will to Know*,
    Harmondsworth: Penguin, 1981, and *Discipline and Punish*,
    Harmondsworth: Penguin, 1982.

28 Examples include C. Booth, *Life and Labour of the People of
    London*, 1889–1903; W. Besant, *South London*, 1899, *East London*,
    1901, *The Thames*, 1903; C.F.G. Masterman, *The Condition of
    England*, 1909; G.R. Sims, *Living London: Its Work and Its Play,
    Its Humour and Its Pathos, Its Sights and Scenes*, London, 1902–3.
    While Sims favoured a fragmentary photojournalist approach,
    historians like Besant researched local histories and commentators
    like Masterman drew on organic metaphors to convey the scale
    and sprawl of London.

29 See Elizabeth Grosz, *Volatile Bodies*, Bloomington and
    Indianapolis: Indiana University Press, 1994, and Foucault, *A
    History of Sexuality*.

30 Lucy Bland, 'Purity, motherhood, pleasure or threat', in
    S. Cartledge and J. Ryan, eds, *Sex and Love: New Thoughts on Old
    Contradictions*, London: Women's Press, 1986, p.134.

31 Cork, *Vorticism and Abstract Art*, vol.II, p.414. Saunders's address
    at 4 Phené Street (c.1912–17) was near Dismorr's at 183 Kings
    Road.

32 Little is known about Lechmere, who, according to Cork, ibid,
    vol.1, p.218, met Lewis at a dinner party c.1912.

33 Dismorr's writings were included in the *Little Review* in 1919. She
    contributed 'Some Russian artists', on Goncharova, Vassilieva,
    Chagall, Archipenko and Lipschitz, and a drawing, *Conversation*,
    to *The Tyro*, no.2, 1922. In the 1920s she exhibited with the

London Group, becoming a member in 1926, and with the Seven and Five group. In the 1930s she was making abstract art and was a contributor to *Axis* no.8, 1937. For some discussion of her work before 1914 see Anna Gruetzner Robins, *Modern Art in Britain, 1910–14*, London: Merrell Holberton, 1997, pp.112–13.

34 Richard Shone, 'The Friday Club', *Burlington Magazine*, May 1975, pp.279–84. In 1916 Saunders exhibited at the AAA and as a non-member with the London Group. For biographical details of Saunders, see Peppin, *Helen Saunders*, and on all four women see Beckett and Cherry, 'Women under the Banner of Vorticism', pp.135–7.

35 *The Introspective Eye: Dorothy Shakespear Pound's Modernist Vision*, Emerson Gallery, Hamilton College, 1997, with a biographical note by Omar Pound; Omar Pound and A.Walton Litz, eds, *Ezra Pound and Dorothy Shakespear Pound: Their Letters, 1910–14*, New York: New Directions, 1984.

36 Lisa Tickner, *The Spectacle of Women: Imagery of the Suffrage Campaign, 1907–1914*, London: Chatto and Windus, 1987.

37 Denise Hooker, *Nina Hamnett, Queen of Bohemia*, London: Constable, 1986, and Elliott and Wallace, *Women Artists and Writers*, pp.140–49.

38 Lisa Tickner, 'The "Left-handed Marriage": Vanessa Bell and Duncan Grant', in *Significant Others*, ed. W.Chadwick and I.de Courtivron, London: Thames and Hudson, 1993; Frances Spalding, *Vanessa Bell*, London: Weidenfeld and Nicolson, 1983; Gretchen Gersina, *Carrington: A Life of Dora Carrington*, Oxford: Oxford University Press, 1990; Jane Hill, *The Art of Dora Carrington*, London: Herbert Press, 1994. For an invaluable analysis of Bloomsbury domesticity see Christopher Reed, '"A Room of One's Own": The Bloomsbury Group's Creation of a Modern Domesticity', *Not at Home*, pp.147–60.

39 Tickner, *The Spectacle of Women*, pp.17–18. Grant was a nephew of suffrage supporter Lady Julia Strachey whose daughter Philippa was the Secretary to the London Society for Women's Suffrage. Elliott and Wallace, *Women Artists and Writers*, p.153.

40 *Souvenir and Handbook of Woman's Kingdom Exhibition*, 11–30 April 1914, Olympia, London; the catalogue has a photograph of Millicent Garrett Fawcett on the cover. A Fine Arts Gallery was intended to show the work of modern women painters, sculptors and craftswomen. Dismorr's *The Square*, priced six guineas, and an untitled drawing were included. Women's Suffrage Collection: Millicent Fawcett Collection, Manchester Public Libraries, M 50/2/13/12.

41 Harriet Shaw Weaver was in 1912 Secretary of the Appeal for the South London Women's Hospital. A subscriber to the *Freewoman* and a member of its discussion circle, she offered £200 for the relaunch of the *New Freewoman* which gave her a controlling interest in the paper. She contributed to *The Egoist* under the pen-name 'Josephine Wright'. See J.Lidderdale and M.Nicholson, *Dear Miss Weaver: Harriet Shaw Weaver, 1876–1961*, London: Faber and Faber, [1962] 1970.

42 Helen McNeil, 'Vortex Marsden: A Little Magazine and the Making of Modernity', [1999] forthcoming 2000. On Marsden see Les Garner, *A Brave and Beautiful Spirit: Dora Marsden, 1882–1960*, Avebury: Gower, 1990, and Bruce Clarke, *Dora Marsden and Early Modernism*, Ann Arbor: University of

Michigan Press, 1996. We are also indebted to Judy Greenway for discussions on Marsden.

43 *New Freewoman*, 15 June 1913, p.5.

44 McNeil, 'Vortex Marsden'; the *New Freewoman*'s offices were in the Theosophical Society's premises in Oakley Street, and most sales came from this source.

45 *New Freewoman*, 23 November 1911, p.2; 2 May 1912, p.482. Helen McNeil has demonstrated how Dora Marsden reprinted passages from Otto Weininger's *Sex and Character*, 1903, translated 1906, precisely to refute it.

46 Rebecca West, 'The Freewoman', *Time and Tide*, 16 July 1926, reprinted in *Time and Tide Wait for No Man*, ed. Dale Spender, London: Pandora, 1984, pp.63–8, quotation p.66.

47 Quoted in Lucy Bland, 'Heterosexuality, Feminism and the *Freewoman* Journal in Early Twentieth-Century England', *Women's History Review*, vol.IV, no.1, 1995, pp.5–21; see also Bland, *Banishing the Beast*.

48 Gruetzner Robins, *Modern Art in Britain*, p.119; Mark Antliff, *Inventing Bergson: Cultural Politics and the Parisian Avant-Garde*, Princeton, N.J.: Princeton University Press, 1993, pp.67–103.

49 Rebecca West, 'Indissoluble Matrimony', *Blast* no.1, pp.98–117. *Blast*, no.1 pronounced, '*Blast* presents an art of Individuals' (p.8).

50 Feminist historians are by no means agreed on the freedoms offered by new city spaces, see Rachel Bowlby, *Just Looking: Consumer Culture in Dreiser, Gissing and Zola*, London and New York: Methuen, 1985; Judith R.Walkowitz, *City of Dreadful Delight: Narratives of Sexual Danger in Late Victorian London*, London: Virago, 1992; and Lynne Walker, 'Vistas of Pleasure: Women as Consumers of Urban Space, 1850–1900', *Women in the Victorian Art World*, ed. C.C.Orr, Manchester: Manchester University Press, 1994, pp.70–85.

51 Helen Saunders, 'Notes on Harriet Weaver', in Lidderdale and Nicholson, *Dear Miss Weaver*, p.120.

52 Cork, *Vorticism and Abstract Art*, vol.1, p.148; vol.2, p.414. According to the prospectus, 'Saturday afternoon meetings of artists' were held from 4 to 6pm, ibid, vol.1, p.158.

53 Wendy Baron, *Miss Ethel Sands and her Circle*, London: Peter Owen, 1977, pp.66–8.

54 An illuminating example of the ways in which this mythology was generated is given in Walter Michel, *Wyndham Lewis: Paintings and Drawings*, London: Thames and Hudson, 1971, p.152, n.11. In reply to an undisclosed question from Michel, Saunders responded, 'You are I am sure right in thinking that Lewis *was* to all extents and purposes *Blast*'; quoted in Cork, *Vorticism and Abstract Art*, vol.1, p.243. It is assumed from this, rather un-questioningly, that 'the indefatigable Lewis' wrote most of *Blast*.

55 Jane Beckett and Deborah Cherry, 'Art, Class and Gender', *Feminist Arts News*, 1987, vol.2, no.6, pp.18–21; Lisa Tickner, 'Men's Work? Masculinity and Modernism', *differences*, vol.IV, no.3, 1992, p.19; quoted in Cork, *Vorticism and Abstract Art*, vol.1, pp.93–4.

56 Geoffrey Pearson, 'From Hooligans to Heroes', *New Society*, 30 June 1983. The unsolicited propositioning by 'male pests' of women walking or shopping in late nineteenth-century London is discussed in Judith Walkowitz, *City of Dreadful Delight*, pp.50–52.

57 West, 'An orgy of disorder', p.98.

58 Kate Lechmere to Wyndham Lewis, 25 July 1914, Cornell University Library.

59 Brigid Peppin, *Helen Saunders*, no.9.

60 In the prospectus, Lewis is named as manager and Lechmere and Lewis as directors, see Cork, *Vorticism and Abstract Art*, vol.1, p.158. There is no doubt from the correspondence between Lechmere and Lewis at Cornell University Library that Lechmere managed the financial and business aspects of the enterprise: on 25 March 1914 she wrote to Lewis sending him his share certificates in the 'Cubist Art Centre Ltd'. The work of women in creating the institutions of Parisian modernism, particularly in setting up and funding salons, meeting-places and publishing houses is well documented in Shari Benstock, *Women of the Left Bank: Paris, 1900–1940*, Austin, Texas: University of Texas Press, 1986; Elliott and Wallace, *Women Artists*; and Gillian Perry, *Women Artists and the Parisian Avant-Garde*, Manchester: Manchester University Press, 1995.

61 'Cubist' and 'Cubism' were highly volatile terms in these years, see Jane Beckett, 'Cubism and Sculpture', *British Sculpture in the Twentieth Century*, London: Whitechapel Art Gallery, 1980.

62 Frank Vane Rutter was the art critic for the *Sunday Times*, editor of *Art News* (1909–12), founder and secretary of the Allied Artists' Association in 1908, curator of Leeds Art Gallery and a collector of modern art. As the selector of 'Post-Impressionists and Futurists' at the Doré Galleries in 1913, which included Lewis, Nevinson and Wadsworth, Rutter was 'blessed' in *Blast* no.1.

63 Kate Lechmere to Wyndham Lewis, 23 July [1914], Cornell University Library.

64 Lechmere's apartment above was, according to *Vanity Fair*, 25 June 1914, decorated with 'black doors in cream walls, and black curtains in addition to the usual orgies of colour'; in addition she painted her window boxes with abstract patterns.

65 'Rebel Art in Daily Life', *Daily News*, 7 April 1914.

66 Cork, *Vorticism and Abstract Art*, vol.1, p.148.

67 ibid, p.147. The painting is now lost.

68 Kate Lechmere to Wyndham Lewis, 19 May [1914], Cornell University Library. Works by Gaudier-Brzeska, Bomberg and Roberts were also shown.

69 Henri Gaudier-Brzeska, *The Egoist*, 15 June 1914, p.228.

70 Kate Lechmere to Wyndham Lewis, 23 July [1914], Cornell University Library. For brochure see Cork, *Vorticism and Abstract Art*, vol.1, p.157.

71 Lechmere's letters to Lewis in Cornell frequently discussed financial matters. She loaned Lewis £100 for the printing of *Blast* in 1914, and petitioned for payment, 'fairness and justice' on several occasions; in 1915 she served a writ on him for repayment. Her letter of 23 July [1914] discusses a tussle between herself, Dismorr and Saunders over the distribution of *Blast*.

72 'Restaurant Art', *Colour Magazine*, April 1916, p.xiv; 'Futurism in Furnishing', ibid, May 1916. A card, dated January 1916, 'to view the room with Paintings and Ornament by Mr Wyndham Lewis', attributes the decoration to Lewis.

73 Richard Cork, *Art Beyond The Gallery in Early 20th-Century England*, New Haven and London: Yale University Press, 1985, p.271.

74 ibid, p.321.

75 Peppin, *Helen Saunders*, nos 14, 15 and 22. *Vorticist Composition in Red and Black*, c.1915–16, no.20.

76 *Daily Mirror*, 2 and 3 December 1913, and *Daily News* both carried photo-features on Futurist gowns in 1914.

77 William C. Wees, *Vorticism and the English Avant Garde*, Manchester: Manchester University Press, 1972, pp.38–9.

78 *Daily Mirror*, 30 March 1914, p.7. The interior was completely rearranged for the photographer of *The Graphic*, 25 April 1914, p.726: a painting by Lewis was hung over the fireplace and another version of *Caprice* was placed over a door.

79 The Omega incident was recollected by Winifred Gill, quoted in Peters Corbett, *The Modernity of English Art*, p.38; Cork, *Vorticism and Abstract Art*, vol.1, p.132.

80 Lisa Tickner, 'Augustus John: Gypsies, Tramps and *Lyric Fantasy*', one of her four Paul Mellon Lectures on Modern Life and Modern Subjects, London, 1996. For Camden Town men in suits see Malcolm Drummond, *Portrait of Charles Ginner*, c.1911, Southampton Art Gallery, and *Nineteen Fitzroy Street*, c.1914, Laing Art Gallery, Newcastle.

81 'A Post-Impressionist flat: what would the landlord think?', *Daily Mirror*, 8 November 1913, p.3. Thanks to Geoff Archer for bringing this to our attention. The other photograph shows a seated woman intent on her sewing, surrounded by cushions; the mood is calm and tranquil and the emphasis is on Omega products and decorative style.

82 'School of Cubist Art', *Evening Standard*, 30 March 1914; Cork, *Vorticism and Abstract Art*, vol.1, p.149.

83 Did Lechmere purchase it in Paris, or like other women artists, design and make her clothes?

84 A photograph of Lechmere and another woman in this attire is reproduced, ibid. According to Lechmere, Lewis set a dress code for women appearing at the Centre of 'simple white blouses and long dark skirts' which in Lechmere's recollection was the attire of 'a high-class shop girl', see Wees, *Vorticism and the English Avant-Garde*, p.146.

85 Peters Corbett, *The Modernity of English Art*, p.41. Countess Drogheda's decorations received extensive press coverage; Violet Hunt commissioned Lewis to provide decorations for Ford Madox Ford's study at South Lodge, and Mrs Percy Harris, wife of the deputy chair of the London County Council, proposed decorations for her Sloane Street home. Lewis was regularly invited to fashionable soirées and dinners, see Cork, *Vorticism and Abstract Art*, vol.1, pp.132–5, 266, 270.

86 Dismorr to Lewis, [?1913], Cornell University Library.

87 Cork, *Vorticism and Abstract Art*, vol.1, p.275.

88 'Vorticists at the Doré Gallery', *Observer*, 4 July 1915, p.9, in which 'Sanders' and 'Dismore' are included in the grouping 'six different men'.

89 Deborah Cherry, 'Carrington: The Exhibition', *Texte zur Kunst*, vol.6, no.2, 1996, pp.190–92.

90 *The Egoist*, 15 June 1914, pp.227–9. For the nineteenth-century categorization of 'woman artist' see Deborah Cherry, *Painting Women*.

91 *The Egoist*, 15 June 1914, p.233; Ezra Pound, 'The New Sculpture', ibid, 16 February 1914, pp.67ff. The numerous references to Africa, and to modern artists as 'savage'/'primitive mercenaries' took place within a colonial/imperialist rhetoric.

92 Jessica Dismorr, 'June Night', *Blast* no.1, pp.67–8.

93 Jessica Dismorr, 'Promenade', ibid, p.69.

94 Richardson sets seven of the thirteen novels of *Pilgrimage* around the area of Fitzrovia/Bloomsbury, precisely that struggled over by modernist art groups. There are several close parallels between Dismorr's prose poems and the early novels of *Pilgrimage*. Woolf's *Night and Day* of 1919 was also set in London.

95 Cork, *Vorticism and Abstract Art*, vol.II, p.417, suggests that 'June Night' is 'a parable of the artist's own conversion from Fauvism to Vorticism'.

96 Michel de Certeau, 'Walking in the City', in *The Practice of Everyday Life*, part 3 'Spatial Practices', Berkeley: University of California Press, 1984, pp.91–110.

97 Woolf, Virginia, 'Street Haunting: A London Adventure', 1930, *Collected Essays of Virginia Woolf*, vol.4, London: Hogarth Press, 1966, pp.155–67. See also Rachel Bowlby, 'Walking, Women and Writing: Virginia Woolf as *Flâneuse*', *New Feminist Discourses*, ed. Isobel Armstrong, London: Routledge, 1992, pp.26–47.

98 In the 1880s Shaftesbury Avenue, Cambridge Circus and Charing Cross Road were developed and Piccadilly Circus enlarged. Aldwych, begun in 1892 on the north side, was not completed until 1905. The construction of Kingsway and its buildings continued until the early 1920s. New buildings adjacent to Trafalgar Square were erected from 1901, including, in 1911, Admiralty Arch; government buildings in Whitehall were constructed from 1898 to 1907.

99 *Blast* no.2, p.65.

100 *Blast* no.1, p.39.

101 Jennifer Bloomer, *Architecture and the Text: The (S)crypts of Joyce and Piranesi*, New Haven and London: Yale University Press, 1993, pp.11,48.

102 Peppin, *Helen Saunders*, nos 12,16.

103 Victoria and Albert Museum, London. Dismorr exhibited a drawing, *Edinburgh Castle*, in the Vorticist exhibition of 1917. A painting of the same title (oil on plywood, 51.5 x 47 cm) was in the collection of R.H.M.Ody. The composition of this massive structure depends on an observation of Assyrian sculptures housed in the British Museum in London. A consideration of the pronounced relations in Vorticism between imperialist collecting and visual culture is beyond the scope of this essay.

104 Peppin, *Helen Saunders*, no.8. Taking Cork's title (*Vorticism and Abstract Art*, vol.1, p.150), Tickner has argued that here 'Saunders probably comes closer than anyone else in the pre-war avant-garde to producing an overtly feminist painting'; see 'Men's Work?', p.22.

105 Saunders's painting entitled *Atlantic City* (now lost) was shown at the Vorticist exhibition of 1915.

106 Cork, *Vorticism and Abstract Art*, vol.2, pp.419–24.

107 City views out of windows include Vanessa Bell, *46 Gordon Square*, c.1909–10 (private collection) and several by the Camden Town painters, who also depicted urban interiors. For a detailed study, see Jane Beckett and Deborah Cherry, 'When Painting Was/As Murder: Walter Sickert and Camden Town', forthcoming.

108 Freud's concept of the unhomely/*unheimlich*, from his essay 'The Uncanny', is developed in relation to visual culture in our forthcoming essay, see note above.

109 Jane Beckett, 'I(s)land Narratives'.

110 Ezra Pound, *Fortnightly Review*, September 1914.

111 Reproduced in Cork, *Vorticism and Abstract Art*, vol.1, p.134.

112 Reproduced, ibid, p.287; *Abstract Composition*, c.1914–15, Hamilton College Collection, Clinton, NY; reproduced in Karin Orchard, ed., *Blast*.

113 Peppin, *Helen Saunders*, no.18.

114 ibid, nos 5, 17. Loss of work makes it difficult to ascertain or reconstruct such processes, but *Hammock c.*1912–13 (no.6) may be an abstraction from a popular Edwardian subject of a young woman reclining in a hammock. Lewis's *Portrait of an Englishwoman* (plate IV), reproduced in *Blast* no.1, utilized architectural and mechanical forms for the rendition of the female body.

115 According to Peppin (*Helen Saunders*, no.5), this drawing was cut down by the artist to its present irregular shape.

116 Cork, *Vorticism and Abstract Art*, vol.1, p.150.

117 Peppin (*Helen Saunders*, no.12) connects this drawing to an exhibit at the Vorticist exhibition of 1915 entitled *Black and Khaki*.

118 ibid, nos 14, 16, 22, 21. Peppin links no.16, one of the few signed with the artist's initials, with *Cannon*, one of the three drawings by the artist which was purchased by John Quinn. Similarly *Monochrome Composition with Ascending Figures*, Peppin, *Helen Saunders*, no.21.

119 ibid, no.7, p.44; Jessica Dismorr, 'Monologue', *Blast* no.2, p.65.

120 Vanessa Bell, *Composition*, c.1914, Museum of Modern Art, New York; *Abstract Painting*, c.1914, Tate Gallery, London. The title of Grant's *Interior at Gordon Square*, 1915 (private collection), signals its London location; in its abstracted forms can be perceived a doorway and an 'Omega' interior.

Notes to 'You Must Speak with Two Tongues', pages 113–120

1 *Blast* no.1, June 1914, p.30.

2 Filippo Tommaso Marinetti, 'The Founding and Manifesto of Futurism' (1909), *Marinetti: Selected Writings*, ed. R.W.Flint, New York: Farrar, Straus and Giroux, 1972, pp.39–44.

3 For discussions of *Enemy of the Stars*, see Reed Way Dasenbrock, *The Literary Vorticism of Ezra Pound and Wyndham Lewis: Towards the Condition of Painting*, Baltimore and London: Johns Hopkins University Press, 1985, pp.127–39; Toby Avard Foshay, *Wyndham Lewis and the Avant Garde: The Politics of the Intellect*, Montreal: McGill-Queen's University Press, 1992, pp.22–33; David Graver, 'Vorticist Performance and Aesthetic Turbulence in *Enemy of the Stars*', *PMLA*, vol.CVII, no.3, May 1992, pp.482–96; Paul Edwards, *Wyndham Lewis: Painter and Writer*, New Haven and London: Yale University Press, 2000, pp.139–65.

4 An exception to this general neglect is Philip Head's essay,

'Vorticist Antecedents', in his book *Some Enemy Fight-Talk: Aspects of Wyndham Lewis on Art and Society*, Borough Green: Green Knight Editions, 1999, pp.87–106.

5 The play is also related to other modernist texts of the time that are not Expressionist, however, notably Marinetti's *La Conquête des étoiles* (1902) and Aleksei Kruchenykh's *Victory over the Sun* (1913), trans. Ewa Bartos and Victoria Ness Kirby, *The Drama Review*, vol.xv, no.4 (fall 1971), pp.92–124.

6 Friedrich Nietzsche, *Complete Works*, Vol.XIII *The Genealogy of Morals*, ed. Oscar Levy, Edinburgh and London: T.N.Foulis, 1910, Essay III, Section 11.

7 'M.M.B.', 'Rebel Art in Modern Life', *Daily News and Leader*, 7 April 1914, p.14. For a discussion of the relevance of this interview to Lewis's designs for Lady Drogheda's drawing-room, see Richard Cork, *Art Beyond The Gallery in Early 20th-Century England*, New Haven and London: Yale University Press, 1985.

8 'Rebel Art in Modern Life', p.14.

9 'A Review of Contemporary Art', *Blast* no.2, July 1915, p.43.

10 Wyndham Lewis, 'Futurism, Magic and Life', *Blast* no.1, p.134.

11 'Fêng Shui and Contemporary Form', *Blast* no.1, p.138.

12 Lewis to Charles Handley-Read, 22 September 1949, *The Letters of Wyndham Lewis*, ed. W.K.Rose, London: Methuen, 1963, pp.504–5.

13 The phrases in quotation marks are from Lewis's 'A Review of Contemporary Art', *Blast* no.2, p.40.

14 T.E.Hulme, 'Modern Art and its Philosophy', 1914; reprinted in *The Collected Writings of T.E.Hulme*, ed. Karen Csengeri, Oxford: Clarendon, 1994, pp.273–4.

15 T.E.Hulme, 'Modern Art III: The London Group', ibid, pp.294–8.

16 'The Improvement of Life', *Blast* no.1, p.146, and 'Manifesto', p.33.

17 The contract is in the Wyndham Lewis collection of the Carl A.Kroch Library, Cornell University.

18 Pound wrote to his (and the Vorticists') patron, John Quinn, on 15 May 1917 that he had collected the manuscript, adding 'It has been lost in the office of dead publisher's ex-landlord for nearly two years'. *The Selected Letters of Ezra Pound to John Quinn, 1915–1924*, ed. Timothy Materer, Durham and London: Duke University Press, 1991, p.112.

19 Wyndham Lewis, 'Inferior Religions', 1917; reprinted in Wyndham Lewis, *The Complete Wild Body*, ed. Bernard Lafourcade, Santa Barbara: Black Sparrow Press, 1982, p.316. (Text corrected by collation with *Little Review* printing).

20 ibid, p.315.

21 Wyndham Lewis, *The Ideal Giant*, 1916; reprinted in Wyndham Lewis, *Collected Poems and Plays*, ed. Alan Munton, Manchester: Carcanet, 1979, p.130.

22 'Wyndham Lewis Vortex No.1: Art Vortex. Be Thyself', *Blast* no.2, p.91.

23 Wyndham Lewis, 'The New Egos', *Blast* no.1, p.141.

24 Ezra Pound, 'Vorticism', 1914; reprinted in Ezra Pound, *Gaudier-Brzeska: A Memoir*, 1916; revised ed. New York: New Directions, 1970, p.92. Pound's point here is not explicitly to deny Lewis's status as a writer; ostensibly he is merely drawing a parallel and making a contrast between writing and painting. But in doing so he reserves centrality for himself and his protégés in the literary branch of the movement.

25 Wyndham Lewis to the editor of *Partisan Review*, April 1949 (perhaps not sent), *The Letters of Wyndham Lewis*, p.492.

26 The proofs of Lewis's 1919 book, *The Caliph's Design: Architects! Where is your Vortex?*, sparsely corrected by Pound and now in the Poetry and Rare Books department of the Library, State University of Buffalo (Map Case, MC4,9), reveal something of both the closeness and slight tension in their relationship. In the Preface, Lewis criticized an 'Art-for-Art's sake dilettantism' in much modern painting, but continued, 'Yet you find [more] vigour and conviction [in that art than in literature]; its exponents, Picasso, Matisse, Derain, Balla, for example, are [more] <very> considerable artists, [more] <very> sure of themselves and of the claims of their business [than most contemporary men of letters].' Pound deleted the words in square brackets and substituted those in angle-brackets. Pound's is the version that was published. It is unlikely that Lewis would have allowed anyone else to alter his meaning like this.

27 Pound, 'Vorticism', pp.91–2.

28 ibid, p.84.

29 Ezra Pound to John Quinn, 13 July 1916, 19 July 1916, *Ezra Pound and the Visual Arts*, ed. Harriet Zinnes, New York: New Directions, 1980, pp.238–9, 240.

30 Wyndham Lewis, 'Futurism, Magic and Life', *Blast* no.1, p.135.

31 *Blast* no.2, p.19. See also Charles Altieri, 'Modernist Abstraction and Pound's First Cantos: The Ethos for a New Renaissance', *Kenyon Review*, new series, vol.VII, no.4, fall 1985, pp.79–105, and Patricia Rae, 'From Mystical Gaze to Pragmatic Game: Representations of Truth in Vorticist Art', *ELH*, vol.LVI, no.3, fall 1989, pp.689–720. Rae's article is particularly germane to the argument in the present essay on account of its delineation of a pragmatist-inspired 'competitive' epistemology for Vorticism.

32 See Christine Froula, *To Write Paradise: Style and Error in Pound's Cantos*, New Haven and London: Yale University Press, 1986. 'Canto IV' was not the first that Pound completed, but Froula shows that work on it was crucial in rethinking the aesthetic of the project. As published, 'Canto IV' is very different from its drafts, and contains no material relating to the modern world; the monologue about the war was dropped. It is possible that Pound's tentative attempts to incorporate modern material into his work at this point were a response to criticism Lewis voiced of his preoccupation with archaic and exotic subject-matter.

33 In his letter of 15 May 1917 to Quinn, Pound states that Lewis's 'Inferior Religions' is 'the best piece of theoretical prose Lewis has ever done'. *Selected Letters*, p.112.

34 Tom Normand, *Wyndham Lewis the Artist: Holding the Mirror up to Politics*, Cambridge: Cambridge University Press, 1992, pp.76–83.

35 *The Ideal Giant*, *Collected Poems and Plays*, pp.131–2.

Biographical Notes

COMPILED BY RICHARD CORK

LAWRENCE ATKINSON 1873–1931

Born 17 January 1873 in Chorlton upon Medlock, near Manchester. Educated at Bowden College, Chester, and then studied singing and music in Berlin and Paris. Taught singing in Liverpool and London, and gave concert performances. Self-taught as an artist, he exhibited in the July 1913 Allied Artists' Association salon, and moved from Fauvism to Vorticism when he joined the Rebel Art Centre early 1914. Signed *Blast* no. 1's manifesto, June 1914, appeared in the 'Invited to Show' section of the June 1915 Vorticist exhibition and published a book of poems called *Aura*, 1915. Exhibited with the London Group, June 1916, and held a one-man show of 'Abstract Sculpture and Painting' at the Eldar Gallery, London, May 1921. Concentrated on sculpture in later life and awarded Grand Prix for his carving *L'Oiseau* at the 1921 Milan exhibition. Died 21 September 1931 in Paris.

DAVID BOMBERG 1890–1957

Born 5 December 1890 in Birmingham, the fifth child of a Polish immigrant leather-worker. Family moved to Whitechapel 1895, and c.1906–7 Bomberg apprenticed to lithographer Paul Fischer, while studying with Walter Bayes at the City and Guilds evening classes. Broke his indentures to become an artist 1908, and attended Sickert's Westminster School evening classes. Studied at the Slade School 1911–13, visited Paris May–June 1913 and included in the 'Cubist Room' section of the 'Camden Town Group and Others' exhibition at Brighton, December 1913–January 1914. Included in the January–February 1913 and the February–March 1914 Friday Club exhibitions at the Alpine Club

Gallery. Founder-member of the London Group, in whose first exhibition he participated, March 1914. Contributed to the Whitechapel Art Gallery's 'Twentieth Century Art' exhibition, which he helped to organize, May–June 1914. One-man show at the Chenil Gallery, Chelsea, July 1914. Included in 'Invited to Show' section of the June 1915 Vorticist exhibition, and enlisted in the Royal Engineers, November 1915. Married Alice Mayes March 1916, transferred to Canadian Regiment December 1917 to paint war picture and returned to England November 1918. One-man show at the Adelphi Gallery, London, September 1919. In later life changed his style completely, travelled widely and married again to Lilian Holt. Died 19 August 1957 in London.

ALVIN LANGDON COBURN 1882–1966

Born 11 June 1882 in Boston, Massachusetts, the son of a shirt manufacturer. Introduced to photography by his cousin, F. Holland Day, 1890. First exhibition in Boston 1898. First one-man show in London Photographic Salon, 1900. Founder-member of Photo-Secession, 1902. Elected to the 'Linked Ring', 1903. Portfolio appeared in *Camera Work*, 1904, when he moved to London and met George Bernard Shaw. One-man show at the Royal Photographic Society, 1906, and included in the 'International Exhibition of Pictorial Photography' at the Albright Gallery, Buffalo, 1910. Visited New York 1912, when he married Edith Clement. Returned to London 1912 and met Ezra Pound 1913. One-man show of 'Camera Pictures' at the Goupil Gallery, London, October 1913, and published portrait collection called *Men of Mark* the same year. Invented Vortoscope late 1916, and exhibited 'Vortographs and Paintings' in one-man show at the Camera Club, London, February 1917. Elected Honorary Fellow of the Royal Photographic Society 1931, and became naturalized British subject 1932. Died 23 November 1966 in Rhos-on-Sea, North Wales.

JESSICA DISMORR 1885–1939

Born 1885 in Gravesend, the fourth child of a land and property investor. From 1910 to 1913 studied painting in Paris at the Atelier La Palette, under Metzinger, Fergusson, Segonzac and Blanche. Contributed illustrations to several issues of *Rhythm* magazine, 1911, and exhibited in the Allied Artists' Association salons of July 1912 and July 1913. Included in the Salon d'Automne, 1913, and met Lewis the same year. Joined the Rebel Art Centre, spring 1914, and signed the manifesto in *Blast* No. 1, June 1914. Participated as a member of the movement in the June 1915 Vorticist exhibition, contributed illustrations and writings to *Blast* no. 2, July 1915, and included in the January 1917 New York Vorticist exhibition. Exhibited with other ex-Vorticists in Group X at the Mansard Gallery, March–April 1920, elected to the London Group 1926 and became completely abstract by the late 1930s, contributing to *Axis* no. 8, 1937. Committed suicide on 29 August 1939 in London.

SIR JACOB EPSTEIN 1880–1959

Born 10 November 1880 in New York, the third child of a Polish immigrant property owner. Studied at the Arts Student League in New York and then at the Académie Julian in Paris. Moved to London 1905 and became a British subject 1907. Between 1907 and 1908 executed his earliest important commission, eighteen figures for the façade of the British Medical Association's building in The Strand, which prompted the first of many public scandals in Epstein's lifetime. Close friendship with Eric Gill. Produced two decorated relief pillars for Madame Strindberg's Cabaret Theatre Club 1912, and installed his monumental *Tomb of Oscar Wilde* at Père Lachaise cemetery, Paris, autumn 1912. Met Modigliani, Picasso, Brancusi and other radical artists in Paris, then returned to England 1913, and settled in Pett Level, Sussex, to carve in isolation. Exhibited at the July 1913 Allied Artists' Association salon, the 'Post-Impressionist and Futurist Exhibition', October 1913, and the 'Cubist Room' section of the 'Camden Town Group and Others' exhibition in Brighton, December 1913–January 1914. One-man show at the Twenty-One Gallery, December 1913–January 1914. Exhibited as founder-member in March 1914 London Group show, participated in the Whitechapel Art Gallery's 'Twentieth Century Art' exhibition, May–June 1914, and contributed two illustrations to *Blast* no. 1, June 1914.

Displayed original version of *Rock Drill* at March 1915 London Group exhibition, and exhibited in March 1916 Allied Artists' Association salon. Held one-man show at the Leicester Galleries, February–March 1917. Called up 1917 and demobilized 1918. In later life modelled many portrait busts, but also continued to produce ambitious monumental carvings. Knighted 1954. Died 19 August 1959 in London.

FREDERICK ETCHELLS 1886–1973

Born 14 September 1886 in Newcastle upon Tyne, the son of an engineer, and educated at Macclesfield Grammar School. Studied at the Royal College of Art c. 1908–11 and afterwards rented a studio in Paris, where he met Picasso, Braque and Modigliani. Participated in Roger Fry's mural scheme for the Borough Polytechnic 1911, while teaching part-time at the Central School, London. Exhibited in Friday Club, February 1912, collaborated with Duncan Grant on mural in Brunswick Square for Adrian Stephen and his sister Virginia (Woolf), and contributed to the 'Second Post-Impressionist Exhibition' at the Grafton Galleries, October 1912–January 1913. Joined Omega Workshops 1913, visited Dieppe with Lewis the same summer and in October walked out of Omega with Lewis and the other rebels. Contributed to the 'Post-Impressionist and Futurist Exhibition', October 1913, and the 'Cubist Room' section of the 'Camden Town Group and Others' exhibition in Brighton, December 1913–January 1914. Founder-member and exhibitor at the London Group exhibition, March 1914, and joined the Rebel Art Centre spring 1914. Contributed illustrations to *Blast* no. 1, June 1914, and participated as a member in the June 1915 Vorticist exhibition. Contributed illustrations to *Blast* no. 2, July 1915, and then included in the January 1917 New York Vorticist exhibition. Did not fight in war on medical grounds, but painted large picture for Canadian War Memorials Fund. Included in the Group X exhibition at the Mansard Gallery, March–April 1920. Soon after gave up painting, took his ARIBA and became an architect. Designed pioneering Crawford building in Holborn and translated Le Corbusier's *Towards a New Architecture*. Married Hester Sainsbury in 1932. Died 16 August 1973 in Folkestone.

HENRI GAUDIER-BRZESKA 1891–1915

Born Henri Gaudier, 4 October 1891 in St-Jean-de-Braye, near Orleans, the son of a carpenter. Visited England on a scholarship 1906 and again 1908. Started work as a sculptor in Paris, 1910, and met Sophie Brzeska, with whom he lived from this time, adding her surname to his own. Settled in London January 1911, where he soon met John Middleton Murry, Alfred Wolmark, Horace Brodzky and Epstein. Aroused controversy by exhibiting in the July 1913 Allied

Artists' Association salon, befriended T. E. Hulme and Ezra Pound and affiliated himself briefly with the Omega Workshops, 1913–14. Exhibited with the Grafton Group at the Alpine Gallery, January 1914, contributed as a founder-member to the March 1914 London Group exhibition and joined the Rebel Art Centre, spring 1914. Participated in the Whitechapel Art Gallery's 'Twentieth Century Art' exhibition, May–June 1914, contributed an illustration and essay to *Blast* no. 1, and signed its manifesto, June 1914. Chairman of artists' committee for July 1914 Allied Artists' Association salon, of which he wrote a preview in *The Egoist*. Included as a member in the June 1915 Vorticist exhibition and contributed an essay and illustration to *Blast* no. 2, July 1915. Killed serving with the French army, 5 June 1915 at Neuville-Saint-Vaast. *Memoir* published by Pound 1916. Memorial exhibition held at the Leicester Galleries, May–June 1918.

CUTHBERT HAMILTON 1884–1959

Born 15 February 1884 in India, the son of a judge. Studied at the Slade School on a Slade scholarship 1899–1903, contemporary with Lewis. Taught art at Clifton College, 1907–10. Collaborated with Lewis on the decorations for Madame Strindberg's Cabaret Theatre Club, 1912–13, and joined the Omega Workshops, summer 1913, accompanying Lewis, Etchells and Wadsworth when they left the Omega in October the same year. Contributed to the 'Post-Impressionist and Futurist Exhibition', October 1913, and to the 'Cubist Room' section of the 'Camden Town Group and Others' exhibition at Brighton, December 1913–January 1914. Participated in the March 1914 London Group exhibition and joined the Rebel Art Centre, spring 1914. Contributed an illustration to *Blast* no. 1, June 1914, and signed its manifesto. Served as a special constable in the First World War and was the most abstract of the artists who exhibited in Group X at the Mansard Gallery, March–April 1920. Also displayed pottery at Group X, made at the Yeoman Potteries which he had founded, and around this time began to experiment with sculpture. Died 13 March 1959 in Cookham.

WYNDHAM LEWIS 1882–1957

Born 18 November 1882 on board his American father's yacht off Amherst, Nova Scotia. His mother was British. Educated at Rugby School, 1897–8, and studied at the Slade School, 1898–1901. Between 1902 and 1908 travelled widely, visiting Madrid with his friend Spencer Gore, Holland, Munich and Paris, spending summer holidays in Brittany. Settled in England 1909, while continuing to visit Paris every year, and published short stories in *The English Review*. Met Pound

1909–10, and contributed as a founder-member to the first Camden Town Group exhibition, June 1911. Showed again in second Camden Town Group exhibition, December 1911, at the July 1912 Allied Artists' Association salon, the 'Second Post-Impressionist Exhibition', October 1912–January 1913, and at the third Camden Town Group show, December 1912. Painted decorations, including *Kermesse*, for Madame Strindberg's Cabaret Theatre Club, 1912. Contributed to the July 1913 Allied Artists' Association salon, joined the Omega Workshops at the same time, and walked out of the Omega, October 1913. Contributed to the 'Post-Impressionist and Futurist Exhibition', October 1913, and wrote a catalogue preface for the 'Cubist Room' section of the 'Camden Town Group and Others' exhibition at Brighton, December 1913–January 1914. Decorated a dining-room for Lady Drogheda, 1913–14. Exhibited as a founder-member in the March 1914 London Group show, and at the same time founded the Rebel Art Centre. Contributed to the Whitechapel Art Gallery's 'Twentieth Century Art' exhibition, May–June 1914, edited and contributed to *Blast* no. 1, June 1914 and exhibited in the July 1914 Allied Artists' Association salon. Included in March 1915 London Group show and wrote catalogue preface for the June 1915 Vorticist exhibition, to which he contributed. Edited and contributed to *Blast* no. 2, July 1915. Decorated a 'Vorticist Room' with Helen Saunders in the Restaurant de la Tour Eiffel, 1915. Joined army as a gunner 1916 and participated in January 1917 New York Vorticist exhibition. Seconded as a War Artist, December 1917, to paint a picture for the Canadian War Memorials Fund, and published first novel, *Tarr*, 1918. Held one-man show at the Goupil Gallery, February 1919, and wrote catalogue preface for Group X exhibition at the Mansard Gallery, March–April 1920. Married Gladys Anne Hoskins 1929, and continued to write and paint prolifically. Lost his sight 1951. Died 7 March 1957 in London.

C. R. W. NEVINSON 1889–1946

Born 13 August 1889, the son of the war correspondent and author H. W. Nevinson. Studied painting at St John's Wood and the Slade School, 1908–12. Exhibited at the July 1911 Allied Artists' Association salon, and the Friday Club exhibitions of February 1912 and January–February 1913 at the Alpine Club Gallery. Studied in Paris at Académie Julian, and the Cercle Russe, summer 1912 to spring 1913, and became friendly with Severini, Modigliani and other radical French artists. Exhibited at the July 1913 Allied Artists' Association salon, the October 1913 'Post-Impressionist and Futurist Exhibition' and the 'Cubist Room' section of the 'Camden Town Group and Others' exhibition at Brighton, December 1913–January 1914. Welcomed Marinetti with a dinner at the Florence Restaurant, November 1913, and exhibited in the February–March 1914 Friday Club show. Contributed as a founder-member to the March 1914 London Group exhibition, and joined the Rebel Art Centre soon afterwards. Included in the Whitechapel Art Gallery's 'Twentieth Century Art' exhibition, May–June 1914, and published with Marinetti in June 1914 the 'Futurist Manifesto: Vital English Art' which the other members of the Rebel Art Centre repudiated. Exhibited in the July 1914 Allied Artists' Association salon, and then showed his first war pictures in the March 1915 London Group exhibition. Married 1915. Included in the 'Invited to Show' section of the June 1915 Vorticist exhibition as a 'Futurist', and contributed an illustration to *Blast* no. 2, July 1915. Served in the Red Cross and the Royal Army Medical Corps 1914–17, and held two very successful one-man shows at the Leicester Galleries, September–October 1916 and March 1918. Painted war picture for the Canadian War Memorials Fund 1918 and renounced Futurism. In later life his work became far more traditional. Died 7 October 1946 in London.

WILLIAM ROBERTS   1895–1980

Born 5 June 1895 in London, the third child of a Hackney carpenter. Apprenticed 1909 to the poster-designing and advertising firm of Sir Joseph Causton Ltd, to learn commercial art. At the same time attended evening classes at St Martin's School of Art. Won a precocious LCC scholarship in drawing to the Slade School, 1910, where he studied for three years. Executed a tempera wall painting for Fulham Girls' Club, 1911, and won a Slade Scholarship 1912. Left the Slade summer 1913, and travelled in France and Italy. Joined the Omega Workshops after Lewis and the other rebels had left, and exhibited with the New English Art Club December 1913. Included in the Grafton Group show at the Alpine Club Gallery, January 1914, and contacted spring 1914 by Lewis, who borrowed two of his pictures to hang in the Rebel Art Centre. Contributed to the Whitechapel Art Gallery's 'Twentieth Century Art' exhibition, May–June 1914, work illustrated in *Blast* no. 1, June 1914, and signed its manifesto. Exhibited in the March 1915 London Group show and as a member in the June 1915 Vorticist exhibition. Contributed illustrations to *Blast* no. 2, July 1915. Joined the Royal Field Artillery 1916, participated in the January 1917 New York Vorticist exhibition and returned to England 1918 to paint a large picture for the Canadian War Memorials Fund. Demobilized 1919, and executed three paintings for the Restaurant de la Tour Eiffel. Contributed to Group X at the Mansard Gallery, March–April 1920, and held first one-man show at the Chenil Gallery in November 1923. Issued a series of pamphlets and books on his early work from 1956 to 1969. Elected a Royal Academician 1966. Died 20 January 1980 in London.

HELEN SAUNDERS   1885–1963

Born 4 April 1885 in London, the daughter of a director of the Great Western Railway. Educated at home in Bedford Park. Studied at the Slade School, 1906–7, and at the Central School. Exhibited in the February 1912 Friday Club exhibition at the Alpine Club Gallery, and in the Allied Artists' Association salons of July 1912 and July 1913. Joined the Rebel Art Centre, spring 1914, and contributed to the Whitechapel Art Gallery's 'Twentieth Century Art' exhibition, May–June 1914. Signed the manifesto in *Blast* no. 1, June 1914, as 'H. Sanders'. Participated as a member in the June 1915 Vorticist Exhibition, and contributed a poem and illustrations to *Blast* no. 2, July 1915. Assisted Lewis with the decoration of the 'Vorticist Room' at the Restaurant de la Tour Eiffel, summer 1915, and exhibited at the July 1916 Allied Artists' Association salon. Included as a non-member in the November–December 1916 London Group exhibition, and then participated in the January 1917 New York Vorticist exhibition. Continued to paint in a more representational style in later life, sometimes close to the work of her friend Jessica Dismorr. Died 3 January 1963 in London.

DOROTHY SHAKESPEAR   1886–1973

Born 14 September 1886 in London, the daughter of a solicitor from India and the minor Edwardian novelist Olivia Shakespear. Educated at Crowborough School, Sussex, and St James's School, Malvern. Self-taught as an artist, and specialized from an early age in landscape watercolours. Met Ezra Pound 1908. Both Dorothy and her mother attended the lectures Pound gave on medieval literature at the Regent Street Polytechnic 1909–10, and he later introduced her to Lewis and Gaudier. Impressed by the Rebel Art Centre when taken there by Pound for Saturday afternoons, spring 1914. Married Pound, April 1914, but always kept her maiden name when painting because she wanted to keep her work separate from her husband's. Lewis encouraged her during the Vorticist period, and she contributed a decoration and an illustration to *Blast* no. 2, July 1915. Always remained an amateur artist, never holding or seeking an exhibition. In later life acknowledged a debt to Vorticism, which can be seen informing the many landscape studies she executed after 1920. Died 8 December 1973 near Cambridge.

EDWARD WADSWORTH   1889–1949

Born 29 October 1889 in Cleckheaton, Yorkshire, the son of a wealthy worsted-spinning magnate. Studied engineering at Munich 1906 but became more interested in painting, attending the Knirr School in his spare time. On returning to England went to the Bradford School of Art, where he gained a scholarship to the Slade School. Studied at the Slade 1908–12. Married Fanny Eveleigh and spent honeymoon in the Canary Islands, April–May 1912, afterwards travelling in France and Spain. Exhibited in the Friday Club at the Alpine Club Gallery, February 1912 and January–February 1913. Included in the last month (January 1913) of the 'Second Post-Impressionist Exhibition'. Joined the Omega Workshops summer 1913 and exhibited in the July 1913 Allied Artists' Association salon. Left the Omega with Lewis and the other rebels October 1913, and contributed to the 'Post-Impressionist and Futurist Exhibition' the same month. Included in the 'Cubist Room' section of the 'Camden Town Group and Others' exhibition at Brighton, December 1913–January 1914, and exhibited as a founder-member in the March 1914 London Group show. Joined the Rebel Art Centre, spring 1914, and participated in the Whitechapel Art Gallery's 'Twentieth Century Art' exhibition, May–June 1914. Contributed illustrations and translations from Kandinsky's *On the Spiritual in Art* to *Blast* no. 1, June 1914, and signed its manifesto. Included in the July 1914 Allied Artists' Association salon, and in the March 1915 London Group exhibition. Contributed as a member to the June 1915 Vorticist exhibition, and reproduced his work in *Blast* no. 2, July 1915. Served in the Royal Naval Volunteer Reserve until invalided out 1917. Included in the January 1917 New York Vorticist exhibition, and then employed designing dazzle camouflage for ships in Bristol and Liverpool. Painted large picture for the Canadian War Memorials Fund, and held a one-man show at the Adelphi Gallery, March 1919. Exhibited in Group X at the Mansard Gallery, March–April 1920, and in later life pursued a more representational style, apart from a period in the 1930s when associated with Unit One. Died 21 June 1949 in London.

Notes on Contributors

DR JANE BECKETT is Senior Lecturer in Art and Visual Culture at the University of East Anglia. She has published extensively on modernism in Europe and Britain and on contemporary British culture. She is currently working on a cultural history of Amsterdam. Recent publications include 'The Bleaching Fields: Dutch Landscape, Modernity and Gender', in *Landscape and Gender*, ed. A. Gruetzner Robins and S. Adams, Manchester University Press, 2000; 'I(s)land Narratives: Englishness, Visuality and Vanguard Culture', in *Modernities and Identities in English Art 1870–1914*, ed. David Peters Corbett, Manchester University Press, 2000; *Plan B: The Work of Lubaina Himid*, Tate Gallery Publications, 2000.

DEBORAH CHERRY is Professor of the History of Art at the University of Sussex. She has written extensively on British art of the nineteenth and twentieth centuries, and her publications include *Painting Women: Victorian Women Artists*, Routledge, 1993, and *Beyond the Frame: Feminism and Visual Culture, Britain 1850–1900*, Routledge, 2000. She co-edited *The Edwardian Era*, Phaidon, 1987, with Jane Beckett.

RICHARD CORK read Art History at Cambridge University, where he was awarded a Doctorate in 1978. He is Chief Art Critic of *The Times*. In 1989–90 he was the Slade Professor of Fine Art at Cambridge. From 1992 to 1995 he was Henry Moore Senior Fellow at the Courtauld Institute, and then served as Chair of the Visual Arts Panel at the Arts Council of England (1995–8). Formerly Art Critic of the *Evening Standard* and *The Listener*, and Editor of *Studio International*, he has delivered the Lethaby Lectures at the Royal College of Art and the Durning-Lawrence Lectures at University College London. A frequent broadcaster on radio and television, he has organized major exhibitions at The Tate Gallery, the Royal Academy, the Hayward Gallery and elsewhere. His exhibition on Art and the First World War, held in Berlin and London, won a National Art Collections Fund Award in 1995. His books include a study of *Vorticism*, awarded the John Llewellyn Rhys Prize in 1976; *The Social Role of Art*, 1979; *Art beyond The Gallery*, which won the Banister Fletcher Award as the best art book of 1985; *David Bomberg*, 1987; *A Bitter Truth: Avant-Garde Art and the Great War*, 1994; *Bottle of Notes: Claes Oldenburg and Coosje van Bruggen*, 1997; and *Jacob Epstein*, 1999. He is now working on a history of British sculpture in the twentieth century.

PAUL EDWARDS is a Senior Lecturer in English at Bath Spa University College. He has published widely on Wyndham Lewis and modernism, and has edited several of Lewis's books for Black Sparrow Press. His *Wyndham Lewis: Art and War* accompanied the Imperial War Museum's exhibition of Lewis's work in 1992. His major study of Lewis, *Wyndham Lewis: Painter and Writer*, was published by Yale University Press in 2000.

DR KARIN ORCHARD studied Art History, History and Literature in Hamburg, Edinburgh and London, completing her PhD on 'Androgyny in Sixteenth Century Art' in 1988. She has published on art in the sixteenth and twentieth centuries. During a traineeship at the Hamburger Kunsthalle she worked on (among other things) the exhibitions 'Zauber der Medusa: Europäische Manierismen' for the Vienna Festival, 1987, and 'Europa 1789: Aufklärung, Verklärung, Verfall', 1989. Since 1991 she has been curator at the Sprengel Museum, Hanover, responsible for such exhibitions as 'Die Erfindung der Natur: Max Ernst, Paul Klee, Wols und das surreale Universum', 1994, 'BLAST: Vortizismus – Die erste Avantgarde in England 1914–1918', 1996, and 'Aller Anfang ist MERZ: Von Kurt Schwitters bis heute', 2000. Since 1994 she has been Director of the Kurt Schwitters Archive in the Sprengel Museum, Hanover, and joint editor of the Kurt Schwitters Catalogue Raisonné.

ANDREW WILSON is an art historian, curator and writer on contemporary culture and art. He is the Deputy Editor of *Art Monthly* and was London Correspondent of *Forum International* (Antwerp), 1990–93. He was awarded a PhD by the Courtauld Institute of Art, London, in 2000. He has published internationally; recent publications include major catalogues for Mark Wallinger (Gegenwartskunst Museum, Basel) and Richard Wilson (Serpentine Gallery, London), and books on Paul Graham (Phaidon Press) and Gustav Metzger (Coracle Press). In 1988 he edited a book of essays on Vorticism (ICSAC, Brussels) and in 1990 organized an exhibition of works on paper by Wyndham Lewis (Austin/Desmond Fine Art, London); he is currently working on major exhibitions of Concrete Poetry and of British abstract painting of the 1930s.

Bibliography

Alley, Ronald, *William Roberts* (exhibition catalogue), London: Arts Council of Great Britain, 1965

Altieri, Charles, 'Modernist Abstraction and Pound's First Cantos: The Ethos for a New Renaissance', *Kenyon Review*, new series, vol.VII, no.4, fall 1985, pp.79–105

Antliff, Mark, *Inventing Bergson: Cultural Politics and the Parisian Avant-garde*, Princeton, N.J.: Princeton University Press, 1993

Baron, Wendy, *Miss Ethel Sands and her Circle*, London: Peter Owen, 1977

—, *The Camden Town Group*, London: Scolar Press, 1979

Beckett, Jane, '*A Terrific Thing*': British Art 1900–1916 (exhibition catalogue), Norwich: Norwich Castle Museum, 1976

—, 'Cubism and Sculpture', *British Sculpture in the Twentieth Century* (exhibition catalogue), London: Whitechapel Art Gallery, 1980

—, 'I(s)land Narratives: Englishness, Visuality and Vanguard Culture 1914–1918', *Modernities and Identities in English Art 1860–1914*, ed. David Peters Corbett, Manchester: Manchester University Press, forthcoming

Beckett, Jane, and Cherry, Deborah, 'Art, Class and Gender', *Feminist Art News*, vol.II, no.6, 1987, pp.18–21

—, 'Women under the Banner of Vorticism', *ICSAC Cahier 8/9: Vorticism*, December 1988, pp.129–43

—, 'Jenseits des Sichtbaren: Frauen, Grossstadtkultur, Vortizismus', *Blast: Vortizismus – Die Erste Avantgarde in England 1914–1918* (exhibition catalogue), ed. Karin Orchard, Berlin: Ars Nicolai, 1997

—, 'Modern Women, Modern Spaces: Women, Metropolitan Culture and Vorticism', *Women Artists and Modernism*, ed. K. Deepwell, Manchester: Manchester University Press, 1998, pp.36–54

Bell, Clive, 'The London Salon at the Royal Albert Hall', *The Athenaeum*, 27 July 1912, pp.98–9

—, 'The English Group', *Second Post-Impressionist Exhibition: British, French and Russian Artists* (exhibition catalogue), London: Grafton Galleries, 1912

—, 'The New Post-Impressionist Show', *Nation*, 25 October 1913, p.173

—, 'The English Group', *Post-Impressionists in England: The Critical Reception*, ed. J.B.Bullen, London and New York: Routledge, 1988, pp.349–51

—, *Art*, 1914; reprinted London: Chatto and Windus, 1928

Bell, Quentin, and Chaplin, Stephen, 'The Ideal Home Rumpus', *Apollo*, vol.LXXX, no.32, October 1964, 284–91

—, 'Rumpus Revived', *Apollo*, vol.LXXXIII, no.47, January 1966, p.75

Benstock, Shari, *Women of the Left Bank: Paris, 1900–1940*, Austin, Texas: University of Texas Press, 1986

Bland, Lucy, 'Marriage Laid Bare: Middle-class Women and Marital Sex, 1880s to 1914', *Labour and Love: Women's Experience of Home and Family*, ed. J.Lewis, Oxford: Blackwell, 1986, pp.123–46

—, 'Heterosexuality, Feminism and The *Freewoman* Journal in Early Twentieth-Century England', *Women's History Review*, vol.IV, no.1, 1995, pp.5–21

—, *Banishing the Beast: English Feminism and Sexual Morality, 1880–1914*, Harmondsworth: Penguin, 1995

Blast no.1, June 1914; reprinted Santa Barbara: Black Sparrow Press, 1981

Blast no.2, July 1915; reprinted Santa Barbara: Black Sparrow Press, 1981

Bloomer, Jennifer, *Architecture and the Text: The (S)crypts of Joyce and Piranesi*, New Haven and London: Yale University Press, 1993

Boccioni, Umberto, Carrà, Carlo, Russolo, Luigi, Balla, Giacomo and Severini, Gino, 'Manifesto of the Futurist Painters', *The Italian Futurist Painters* (exhibition catalogue), London: Sackville Gallery, 1912

Bomberg, David, Foreword, *David Bomberg* (exhibition catalogue), London: Chenil Gallery, 1914, n.p.

Bowlby, Rachel, *Just Looking: Consumer Culture in Dreiser, Gissing and Zola*, London and New York: Methuen, 1985

—, 'Walking, Women and Writing: Virginia Woolf as *Flâneuse*', *New Feminist Discourses*, ed. Isobel Armstrong, London: Routledge, 1992, pp.26–47

Brodzky, Horace, *Henri Gaudier-Brzeska, 1891–1915*, London: Faber and Faber, 1933

Bullen, J.B., ed., *Post-Impressionists in England: The Critical Reception*, London and New York: Routledge, 1988

Bürger, Peter, *Theory of the Avant-Garde*, 1974; reprinted Minneapolis: University of Minnesota Press, 1984

Causey, Andrew, 'Wadsworth in the Early Twenties', *A Genius of Industrial England: Edward Wadsworth, 1889–1949* (exhibition catalogue), ed. Jeremy Lewison, London: Arkwright Arts Trust, 1990, pp.30–48

de Certeau, Michel, *The Practice of Everyday Life*, Berkeley: University of California Press, 1984

Cherry, Deborah, *Painting Women: Victorian Women Artists*, London and New York: Routledge, 1993

—, 'Carrington: The Exhibition', *Texte zur Kunst*, vol.6, no.2, 1996, pp.190–92

Cianci, Giovanni, 'Futurism and the English Avant Garde: The Early Pound between Imagism and Vorticism', *Arbeiten aus Anglistik und Amerikanistik*, Band 6, Heft 1/81, 1981, pp.3–39

—, 'Un Futurismo in panni neoclassici: sul primo Wyndham Lewis vorticista', *Wyndham Lewis: Letteratura/Pittura*, ed. Giovanni Cianci, Palermo: Sellerio, 1982, pp.25–66

Clarke, Bruce, *Dora Marsden and Early Modernism*, Ann Arbor: University of Michigan Press, 1996

Clutton-Brock, A., 'Process or Person', *Essays in Art*, London: Methuen, 1919, pp.98–9

Coburn, Alvin Langdon, *Alvin Langdon Coburn, Photographer: An Autobiography*, ed. Helmut and Alison Gernsheim, 1966, reprinted New York: Dover, 1978

Cohen, Milton A., 'The Futurist Exhibition of 1912: A Model of Prewar Modernism', *European Studies Journal*, vol.XII, no.2, 1995, pp.1–31

Colomina, Beatriz, ed., *Sexuality and Space*, Princeton, N.J.: Princeton Architectural Press, 1992

Corbett, David Peters, *The Modernity of English Art, 1914–30*, Manchester: Manchester University Press, 1997

—, ed., *Wyndham Lewis and the Art of Modern War*, Cambridge: Cambridge University Press, 1998

Cork, Richard, *Vorticism and its Allies* (exhibition catalogue), London: Arts Council of Great Britain, 1974

—, *Vorticism and Abstract Art in the First Machine Age*: vol.I *Origins and Development*; vol.II *Synthesis and Decline*, London: Gordon Fraser, 1976

—, 'The Cave of the Golden Calf', *Artforum*, December 1982, pp.56–82

—, 'Wyndham Lewis and the Drogheda Dining Room', *Burlington Magazine*, October 1984, pp.610–19

—, *Art Beyond The Gallery in Early 20th-Century England*, New Haven and London: Yale University Press, 1985

—, 'The Vorticist Circle, Bomberg and the First World War', *British Art in the Early Twentieth Century* (exhibition catalogue), ed. Susan Compton, London: Royal Academy of Arts; Munich: Prestel Verlag, 1987

—, *David Bomberg*, New Haven and London: Yale University Press, 1987

—, *A Bitter Truth: Avant-Garde Art and the Great War*, New Haven and London: Yale University Press, 1994

—, *Jacob Epstein*, London: Tate Gallery Publishing, 1999

Dasenbrock, Reed Way, *The Literary Vorticism of Ezra Pound and Wyndham Lewis: Towards the Condition of Painting*, Baltimore and London: Johns Hopkins University Press, 1985

Durman, Michael, and Munton, Alan, 'Wyndham Lewis and the Nature of Vorticism', *Wyndham Lewis: Letteratura/Pittura*, ed. Giovanni Cianci, Palermo: Sellerio, 1982, pp.111–18

Ede, H.S., *Savage Messiah: A Life of Gaudier-Brzeska*, London: Heinemann, 1931

Edwards, Paul, *Wyndham Lewis: Art and War*, London: The Wyndham Lewis Memorial Trust in association with Lund Humphries, 1992

—, 'Wyndham Lewis's *Timon of Athens* Portfolio: The Emergence of Vorticist Abstraction', *Apollo*, vol.CXLVIII, no.439, October 1998, pp.34–40

—, *Wyndham Lewis: Painter and Writer*, New Haven and London: Yale University Press, 2000

Elliott, Bridget, and Wallace, Jo-Ann, *Women Artists and Writers: Modernist (Im)positionings*, London and New York: Routledge, 1994

Epstein, Jacob, *Let There Be Sculpture*, London: Michael Joseph, 1940

Etchells, Frederick, 'A Note', *Exhibition of Original Woodcuts and Drawings by Edward Wadsworth* (exhibition catalogue),

London: Adelphi Gallery, 1919; reprinted in Frances Carey and Anthony Griffiths, *Avant-Garde British Printmaking 1914–1960*, London: British Museum, 1990, p.31

Foshay, Toby Avard, *Wyndham Lewis and the Avant Garde: The Politics of the Intellect*, Montreal: McGill-Queen's University Press, 1992

Foucault, Michel, *History of Sexuality*: vol.I *The Will to Know*, Harmondsworth: Penguin, 1981

Freyer, Grattan, 'Blast and Counter-Blast', *Irish Times*, 12 August 1972

Froula, Christine, *To Write Paradise: Style and Error in Pound's Cantos*, New Haven and London: Yale University Press, 1986

Fry, Roger, Introduction, *Manet and the Post-Impressionists* (exhibition catalogue), London: Grafton Galleries, 1910

—, 'The Allied Artists at the Albert Hall', *Nation*, 20 July 1912, p.583

—, 'The French Group', *Second Post-Impressionist Exhibition: British, French and Russian Artists* (exhibition catalogue), London: Grafton Galleries, 1912

—, *Vision and Design*, 1920; revised edition 1925; reprinted London: Chatto and Windus, 1929

—, *The Letters of Roger Fry*, ed. Denys Sutton, London: Chatto and Windus, 1972

Garner, Les, *A Brave and Beautiful Spirit: Dora Marsden, 1882–1960*, Avebury: Gower, 1990

Gaudier-Brzeska, Henri, 'Allied Artists' Association Ltd., Holland Park Hall', *The Egoist*, 15 June 1914, p.228

—, 'Vortex. Gaudier-Brzeska', *Blast* no.1, June 1914, pp.155–8

Gersina, Gretchen, *Carrington: A Life of Dora Carrington*, Oxford: Oxford University Press, 1990

Goldring, Douglas, *South Lodge*, London: Constable, 1943

Graver, David, 'Vorticist Performance and Aesthetic Turbulence in *Enemy of the Stars*', *PMLA*, vol.CVII, no.3, May 1992, pp.482–96

Green, Christopher, ed., *Art Made Modern: Roger Fry's Vision of Art* (exhibition catalogue), London: Courtauld Galleries in association with Merrell Holberton, 1999

Grosz, Elizabeth, 'Bodies/Cities', *Sexuality and Space*, ed. Beatriz Colomina, Princeton, N.J.: Princeton Architectural Press, 1992, pp.241–53

Harrison, Charles, *English Art and Modernism*, London: Allen Lane, 1981

Head, Philip, 'Vorticist Antecedents', *Some Enemy Fight-Talk: Aspects of Wyndham Lewis on Art and Society*, Borough Green: Green Knight Editions, 1999, pp.87–106

Hill, Jane, *The Art of Dora Carrington*, London: Herbert Press, 1994

Holmes, C.J., *Notes on the Post-Impressionist Painters. Grafton Galleries 1910–1911*, London: Philip Lee Warner, 1910

Honer, J., ed., *C.R.W. Nevinson: The Twentieth Century* (exhibition catalogue), London: Merrell Holberton in association with the Imperial War Museum, 1999

Hooker, Denise, *Nina Hamnett, Queen of Bohemia*, London: Constable, 1986

Hulme, T.E., 'Contemporary Drawings, 2', *The New Age*, 2 April 1914, p.688

—, 'Modern Art III: The London Group', *The New Age*, 26 March 1914, p.661

—, 'Modern Art IV: Mr David Bomberg's Show', *The New Age*, 9 July 1914, pp.230–31

—, *Speculations: Essays on Humanism and the Philosophy of Art*, ed. Herbert Read, London: Routledge and Kegan Paul, 1924

—, *The Collected Writings of T. E. Hulme*, ed. Karen Csengeri, Oxford: Clarendon Press, 1994

Humphreys, Richard, *Pound's Artists: Ezra Pound and the Visual Arts in London, Paris and Italy* (exhibition catalogue), London: Tate Gallery Publications, 1985

Huyssen, Andreas, 'Mass Culture as Woman: Modernism's Other', *After the Great Divide: Modernism, Mass Culture, Post-Modernism*, Bloomington: Indiana University Press, 1986

Hynes, Samuel, *A War Imagined: The First World War and English Culture*, London: Bodley Head, 1990

Ind, Rosemary, 'Frederick Etchells: Plain Home Builder: Where is your Vortex?', *ICSAC Cahier 8/9: Vorticism*, December 1988, pp.145–67

Internationaal Centrum voor Structuuranalyse en Constructivisme (ICSAC), *Cahier 8/9: Vorticism*, ed. Andrew Wilson, Brussels, 1988

Kenner, Hugh, *The Pound Era: The Age of Ezra Pound, T. S. Eliot, James Joyce and Wyndham Lewis*, London: Faber and Faber, 1972

Krauss, Rosalind, *The Originality of the Avant-Garde and Other Modernist Myths*, Cambridge, Mass.: MIT Press, 1985

Kruchenykh, Aleksei, *Victory over the Sun*, (1913), trans. Ewa Bartos and Victoria Ness Kirby, *The Drama Review*, vol.xv, no.4, fall 1971, pp.92–124

Langhan, Mary, and Schwartz, Bill, eds, *Crises in the British State, 1880–1920*, London: Hutchinson, 1985

Lewis, Wyndham, 'The Cubist Room', *Exhibition by the Camden Town Group and Others* (exhibition catalogue), Brighton: Public Art Galleries, 1913

—, Foreword, *Guns* (exhibition catalogue), London: Goupil Gallery, 1919

—, *The Caliph's Design: Architects! Where is your Vortex?*, 1919; reprinted, ed. Paul Edwards, Santa Barbara: Black Sparrow Press, 1986

—, 'The Children of the New Epoch', *The Tyro*, no.1, [April] 1921, p.3

—, *The Lion and the Fox: The Role of the Hero in the Plays of Shakespeare*, London: Grant Richards, 1927

—, *Time and Western Man*, 1927; reprinted, ed. Paul Edwards, Santa Rosa: Black Sparrow Press, 1993

—, *Enemy of the Stars*, London: Desmond Harmsworth, 1932

—, *Blasting and Bombardiering*, London: Eyre and Spottiswoode, 1937; revised edition London: John Calder, 1982

—, 'Early London Environment', *T. S. Eliot*, ed. Richard March and Tambimuttu, London: Editions Poetry, 1948, pp.24–32

—, *Rude Assignment: A Narrative of my Career up-to-date*, London: Hutchinson, 1950

—, *Wyndham Lewis and Vorticism* (exhibition catalogue), London: Tate Gallery, 1956

—, *The Letters of Wyndham Lewis*, ed. W. K. Rose, London: Methuen, 1963

—, *Wyndham Lewis on Art: Collected Writings*, ed. C. J. Fox and Walter Michel, London: Thames and Hudson, 1969

—, 'Letters to Thomas Sturge Moore', ed. Victor Cassidy, *Lewisletter*, no.7, October 1977, pp.8–23

—, *Collected Poems and Plays*, ed. Alan Munton, Manchester: Carcanet, 1979

—, *The Complete Wild Body*, ed. Bernard Lafourcade, Santa Barbara: Black Sparrow Press, 1982 (incorporates *The Wild Body*, 1927)

—, *Creatures of Habit and Creatures of Change: Essays on Art, Literature and Society, 1914–1956*, ed. Paul Edwards, Santa Rosa: Black Sparrow Press, 1989

— and Pound, Ezra, *Pound/Lewis: The Letters of Ezra Pound and Wyndham Lewis*, ed. Timothy Materer, New York: New Directions, 1985

Lewison, Jeremy, ed., *Henri Gaudier-Brzeska, 1891–1915* (exhibition catalogue), Cambridge: Kettle's Yard Gallery, 1983

Lidderdale, J., and Nicholson, M., *Dear Miss Weaver: Harriet Shaw Weaver, 1876–1961*, 1962; reprinted London: Faber and Faber, 1970

McNeil, Helen, 'Vortex Marsden: A Little Magazine and the Making of Modernity', 1999, forthcoming 2000

Manson, J.B., 'Introduction: Rooms I.–II.', *Exhibition by The Camden Town Group and Others* (exhibition catalogue), Brighton: Public Art Galleries, 1913

Marinetti, Filippo Tommaso, *La Conquête des étoiles*, Paris: Editions de la Plume, 1902

—, 'Futurist Venice', *The Tramp: An Open Air Magazine*, August 1910, pp.487–8

—, 'Initial Manifesto of Futurism', *The Italian Futurist Painters* (exhibition catalogue), London: Sackville Gallery, 1912

—, *Zang Tumb Tumb: Parole in Libertà*, Milan: Edizioni Futuriste di 'Poesia', 1914

—, *Teoria e Invenzione Futurista*, ed. L. De Maria, Milan: Mondadori, 1968

—, *Marinetti: Selected Writings*, ed. R.W. Flint, trans. Flint and Arthur A. Coppotelli, New York: Farrar, Straus and Giroux, 1972

Materer, Timothy, *Vortex: Pound, Eliot and Lewis*, Ithaca and London: Cornell University Press, 1979

Meyers, Jeffrey, *The Enemy: A Biography of Wyndham Lewis*, London: Routledge, 1980

Michel, Walter, *Wyndham Lewis: Paintings and Drawings*, London: Thames and Hudson, 1971

'M. M. B.', 'Rebel Art in Modern Life', *Daily News and Leader*, 7 April 1914, p.14

Nevinson, C.R.W., 'Vital English Art', *The New Age*, 18 June 1914, pp.160–2

—, *Paint and Prejudice*, London: Methuen, 1937

Nevinson, Margaret, 'Futurism and Women', *The Vote*, 31 December 1910, p.112

Nietzsche, Friedrich, *Complete Works*: vol.xiii *The Genealogy of Morals*, ed. Oscar Levy, Edinburgh and London: T. N. Foulis, 1910

Normand, Tom, *Wyndham Lewis the Artist: Holding the Mirror up to Politics*, Cambridge: Cambridge University Press, 1992

d'Offay Couper Gallery, *Abstract Art in England 1913–1915* (exhibition catalogue), London, 1969

O'Keeffe, Paul, 'The Troubled Birth of *Blast*: December 1913–June 1914', *ICSAC Cahier 8/9: Vorticism*, December 1988, pp.43–57

Orchard, Karin, ed., *Blast: Vortizismus – Die Erste Avantgarde in England 1914–1918* (exhibition catalogue), Berlin: Ars Nicolai, 1997

Pearson, Geoffrey, 'From Hooligans to Heroes', *New Society*, 30 June 1983

Peppin, Brigid, *Helen Saunders, 1885–1963* (exhibition catalogue), Oxford: Ashmolean Museum, 1996

Perry, Gillian, *Women Artists and the Parisian Avant-Garde*, Manchester: Manchester University Press, 1995

Poggioli, R., *The Theory of the Avant-Garde*, 1962; reprinted Cambridge, Mass.: Harvard University Press, 1968

Pound, Ezra, *A Lume Spento*, Venice: Antonini, 1908

—, 'Prologemena', *Poetry Review*, February 1912, p.76

—, 'The New Sculpture', *The Egoist*, 16 February 1914, pp.67–8

—, 'Vortex Pound', *Blast* no.1, June 1914, p.153

—, 'Edward Wadsworth, Vorticist', *The Egoist*, 15 August 1914, p.306

—, 'Vorticism', *Fortnightly Review*, 1 September 1914, pp.461–71

—, 'Preliminary Announcement of the College of Arts', *The Egoist*, 2 November 1914, 413–14

—, 'Affirmations II: Vorticism', *The New Age*, 14 January 1915, pp.277–8

—, 'Affirmations III: Jacob Epstein', *The New Age*, 21 January 1915, pp.311–12

—, 'Affirmations IV: As for Imagisme', *The New Age*, 28 January 1915, p.349

—, *Gaudier-Brzeska: A Memoir*, London: John Lane, 1916; revised edition 1970, New York: New Directions, 1974

—, 'Prefatory Note', *A Memorial Exhibition of the Work of Henri Gaudier-Brzeska* (exhibition catalogue), London: Leicester Galleries, 1918

— (as 'B.H.Dias'), 'Art Notes', *The New Age*, 27 March 1919, p.342

—, *The Letters of Ezra Pound, 1907–1941*, ed. D.D.Paige, London: Faber and Faber, 1951

—, *Ezra Pound and the Visual Arts*, ed. Harriet Zinnes, New York: New Directions, 1980

—, *The Selected Letters of Ezra Pound to John Quinn, 1915–24*, ed. Timothy Materer, Durham and London: Duke University Press, 1991

Pound, Omar, *The Introspective Eye: Dorothy Shakespear Pound's Modernist Vision* (exhibition catalogue), Clinton NY: Emerson Gallery, Hamilton College, 1997

—, and Litz, A.Walton, eds, *Ezra Pound and Dorothy Shakespear Pound: Their Letters, 1909–1914*, New York: New Directions, 1984

Rae, Patricia, 'From Mystical Gaze to Pragmatic Game: Representations of Truth in Vorticist Art', *ELH*, vol.LVI, no.3, fall 1989, pp.689–720

Reed, Christopher, '"A Room of One's Own": The Bloomsbury Group's Creation of Modernist Domesticity', *Not at Home: The Suppression of Domesticity in Modern Art and Architecture*, ed. C.Reed, London: Thames and Hudson, 1996, pp.147–60

Roberts, William, *The Vortex Pamphlets, 1956–1958*, London: Canale, 1958

Robins, Anna Gruetzner, *Modern Art in Britain 1910–1914* (exhibition catalogue), London: Merrell Holberton in association with Barbican Art Gallery, 1997

Rothenstein, John, *Modern English Painters*: Vol.1 *Sickert to Grant*, London: Arrow, 1962

Rutter, Frank, Foreword, *Post-Impressionists and Futurists* (exhibition catalogue), London: Doré Galleries, 1913, n.p.

Sackville Gallery, *Exhibition of Works by the Italian Futurist Painters* (exhibition catalogue), London, 1912

Saunders, Helen, 'Notes on Harriet Weaver', Lidderdale, J., and Nicholson, M., *Dear Miss Weaver: Harriet Shaw Weaver,*

1876–1961, 1962; reprinted London: Faber and Faber, 1970

Sellwood, Sara, 'The Dissemination of Ideas about Abstract Art in England and America', *Towards a New Art: Essays on the Background to Abstract Art, 1910–1920*, ed. Michael Compton, London: Tate Gallery, 1980, pp.207–9

Shipp, Horace, *The New Art: A Study of the Principles of Non-Representational Art and their Application in the Work of Lawrence Atkinson*, London: C.Palmer, 1922

Shone, Richard, 'The Friday Club', *Burlington Magazine*, May 1975, pp.279–84

—, *The Art of Bloomsbury: Roger Fry, Vanessa Bell and Duncan Grant* (exhibition catalogue), London: Tate Gallery Publishing, 1999

Silber, Evelyn, *The Sculpture of Epstein*, Oxford: Phaidon, 1986

—, *Gaudier-Brzeska: Life and Art*, London: Thames and Hudson, 1996

Speight, Margot, 'The Women in the Picture', *Enemy News*, no.9, 1978, pp.7–11

Suleiman, Susan R., *Subversive Intent: Gender, Politics and the Avant-Garde*, Cambridge, Mass.: Harvard University Press, 1990

Tickner, Lisa, *The Spectacle of Women: Imagery of the Suffrage Campaign, 1907–1914*, London: Chatto and Windus, 1987

—, 'Men's Work? Masculinity and Modernism', *differences*, vol.IV, no.3, 1992, pp.1–37

—, 'The "Left-handed Marriage": Vanessa Bell and Duncan Grant', *Significant Others*, ed. W.Chadwick and I. de Courtivron, London: Thames and Hudson, 1993, pp.65–81

—, *Modern Life and Modern Subjects: British Art in the Early Twentieth Century*, New Haven and London: Yale University Press, 2000

Wadsworth, Edward, *The Black Country*, London: Ovid Press, 1920

Walker, Lynne, 'Vistas of Pleasure: Women as Consumers of Urban Space, 1850–1900', *Women in the Victorian Art World*, ed. C.C.Orr, Manchester: Manchester University Press, 1994, pp.75–85

Walkowitz, Judith R., *City of Dreadful Delight: Narratives of Sexual Danger in Late Victorian London*, London: Virago, 1992

Waugh, Rosa, *An Interplay of Life and Art*, Broxbourne, 1957

Weeks, Jeffrey, *Sex, Politics amd Society*, London: Longman, 1981

Wees, William C., *Vorticism and the English Avant-Garde*, Manchester: Manchester University Press, 1972

West, Rebecca, 'The *Freewoman*', *Time and Tide*, 16 July 1926; reprinted in *Time and Tide Wait for no Man*, ed. Dale Spender, London: Pandora, 1984, pp.63–8

Wilson, Andrew, 'Demobilisation: The End of Vorticism or another "Blast"? 1919–1921', *ICSAC Cahier 8/9: Vorticism*, ed. Andrew Wilson, Brussels, 1988, pp.205–30

Woolf, Virginia, 'Mr Bennett and Mrs Brown', 1924; reprinted in *Collected Essays of Virginia Woolf*, vol.1, London: Hogarth Press, 1966, pp.319–37

—, 'Street Haunting: A London Adventure', 1930; reprinted in *Collected Essays of Virginia Woolf*, vol.4, London: Hogarth Press, 1966, pp.155–67

Worringer, Wilhelm, *Abstraction and Empathy: A Contribution to the Psychology of Style*, 1908; trans. M.Bullock, London: Routledge and Kegan Paul, 1953

Index

Numbers of black and white figures are given in **bold**; references to colour plates are in the form **pl.**xv